ROBERT BRIDGES

A Study of Traditionalism in Poetry

ROBERT BRIDGES

A Study of Traditionalism in Poetry

BY

ALBERT GUÉRARD, Jr.

NEW YORK

RUSSELL & RUSSELL · INC

1965

FOR
ARTHUR YVOR WINTERS
A great teacher and a dear friend

PREFACE

TODAY the work of Robert Bridges seems even more remote from the contemporary poetic situation than it did at the time of his death eleven years ago. It is not surprising that no exhaustive critical study of Bridges' work has appeared during the intervening years. Poets and critics of the thirties, with their allegiance already divided between socially conscious "left wing" poets and the various enthusiasms inculcated by T. S. Eliot, had little time to devote to the author of a long philosophical poem and of a few graceful and mild lyrics appearing at the end of anthologies of English poetry. The present author has frequently been asked why he devotes so much attention to a poet so old-fashioned and traditional, and withal so completely uninfluenced by the only ancestors who can confer legitimacy today, the French Symbolists and the English Metaphysicals.

I cannot answer this question adequately without summarizing the contents of this book. Like Jonson, Herbert and even Donne, Bridges has suffered severely at the hands of the very anthologists who have brought his poetry a wider public. The poems which everyone knows, such as "A Passer-By" and "On a Dead Child," are indeed quiet and lovely lyrics, but compared with the more intense and more serious poems which have not been reprinted they have little importance. Far from being a learned formalist, primarily interested in prosodic exercises, Bridges seems to me to have been one of the most impressive as well as one of the most serious poets of the last hundred years. The present book was written, above all, to establish the grounds for this rather heretical opinion.

It also seemed to me that a poet so far removed from the poetic fashions of the day might have much to tell us about our present literary failings. Although several important poets have reminded

us of their indebtedness to various schools of poetry in the seventeenth and nineteenth century, few ages have made such a complete break with the past as has our own. In a time of radical
innovators and dubious allies of traditionalism, the study of a
poet who was naturally and unostentatiously traditional should
be of value. The way in which Bridges used very diverse masters
in his lyrics, plays and philosophical poem may illustrate not only
the manner in which a poet perfects his style but also some of the
workings of the creative imagination.

The present book therefore proposes to make the first exhaustive critical study of Bridges' poetry, and to make a study and
defense of traditionalism as well. It is in no sense a life of the poet.
A biography would offer interesting confirmation of Ruskin's
theories concerning the relationship between an artist's character
and his work. Unfortunately Bridges, who throughout his life
shunned any form of publicity, requested in his will that no biography be written. In view of the concentration on the poetry
itself which this request demanded, I have given little attention
to Bridges' hymns and studies of music or to his work in connection with the Society for Pure English. The critical essays are examined only insofar as they throw light on the poetry. (It should
be noted in this connection that in his *Selected Essays, Papers, etc.*
Bridges experimented with a system of phonetic spelling which
added several new letters to the alphabet. Wherever I quote from
the essays, I have restored the normal spelling. In *The Testament
of Beauty* Bridges employed a much simpler system of phonetic
spelling. In quoting from this poem I have retained Bridges'
spelling, omitting only the distinctions which he makes, through
the use of typographical innovations, between the qualities of
vowels.)

The division of the book into considerations of the lyric, dramatic and philosophical poetry was necessary to a thorough study
of the poetry, but may prove a trifle misleading. It must be kept
in mind that the majority of Bridges' best lyrics were written be-

tween 1875 and 1900, while *The Testament of Beauty* was begun not earlier than 1925. Eight of Bridges' ten plays were written between 1882 and 1888; thus the dramatic poetry did not follow upon the lyric poetry or immediately precede *The Testament of Beauty*. During the quarter century in which he wrote little of poetic importance, 1900–1925, Bridges was occupied with experiments in classical prosody, studies of Milton's versification, the preparation of essays and anthologies, and investigations for the Society for Pure English.

The present book is intended to meet the demands of the scholar as well as of the general reader. It therefore contains much material on sources and analogues. Wherever this material seems to have general pertinence, it has been included in the text; otherwise, it has been removed to the notes (collected at the back of the book) or to an appendix on sources and analogues. In the case of *The Testament of Beauty*, however, the notes are an integral part of the study, and the reader is asked to consult them as frequently as his time and patience permit. A more detailed study of Bridges' versification than would have been proper in the general chapters has also been reserved for an appendix on prosody, while information on the dating of Bridges' lyrics will be found in still a third appendix.

Of the six published books concerning Robert Bridges and his work, two should be in the hands of any serious student of the poems: G. L. McKay's excellent *A Bibliography of Robert Bridges* (New York, 1933) and Nowell Charles Smith's compact and detailed commentary, *Notes on The Testament of Beauty* (London, 1931). Although a very inadequate guide to the philosophy of the poem, Smith's book records many instances of literary conveyance and explains many obscure allusions. It was obviously a labor of love on the part of a very learned man. Francis Brett Young's *Robert Bridges: A Critical Study* (London, 1914) offers a sympathetic popularized discussion of the lyrics, but shows little understanding of the plays. T. M. Kelshall's *Robert Bridges: Poet Laureate* is an exceedingly brief and to my mind very unreliable survey. It is even more sympathetic than Brett Young's book, however. Mabel L. Hughes' *Everyman's Testament of Beauty: A Study in The Testament of Beauty* (London, 1932) is a work of religious propaganda which offers nothing of interest to the serious student. Tatsu Sasaki's *On the Language of Robert Bridges' Poetry* (Tokyo, 1932) is a dissertation devoted to minute analysis of grammar and syntax. In addition to the above, I also consulted Alexander Brede's unpublished dissertation (Stanford University, 1931), "Studies in Contemporary Poetry: I. Robert Bridges."

Of many debts, the greatest is to Dr. Yvor Winters of Stanford University, who first called my attention to Bridges' poetry. I could record at length the indefatigable care and extraordinary patience with which he assisted me past many obstacles in the writing of this book. The impress of Dr. Winters' own writings, especially his essays on Bridges and his philosophical defense of traditionalism, *Primitivism and Decadence* (New York, 1937), may be found on nearly every page. Again, I could argue my conviction that Dr. Winters stands almost alone among the critics of our day. But I prefer to recall the long autumn and winter evenings of my undergraduate years when a young teacher of English composition developed, in a much younger student, a love of clear thinking, firm poetry and cool prose.

I am also grateful to Professors Howard Mumford Jones and Robert Hillyer of Harvard University and Hardin Craig of Stanford for much valuable advice. My father and mother, Dr. Howard Baker of Harvard, Mr. John Isaacs of King's College, London, and Professor John McClelland of Stanford read all or parts of the manuscript and offered helpful suggestions. I am particularly anxious to record my deep gratitude to Mrs. Robert Bridges and to Elizabeth Daryush, the poet's daughter, for their kind hospitality and invaluable assistance. Also to the officials of the Bodleian Library, the British Museum, the Stanford University Library, and the Harvard College Library for the facilities which they placed at my disposal. I am much indebted to the Clarendon Press, Oxford, for permission to quote so extensively from *The Shorter Poems of Robert Bridges*, the six-volume *Poetical Works of Robert Bridges*, and *The Testament of Beauty*. A generous grant from the American Council of Learned Societies made possible the book's publication.

A. J. G.

Harvard University
February 17, 1941

CONTENTS

PART ONE: LYRIC POETRY

PART TWO: DRAMATIC POETRY

PART THREE: THE TESTAMENT OF BEAUTY

CONCLUSION

xiv CONTENTS

BIOGRAPHICAL NOTE

ROBERT SEYMOUR BRIDGES was born at Walmer (Kent) on October 23, 1844, the fourth son and the eighth of nine children of John Bridges and Harriet Affleck. "The Bridges family had been substantial yeomen in the Isle of Thanet since the sixteenth century. . . . Most of the family property came into the hands of Robert Bridges' grandfather and so to his father, and was sold under the will of the latter . . . in 1853 . . . when Robert was only nine years old. Thus Robert grew up under no necessity of earning a livelihood." *

In September 1854 Bridges was sent to Eton, and during his later school years "his mind was exercised by religious problems and drawn towards 'Puseyite' views. . . ." He went to Oxford in October 1863, as a commoner of Corpus Christi College, and took a second class in *literae humaniores* in the Michaelmas term of 1867. At Oxford, Bridges was chiefly known as a distinguished oarsman: he stroked the Corpus boat to second on the river in 1867.

During his undergraduate years Bridges' interests were shifting from religion to natural science, and in 1869 he entered St. Bartholomew's Hospital as a medical student; he spent much time in travelling on the continent and in Egypt, however, and did not actually begin his medical studies until 1871. He graduated M.B. in 1874, and was house physician at St. Bartholomew's for one year (1875–6). In 1877 he was appointed casualty physician, and in 1878 assistant physician in the Hospital for Sick Children, Great Ormond Street. In June 1881 an attack of pneumonia and empyema ended his medical career; he had, however, "intended to retire at the age of forty. . . ."

In 1882 Bridges moved to the Manor House, Yattendon, Berkshire, and here in 1884 he married Monica, eldest daughter of the architect Alfred Waterhouse. He lived at Yattendon until 1904, and in 1907 settled at Chilswell House, on Boar's Hill near Oxford. During the Yattendon years he produced, in collaboration with Harry Ellis Wool-

* All the quotations in the Biographical Note are from the article on Bridges in the *Dictionary of National Biography, 1922–30*.

dridge, *The Yattendon Hymnal* (1895–9). "In 1895 he was invited by a strong list of supporters to stand for election to the chair of poetry at Oxford. This he declined to do." In 1913, the year in which he was appointed Poet Laureate to succeed Alfred Austin, he founded the Society for Pure English, collaborating in this work with Henry Bradley, Sir Walter Raleigh and Logan Pearsall Smith.

In 1924 Bridges and his wife spent three months at Ann Arbor as guests of the University of Michigan. *The Testament of Beauty*, his last poem, was published in 1929 on the poet's eighty-fifth birthday. He died at Chilswell on April 21, 1930.

Bridges received the Order of Merit in 1929. He was an honorary D.Litt. of Oxford University and an honorary LL.D. of St. Andrews, Harvard and Michigan. From 1895 he was an honorary fellow of Corpus Christi College.

PART ONE

Lyric Poetry

He who in radiant blindness saw that fair
Plesaunce which lay beyond the dolorous gate,
Nor in their banishment allowed despair
To those proud children God had doomed ingrate:
Milton, thy subtle rhythms did prepare
For later minds a plentiful estate.
Thou stood'st beside young Keats, thy lovely heir,
Brooding on homeless Ruth disconsolate;
And most by him whose chiselled lines and bare
Marmoreal form, whose passion temperate
The fires of love cherished with scholar's care,
Bridges, of beauty's realm the Laureate.
These glorious crowns today are thine to wear.
Is this thy pain? Is this to stand and wait?

A. J. G.

CHAPTER ONE

Traditionalism and Autonomy

How, with a fancy so unkind to mirth,
A sense so hard, a style so worn and bare,
Look ye for any welcome anywhere
From any shelf or heart-home on the earth?

— *The Growth of Love*

ENGLISH CRITICISM has seldom been favorably disposed toward Addison's second class of genius,[1] toward poets who are not only traditionalists, but primarily craftsmen. "In England poetry is not commonly thought of as an art but rather as a sort of spontaneous ebullition of emotion, with something of an implicit antithesis between art and inspiration,"[2] and the unprofessional reader likes to think, with Shelley, that this inspiration "acts in a divine and unapprehended manner, beyond and above consciousness."[3] In some ways Robert Bridges was as English as Chaucer, but as a writer he was rather a Latin or Greek: his subject matter was often more intellectual than emotional, his mood more reflective than intuitive, and like Milton he was first an artist, and only afterward a poet in the Shelleyan sense of the word. He never felt, as did Ruskin and Browning, that formal perfection was degrading. Comparing his own inclination toward poetry with that of his Eton friend Digby Dolben, he wrote:

Our instinctive attitudes toward poetry were very dissimilar, he regarded it from the emotional, and I from the artistic side; and he was

thus of a much intenser poetic temperament than I, for when he began
to write poetry he would never have written on any subject that did
not deeply move him, nor would he attend to poetry unless it expressed his own emotions. . . . What led me to poetry was the inexhaustible satisfaction of form, the magic of speech, lying as it seemed to
me in the masterly control of the material.[4]

The passage has been quoted frequently, but usually with the
final words — "the masterly control of the material" — omitted.
This statement of poetic doctrine, thus incompletely rendered, has
probably contributed much to the legend that Bridges was merely
a formalistic technician, a poet who had nothing to say and said
it with consummate skill and ingenuity. Yet the final words are
the most important of all, suggesting as they do a central belief
of Bridges as a poet and philosopher: that the creative imagination is autonomous, and independent of primary experience. Far
from regarding poetry as an amusing and complicated game,
Bridges found it the best means of seeking "the principle of
beauty in all things"; poetry cannot be dissociated from his personal conception of religion. Yet an austere reticence prevented
him from writing about poetry other than as an art or craft; his
prose is heavily freighted with technical discussion, and there are
no more minute studies of prosody and diction than the essays on
Milton and the articles written for the Society for Pure English.
It is nevertheless possible to extract from his book reviews, published lectures and particularly from his short book on Keats
sufficient material to form a reasoned and illuminating catena of
thought on the less formal aspects of his poetic ideal.

The central affirmation, and one which has probably amused or
bewildered younger poets, appears in the essay on Mary Coleridge: "It may be difficult to say what the artistic requirements of
modern poetry are or should be, but two things stand out, namely,
the Greek attainment and the Christian ideal; and art which nowa-
days neglects either of these is imperfect; that is, it will not command our highest love, nor satisfy our best intelligence." [5] In these

lines, which were part of a commentary on Heine, Bridges meant by the Greek attainment, artistic perfection; by the Christian ideal, rightness of feeling. Without the Christian ideal we would not have had that idealization or "growth of love" which resulted in

> Passion with peace . . . desire at rest, —
> A grace of silence by the Greek unguesst,
> That bloom'd to immortalize the Tuscan style.

This Christian-Platonic-Florentine conception of love, while rightly suggesting affinities with Spenser and others, defines Bridges' isolation from the more intense romantic spirit which infused the poetry of the nineteenth century giants, as well as that of many sixteenth and seventeenth century poets. The essays on "The Influence of the Audience on Shakespeare's Drama" and on Keats show even more clearly how different was Bridges' austere attitude toward art from that of most English poets and critics. He censures where others praise or condone: Shakespeare for the depths of "dusty damn'd experience" to which he descends, his obscenity and brutality; Keats for his "want of restraint," [6] the "unworthy treatment of his ideal female characters," [7] his lack of "dignified passion." [8] The objection to Keats reveals an idealized conception of love and an Aristotelian insistence on self-control; the objection to Shakespeare, an insistence on good taste. This love of good taste, as much as natural restraint, accounts for the reticence of Bridges' poetry. The hatred of vulgarity is an essential part of his aesthetic philosophy: "Vulgarity — that is our national blemish and sin. . . . It is blindness to values; it is spiritual death." [9] In his emphasis on good taste Bridges is not unique among English poets, certainly not unique among Victorian poets; yet good taste would have been considered a primary and indispensable poetic virtue by very few of his predecessors. Even Spenser, in fashioning his gentleman, wrote many lines which Bridges must have censured severely.

In one further way Bridges is not, if such an abstraction is possible, "a typical English poet," and that is in his refusal to conceive of life as tragedy. William Butler Yeats refers to "the profound hereditary sadness of English genius,"[10] and the question of whether the tragic view of life is essential to a great poet is an important one. We cannot imagine a Shakespeare who does not express the despair of the late Renaissance; a Webster who does not see the world as a charnel-house; a Hardy showing Victorian optimism. And finally, to take the example of Bridges' chief master — what value other than formal would *Samson Agonistes* have for us if it did not contain the distilled misery, the savage fury of Milton's rebellion? The quarrel of the contemporary Websters and Donnes with Bridges and others who have preserved a serene attitude toward life is not merely literary: they maintain that a poet cannot see things as they really are without sharing their tragic philosophy.

Certainly there is no body of love poetry so devoid not only of animal passion but of frustration and despair as that of Bridges, and he himself was not unaware of the difficulties which this involved. He quotes Richard Watson Dixon as saying that "the passion of love cannot be depicted in narrative without obstacles,"[11] and in his early volumes Bridges appears to have erected, for this reason, certain rather arbitrary and artificial obstacles. A quiet and not uncherished melancholy, like that of the early Milton, broods over the 1873 *Poems* and over the sonnet-sequence, *The Growth of Love*, but many later lyrics express a direct rejection of this mood:

> For howso'er man hug his care,
> The best of his art is gay.

Already it is possible to observe several marked characteristics. These characteristics — emphasis on artistic skill rather than on intensity of emotion, reticence and restraint, good taste, a tempered optimism — suggest that Bridges was unmistakably the child of his time, a suggestion the more telling if we consider his patriotism and insular pride, and the incorporation of scientific theory in his poetry. Yet Bridges' resemblances to other Victorian poets (to Tennyson especially) were largely coincidental. While his style "represents the finest development of the intellectual, and anti-romantic tendency of the nineteenth century, a tendency illustrated by the Wordsworth of the 'Ode to Duty,' by Bryant, by Landor, and by Arnold," [12] his work would probably have revealed the same general characteristics had Bridges appeared in another age. The essentials of Raleigh and Ben Jonson are indistinguishable from those of Landor and Arnold: there have been few changes in the authentic classical style.

We have Bridges' own comments on the age or ages through which he passed. He referred to the audience "whom Tennyson educated to be specially observant of blemishes, and who came to regard finish not only as indispensable, but as the one satisfying positive quality." [13] Mere correctness and finish by no means define Bridges' own idea of artistic perfection, and his earliest metrical experiments may be regarded as reactions against the monotonous and facile smoothness of Tennyson's meters. Tennyson was certainly a fine craftsman, so ingenious a craftsman that his own skill in accentual-syllabic verse had the same effect on subsequent poetry as Milton's mastery of blank verse: it discouraged further attempts in the same manner. The difference, broadly speaking, between Tennyson and Bridges as prosodists, and the superiority of the younger poet, is that Tennyson explored metrical variation for its own sake; Bridges for the sake of new and enriched perception. Tennyson's great technical ingenuity never seemed to be at the service of his material, while Bridges, in trying to capture speech rhythms and give new life to exhausted meters, never forgot that meters, like words, are the servants of emotion and idea.

Another characteristic of Bridges' art shared by few Victorian poets is its simplicity, its refusal to embellish. He shunned the ornate which Bagehot found in Tennyson [14] as firmly as he shunned the grotesque of Browning. His use of natural speech-rhythm, his unreflective descriptions of the English countryside, and particularly his purity of diction were in sharp contrast to the highly literary conventions of the age. The reaction which we see in his poetry against the gilt adornments of diction and imagery used by his contemporaries reminds us of Collins' rejection of the Augustan style: "here the lovely English words are allowed to speak for themselves," [15] and here too the English countryside is allowed to speak for itself. The peacefulness of Bridges' best nature poems, their color and variety, show them to be the poetry of the south of England, as definitely as the wilder majesty of Wordsworth's reveal their northern origin. And it is this quieter countryside which had been lost to English poetry since Collins and Keats, or had peered only occasionally through the huge glooms and cataracts of the early nineteenth century.

Bridges' optimism is also different from that of his contemporaries, and finds expression in a kind of *joy* absent from English poetry since Shelley, a quiet ecstasy wholly different from Browning's *élan vital*. There is no "Determined Cheerfulness" in Bridges' enjoyment of life. A comparison of his attitude toward science with that of his contemporaries shows the same superficial resemblance and the same underlying difference, though there is some of the optimism of Meredith's "Woods of Westermain" in "Wintry Delights." In various poems Bridges declared himself to be in revolt against "the worried congestion of our Victorian era" and against the attitude which involved an enthrallment of the imagination by science:

> I will be what God made me, nor protest
> Against the bent of genius in my time,
> That science of my friends robs all the best,
> While I love beauty, and was born to rhyme.
>   Be they our mighty men, and let me dwell
> In shadow among the mighty shades of old,
> With love's forsaken palace for my cell;
> Whence I look forth and all the world behold.

> And say, These better days, in best things worse,
> This bastardy of time's magnificence,
> Will mend in fashion, and throw off the curse,
> To crown new love with higher excellence.
> Curs'd tho' I be to live my life alone.
> My toil is for man's joy, his joy my own.

Of the Preraphaelites he wrote, ". . . it was the liberty of their ideal, the vagueness of their aspiration, the rebellion against convention, the boyish contempt for authority and discipline that animated their mutual affection and made the charm of their life";[16] but these were qualities foreign to his own temperament. In 1890 William Watson described his poetry as "free from all taint of the literary vices of our time."[17] It was, or was soon to be, the time of "the irresponsible wit of Wilde, the 'evil' line of Beardsley, Dowson's pretty frailty, Davidson's dogged revolt, the aesthetics of Symons, and the precious distilled mystery of the early Yeats,"[18] and for this period Bridges has his own commentary:

> our art
> Self-consciously sickens in qualms of an aesthetic aura,
> Noisily in the shallows splashing and disporting uninspir'd.[19]

His isolation became more pronounced with the new century, and increased as every year brought a further breakdown of traditional forms. Bridges recognized long before "free verse" the necessity of devising new rhythms to compensate for the relative exhaustion of some of the traditional meters, but he was unwilling to accept disintegration of form as the necessary medium for poetry in a disintegrating society. All his criticism insists on the autonomy of form. He knew that "formlessness can have no place in Art,"[20] and one of the chief faults he finds with Dolben as a poet is that he "varies his form more than he masters it."[21]

Much as he was out of sympathy with the disintegrating technical aspects of modern poetry, he was even farther removed from the spirit of that poetry. His own poetry does not give, as many critics believe poetry should give, the "feeling of contemporary life," the sense of the age. He would not accept surrender to futility and boredom, moral anarchy and loss of individualism, revolt against the aristocratic view of life. No great poet can wholly ignore the problems of his age, and there are long passages in the philosophical poems on the first World War, on education, and on other problems of our own century, but unlike his contemporaries Bridges examined these problems as he examined those of technique: in detached tranquillity, and in the context of two thousand years of inherited wisdom and learning. But he refused to become the passive voice and echo of an age "wanting in moral grandeur." [22]

It is therefore impossible to assign Bridges to any particular school, just as it is impossible to assign the detached and lengthening shadow of Henry James to a particular school. As he saw the problems of the day *sub specie aeternitatis*, so he saw the problems of art, if not in the aspect of eternity, at least in the light of all that earlier poetry could teach him. He sought his literary models in various ages and various literatures, and his poetry is therefore *traditional* in the best sense: "that type of poetry which displays at one and the same time the greatest possible distinction with the fewest possible characteristics recognizable as the marks of any particular school, period, or man; ... in brief, that type of poetry which displays the greatest polish of style and the smallest trace of mannerism." [23] Bridges was as little the contemporary of Browning and Swinburne in 1873 as he was of T. S. Eliot and Carl Sandburg in 1930; he was, throughout his career, more truly the contemporary of Arnold and Landor, even of Milton, Herbert and Jonson. He belongs to a particular school only in the sense that these five restrained and classical artists, with a half a dozen of their peers, belong to a particular school.

The first sonnet of *The Growth of Love*,

> They that in play can do the thing they would,
> Having an instinct throned in reason's place,

might well be interpreted as Bridges' admission that he was a
poet not born, but made. In any case, his talent had a very late
flowering. In the Dolben memoir he speaks of writing poetry at
Eton,[24] but there is nothing signed by him, or bearing any marks
of his style, in the various Eton "ephemerals" of the day. The only
lines preserved from his undergraduate years are "Love is up at
break of day" (1862, corrected 1873)[25] and a sonnet, "Sick of
my joyless journey I looked round" (1865, rewritten 1873).[26]
Bridges' earliest poem, written when he was eighteen, is not, in
its corrected form at least, his worst. Sensitive variety of rhythm
and deliberate moulding of impulse betoken the poet he was to
become. The second stanza foreshadows an indolence of mood
which was to be characteristic of many of the *Shorter Poems*:

> Whilst before their busy blade
> At noon the tall corn rattles,
> Love is sleeping in the shade
> Beside the brook, that prattles
> Dreamy music in the shade.

"Sick of my joyless journey" is interesting chiefly because it shows
the influence of Milton and Vergil[27] already at work:

> . . . straight I thought of how Odysseus saw
> Tityos in Hades: bulk incredible
> Covering nine roods he lies. . . .

The earliest uncorrected poem, dating from Bridges' twenty-
fourth year, is an undistinguished piece of didacticism of 108 lines,
"Beatus Ille."[28] The distrust of passion has a more Victorian ring
than in later poems, and there are several stanzas expounding the
Aristotelian doctrine that self-control and the reining in of impulse
should be made habitual:

> And many a practice, strong to storm
> The holds of sin he will invent,
> And never cease until he form
> A habit to oppose his bent.

The central idea of the poem, which is developed with greater distinction in the fourth book of *The Testament of Beauty* sixty years later, is that the young man should form an ideal for himself toward which he will guide his future action, and by which he will be sustained.

In January 1868 Bridges went to Egypt with Lionel Muirhead, and spent the spring travelling on the Nile; from this trip there remains only a small pencil drawing: "R. B. as he appeared when he composed his Ode." [29] There are only three poems dating from 1869; none from 1870 and 1871. Of these three poems, two are best served by their present obscurity, but the third, "I heard a linnet courting," is Bridges' earliest poem, after revision, to find a place in his final canon. Curiously enough W. B. Yeats selects for quotation in his survey of modern poetry the one unchanged stanza from this earliest preserved poem to illustrate the virtues of Bridges' style:

> I heard a linnet courting
>   His lady in the spring:
> His mates were idly sporting,
>   Nor stayed to hear him sing
>   His song of love. —
> I fear my speech distorting
>   His tender love.

Thus Yeats: "Every metaphor, every thought a commonplace, emptiness everywhere, the whole magnificent." [30] Even if this extravagant praise is allowed, we find Bridges at twenty-seven with some two hundred lines of poetry, of which thirty or forty lines are readable. At twenty-seven Milton had *Comus* behind him, Shelley was publishing *The Cenci*, and Keats was dead.

In 1872 and 1873, he wrote fifty poems which were published in his first book, and of these sixteen find a place in the definitive first book of *Shorter Poems*. Thirty-two of these are dated in

Bridges' own copy of the 1873 *Poems* by month as well as year, [31] and from this information we see the periods of creative activity to have been June–September, 1872; February 1873, and July and August 1873. Like many poets, Bridges wrote a great deal in brief periods of creative activity, and very little during the time which intervened.

Poems (1873), by "Robert Bridges / Bachelor of Arts in the University / of Oxford," bears the significant epigraph: "Parva seges satis est." The volume as a whole is incredibly uneven. It contains one of the great threnodies in English poetry, the Spenserian "Elegy on a Lady Whom Grief for the Death of her Betrothed Killed," two very good lyrics in the Jacobean manner ("Dear lady, when thou frownest" and "I will not let thee go"), two excellent imitations of Heine ("I found to-day out walking" and "A poppy grows upon the shore"), the lovely song,

> I made another song,
> In likeness of my love,

and a not unhappy elegy, "Clear and gentle stream," which shows Bridges at his most graceful. All of these poems reveal a delicate mastery of rhythmical variety and a pure unmannered diction. The number of very bad poems is therefore surprising. The greatest stylistic weakness is a total lack of control over the treacherous anapest, a meter he never used again. In this volume alone Bridges succumbs to the worst literary vices of his time. Victorian melodramatic humanitarianism appears in "Capital Punishment": [32]

> Now retribution, so long time
> Asleep, has met him at his prime,
> To match his final crime with crime.

The childish medievalism of "A lady sat high on a castle-tower" [33] and the dank melancholy of "The wood is bare: a river-mist is steeping"[34] are less shocking than the almost unparalleled bathos and clumsiness of "Histoire de la Mère Jary":[35]

> "Then know that his name is John," he cried
> With words that his life expended;
> "Our child is a foundling," he said and died,
> And his earthly sorrows were ended.

It is not surprising that the book received only one review of more than a few lines, and that one by Bridges' friend, Andrew Lang: "Faint memories are awakened, a music long silent is revived — a careless music, rough and full of sudden breaks of melody and of sweet surprises . . . these lyrics . . . show at once true feeling and reticence."[36]

With this review, and especially with his brief mention of Bridges in *Letters on Literature* (1883), Lang was probably more responsible for making Bridges known to a wider public than any other critic. Yet it is clear that the poet went out of his way to avoid publicity; that he cared more to find a fit audience among his Oxford peers than to achieve wide acclaim:

> . . . 'Twere something yet to live among
> The gentle youth beloved, and where I learn'd
> My art, be there remember'd for my song.

Bridges tried to buy up or suppress all copies of the 1873 volume and of *The Growth of Love*; the sonnet-sequence and the 1879 and 1880 *Poems* were published anonymously, and many of the early books were privately printed by Henry Daniel in very small editions. An *Academy* reviewer[37] and Gerard Hopkins[38] in 1881, William Watson in 1890,[39] and John Bailey as late as 1913,[40] all accused Bridges of a perverse desire "to guard against the profanation of being read."[41]

The first edition of *The Growth of Love* (1876), which received a dozen lines of commentary in all, was a small anonymous pamphlet of twenty-four sonnets. There was a later edition of seventy-nine sonnets (1889), and from these the final selection of sixty-nine sonnets (1898) was made. *The Growth of Love*, considered in any of its three versions, is one of the few works by Bridges which require any elucidation. The interpretation which follows is of the final edition, but the explanatory sonnet prefixed to the 1876 edition is helpful. It is unfortunate that something of a kindred nature was not used at the head of the revised sequence, as it would have defined the nature of the series, and forestalled critics who, regarding the whole series as the history of a personal love, found its apparent digressions from this theme irrelevant, and the love poems singularly lacking in earthly passion:

> Love o'er the noble heart will ne'er abate
>   His empire; he will enter by surprise,
> To conquer till his foes be sworn allies,
> And heart and he become incorporate.
>   So the perfected soul, now her own mate,
> Has for her solace neither voice nor eyes,
> Unless the memory of her first disguise
> Quicken the speech of an abolished date.
>
>   I pray you, ye that read me, when ye con
> The terms of fancy, question not, nor say
> Who was perchance the lady he looked on.
>   I tell you she is not of mortal clay:
> Once she was truly, but she died unwon,
> By death transfigured to the light of day.

In the second quatrain we are told that love, once external to the mind or soul, in the form of a personal or objective embodiment, has become part of the soul. "Her first disguise" is the earthly incarnation which the Idea or "Essence" of love assumed, and through which it was first apprehended by the poet: perhaps the lady who "died unwon." This lady has been transfigured; the poet has climbed higher on the Platonic ladder, [42] and his poems are thus addressed not to an earthly mistress, but to an ideal, to Absolute Beauty or Love. Whereas Bridges' idealization of love in *The*

Testament of Beauty oscillates between Christian Platonism, a conception based on the idealization of marriage, and true Platonism, in which the ladder "is a ladder in the strictest sense; you reach the higher rungs by leaving the lower ones behind," [43] in *The Growth of Love* it remains consistently on the true Platonic plane.

The sixty-sixth sonnet of the final edition really summarizes the whole sequence:

> My wearied heart, whenever, after all,
> Its loves and yearnings shall be told complete,
> When gentle death shall bid it cease to beat,
> And from all dear illusions disenthrall:
> However then thou shalt appear to call
> My fearful heart, since down at others' feet
> It bade me kneel so oft, I'll not retreat
> From thee, nor fear before thy feet to fall.
>
> And I shall say, 'Receive this loving heart
> Which err'd in sorrow only: and in sin
> Took no delight; but being forced apart
> From thee, without thee hoping thee most to win,
> Most prized what most thou madest as thou art
> On earth, till heaven were open to enter in.'

The meaning of this address to the "Essence" of Beauty or Love should be obvious. The lover, unable to wed an immortal Idea, has worshipped it in its various earthly incarnations. The immortality assumed is the ideal and disinterested immortality described by Spinoza and other naturalistic philosophers from Lucretius to Santayana. The "dear illusions" are the various transient earthly loves, each embodying some aspect of the eternal "essence": "A mother is followed by a boyish friend, a friend by a girl, a girl by a wife, a wife by a child, a child by an idea. A divinity passes through these various temples; they may all remain standing, long after the god has fled from the last into his native heaven." [44]

The various sonnets in *The Growth of Love* record their creator's successes or failures in his pursuit of the elusive divinity. Many sonnets which do not seem to come within the general scheme are addressed to various embodiments of Beauty and Love. Thus the sonnets to the Muse, culminating in the sixty-eighth sonnet, "Away now, lovely Muse, roam and be free," are brought within the general scheme by the idea that poetry is the best means of doing reverence:

> But of this wonder, what doth most amaze
> Is that we know our love is held for praise.

One of the recurrent themes is the struggle between earthly and spiritual love. The octave of the thirty-fifth sonnet is almost a paraphrase of Plato's ladder: it establishes, in impersonal terms, the ideal; the sestet tells of the poet's own failure to attain it:

> All earthly beauty hath one cause and proof,
> To lead the pilgrim soul to beauty above:
> Yet lieth the greater bliss so far aloof,
> That few there be are wean'd from earthly love. .
>   Joy's ladder it is, reaching from home to home,
> The best of all the work that all was good;
> Whereof 'twas writ the angels aye upclomb,
> Down sped, and at the top the Lord God stood.
>
>   But I my time abuse, my eyes by day
> Center'd on thee, by night my eyes on fire —
> Letting my number'd moments run away —
> Nor e'en 'twixt night and day to heaven aspire:
>   So true it is that what the eye seeth not
> But slow is loved, and loved is soon forgot.

The sonnets, which were consciously modelled on Milton's,[45] are like no others in Victorian poetry. They could not be farther removed, in their quiet tone, lucid controlled statement, and chiselled form, from "Modern Love" or "Sonnets from the

Portuguese." While they reminded Hopkins of Shakespeare's [46] (and there are indeed several Shakespearean echoes), they seem closer in tone and style to the lovely and neglected sonnets of Drummond — "That learned Grecian, who did so excel" and "Sleep, silence' child, sweet father of soft rest," for instance — than to any others in English poetry. Bridges' performance was more consistently fine than Drummond's, however, and of the sixty-nine sonnets at least nine seem to me to deserve place with the best in the language: "Where San Miniato's convent from the sun" (18), "I would be a bird, and straight on wings I arise" (22), "Spring hath her own bright days of calm and peace" (24), "The fabled sea-snake, Old Leviathan" (27), "Thus to be humbled: 'tis that ranging pride" (32), "*O my goddess divine* sometimes I say" (34), "Come gentle sleep, I woo thee: come and take" (48), "I heard great Hector sounding war's alarms" (53) and "Away now, lovely Muse, roam and be free" (68).

In the year of the first edition of *The Growth of Love*, Bridges also published a Latin poem relating the history of St. Bartholomew's Hospital, *Carmen Elegiacum . . . de Nosocomio Sti. Bartolomae Londinensi.* In 1878 he was evidently much harassed by his duties at the hospital as Casualty Physician: in a long and humorous essay, "An Account of the Casualty Department," [47] he complained of overcrowding. He had so many patients to see that he was forced to spend an average of only 1.28 minutes with each patient. In June 1881 he contracted pneumonia, and in November retired from medicine, as he had planned to do in any case at the age of forty. After a trip to Italy and Sicily he took up residence in Yattendon, Berkshire, where he was living by the end of October 1882.[48] He moved to Chilswell House, near Oxford, twenty-four years later; the period at Yattendon was the most productive of his career.

In the extraordinary unevenness of the lyrics written during 1872 and 1873 the reader sees the efforts of a poet learning to write. In addition, too many of the poems were written in the last month before the book went to press, probably to fill out the volume. Bridges evidently pruned his work far more severely in preparing it for the anonymous 1879 and 1880 volumes: there are only thirty-nine lyrics in all, but nearly all of them are good, and show a control of form and material which he was to excel only occasionally in later volumes. To the 1879 volume belong "A Passer-By," the two odes to "Spring," "The Downs" and "Dejection." In the 1880 *Poems* are such popular favorites as "London Snow" and "On a Dead Child," as well as eleven sonnets which were ultimately to take their place in the final edition of *The Growth of Love*. The 1879 *Poems* received little notice, but by 1880 the veils of anonymity had apparently been lifted, for the *Academy* reviewer, without mentioning Bridges, commented that the author had been fully identified by "many persons who have never been formally admitted into his confidence." [49] The stylistic feature of these two volumes is their use of a chastened sprung-rhythm, but the new meter aroused no interest among critics.

Poems (1884) contained six new lyrics, and in 1890 the first collected edition of *Shorter Poems* completed what is now Books I–IV. *Shorter Poems: Book V* appeared in 1893. The 1890 *Shorter Poems* was the first book to sell at all, a new edition being required in a month. "It was about 1890," according to T. H. Warren, "that he began to take his real rank. It was this little volume that made him more widely known." [50]

The five books of *Shorter Poems* constitute Bridges' main achievement as a lyric poet, and form a fairly unified whole. It is impossible to trace any development of interest or style between the volumes of 1879 and 1893, other than the early abandonment of sprung-rhythm: the characteristics of these volumes will therefore be considered in detail in subsequent chapters, rather than in the course of this brief survey of Bridges' career. But the decade of 1880–90, by far the most fruitful of the six during which Bridges was writing, included not only many lyrics and most of *The Growth of Love* sonnets, but also two masques and six (perhaps seven) full-length plays,[51] two studies of Milton's prosody, *Eden*, an oratorio of little interest to a student of the poetry, as well as the long narrative poem *Eros and Psyche*, an adaptation of Apuleius in 2,557 lines.

Eros and Psyche, written in a seven-line stanza reminiscent of Spenser and often Spenserian in diction as well, is not an unqualified success. There are individual passages of great beauty, but the stanza form exerts a rigid tyranny. Although Bridges declared in a note to the poem that he had "never read any English version of the story," [52] his poem was naturally compared with William Morris' treatment of the story in *The Earthly Paradise*. As we shall see later,[53] a comparison of *Eros and Psyche* with the original reveals in an illuminating way the fashion in which Bridges' imagination worked on his reading. A note to the first edition, not later reprinted, gives a more general idea of the poet's alterations, and shows a conscious attempt to effect that fusion of Greek attainment and Christian ideal which he considered essential to the highest art:

The beautiful story is well known, and the version of Apuleius has been simply followed. Such variations and ornaments as are introduced perhaps fall short of what a poetic reader might expect from a poet of this time. The location of the fable, a gentler handling of motive, and the substitution of Hellenism for Latin vulgarity are examples of these liberties, which will be readily allowed. . . .[54]

There is an interesting parallel between the chastening of Eros' lawless love through marriage in the final stanzas of Bridges' poem and "the final defeat of courtly love by the romantic conception of marriage" [55] in the third and fourth books of *The Faerie Queene*. Cupid is married at the end of Apuleius' story, but merely so that he will be kept out of mischief; not, as in Bridges' version, that his love may be spiritualized. Surprisingly enough, Bridges avoids the danger of ruining his story by the untimely intrusion of moralizing, and the significant translation of *voluptate* by JOY comes almost without shock in the final stanza. The attempt to rewrite Apuleius from a Christian point of view was audacious, but not, I think, unsuccessful. The point of view is assumed at the very beginning of the poem, and held consistently throughout, and since Bridges professed to give an adaptation, rather than a translation of Apuleius, he was free to take this kind of liberty.

It is evident from the earliest stanzas that his is neither Apuleius' Psyche nor even Keats'

> . . . latest born, and loveliest vision far
> Of all Olympus' faded hierarchy.

The first description establishes the tone for Bridges' idealization:

> Her vision rather drave from passion's heart
> What earthly soil it had afore possest;
> Since to man's purer unsubstantial part
> The brightness of her presence was addrest:
> And such as mock'd at God, when once they saw
> Her heavenly glance, were humbl'd, and in awe
> Of things unseen, return'd to praise the Best.

This is of course an interpolation in the original, as is the pendant description of Eros, which shows what qualities he lacked, and was to gain through marriage:

> His thickly curling hair, his ruddy cheek,
> And pouting lips, his soft and dimpled chin,
> The full and cushion'd eye, that idly speaks
> Of self content and vanity within,
> The forward, froward ear, and smooth to touch
> His body sleek, but rounded overmuch
> For dignity of mind and pride akin.

The reason for the success of *Eros and Psyche* is a very general one which can nevertheless be proved by illustration: the poet's faith in his own fable. There is none of the condescension which vitiates so many modern renderings of classical mythology. In *The Growth of Love* the reader is conscious of the poet's strain; the sequence bears the traces of hard and at times uncongenial work. In many of the lyrics, on the other hand, and throughout *The Testament of Beauty*, the reader is conscious of the delight Bridges took in writing. This underlying joy in the consciousness of felicitous imagery or phrasing is evident throughout *Eros and Psyche*; if the tyranny of the seven-line stanza sometimes slowed the narrative, it also invited many full stanza descriptions or similes. In stanzas such as the following, Bridges not only succeeds in making his faded Olympian hierarchy human, but takes obvious pleasure in doing so:

> Then on his head he closely set his cap
> With earèd wings erect, and o'er his knee
> He cross'd each foot in turn to prove the strap
> That bound his wingèd sandals, and shook free
> His chlamys, and gat up, and in his hand
> Taking his fair white-ribbon'd herald's wand,
> Lept forth on air, accoutred cap-a-pè.

> And piloting along the mid-day sky,
> Held southward, till the narrow map of Crete
> Lay like a fleck of azure 'neath his eye;
> When down he came, and as an eagle fleet
> Drops in some combe, then checks his headlong stoop
> With wide-flung wing, wheeling in level swoop
> To strike the bleating quarry with his feet.

In the first stanza, the poet's delight is the result of a complete visualization of his creation, a true suspension of disbelief; in the second stanza, the delight is in the nervous experience of stylistic execution. Yet this pleasure, which the reader shares, is obviously gained at the cost of one primary narrative virtue: compared with Apuleius' version, or with all but the fifth book of *The Faerie Queene*, *Eros and Psyche* lacks the straightforward progress of incident and speed of tempo which carry the reader eagerly forward. *Eros and Psyche* should have its greatest appeal to the reader who is familiar with the story, and is willing to interrupt the narrative to read the best stanzas half a dozen times.

After the publication of the fifth book of *Shorter Poems* in 1893 (if we may be guided by the absence of published poems written in other years), Bridges felt the impulse to write lyric poetry only three times: in 1899, 1913, and 1921. *New Poems* (1899) was his last important collection of lyric poetry in traditional accentual-syllabic meters. But between the appearance of the 1893 *Shorter Poems* and 1899, Bridges had passed from relative obscurity to the position of a minor living classic. Most important to the growth of his reputation was the dedication to him of the eighth volume of Miles' *The Poets and the Poetry of the Century*. This volume appeared in 1892, and was entitled *Robert Bridges and Contemporary Poets*. An extensive selection of the poems was introduced by T. H. Warren, in the first really comprehensive essay on his work: Warren emphasized, as no critic had previously done, Bridges' traditionalism.[56] In 1895, Edward Dowden's long appreciative article established the tone which later criticism would take:

Elements of many kinds enter into his volume of 'Shorter Poems' — delicate observation, delight in external nature, delight in art, delight in love, gladness and grief, ethical seriousness, pensive meditation, graceful play of fancy. But all are subdued to balance, measure, harmony; and sometimes our infirmity craves for some fine extravagance, even some splendid sins.[57]

The publication of the first of the six volumes of *Poetical Works* in 1898 further emphasized Bridges' position as an established poet; in February of that year *The Academy* had referred to Bridges as though his career were over: "He has left the English lyric a far more flexible thing than he found it."[58] *New Poems*, published in the second volume of the *Poetical Works* (four of the six volumes were to be devoted to the plays), is characterized by the use of the simplest and most traditional metrical forms. In a note dated September 1899 Bridges says that some of the poems "were

written this year for this volume," [59] which would lead the reader
to look for task-work meant to pad the book. But among the
poems written in this year were "Eros," "The Summer House
on the Mound," and "The Isle of Achilles," three poems which
challenge comparison, for purity of style and richness and complexity of feeling, with any of the earlier poetry. "Eros" is in
octosyllabic couplets; the other two in heroic couplets. *New
Poems* contains proportionately fewer purely descriptive nature
poems than the earlier volumes, and more poems with serious
human themes. Otherwise it could be considered, for purposes
of criticism, a sixth volume of *Shorter Poems.*

Though the collection now called *Later Poems* was first published in the one-volume *Poetical Works* of 1913, all of the poems
which can be dated were written between 1895 and 1906, with
the exception of one written in 1880 and one in 1910. The latter,
"In still midsummer night," is therefore the only lyric poem in
traditional meters known to have been written between 1906 and
1913, and "Melancholia," a sonnet, the only one between 1901
and 1910. "Recollections of Solitude" (1900) is an autobiographical "elegy," and is the most important poem in the collection.
Otherwise the volume is composed of occasional sonnets, two
odes written to music, and two philosophical poems, "La Gloire
de Voltaire" and "To Robert Burns, An Epistle on Instinct." The
odes to music, written in a variety of meters, obviously suffer
from the requirements of their setting. The "Ode to Music Written for the Bicentenary Commemoration of Henry Purcell" is
clearly inferior to either of Dryden's two odes, while "A Hymn
of Nature" has almost no redeeming features. The two philosophical poems are interesting only because they anticipate lines in *The
Testament of Beauty*:

> Whereas the least philosophy may find
> The truths are the ideas; the sole fact
> Is the long story of man's growing mind. [60]

. . . . . .

But rakel Chance and Fortune blind
Had not the power: — Eternal Mind
Led man upon a way design'd,
　By straight selection
Of pleasurable ways, to find
　Severe perfection.[61]

Though these were inactive years, so far as lyric poetry was concerned, it is evident that Bridges became more widely known to the general public between 1899 and 1913, when he was appointed Poet Laureate. In 1912, probably believing that Bridges, who was now almost seventy, would add nothing of importance to his canon, the Oxford University Press published a collected edition in the Oxford Poets series, and in the same year Oxford gave him the degree of Doctor of Letters. In June 1913 *The Journal of Education* offered a prize for a list of the "three greatest poets in order of excellence." The winning list was determined by plebiscite, and the votes were sent in before the appointment to the Laureateship. The vote gave first place to Kipling, second place to Watson, and third place to Bridges.[62]

The appointment to the Laureateship was naturally the occasion for a large number of articles, and for one book, F. E. Brett Young's readable survey, *Robert Bridges: A Critical Study*. The popular reaction to Bridges' appointment is familiar history; it was a reaction even more severe in the United States than in England. The following is typical of many American press comments:

Had Mr. Bridges been able to cast in his lot with the daring young poets who assail society in behalf of the under men, who argue for new forms of pageantry in which the beaten down men shall carry their banners in the procession, the honor now suggested for him must necessarily have passed him by.[63]

Bridges' lyric poetry later than the 1913 *Poetical Works*, embodied in *October* (1920) and *New Verse* (1925), is chiefly interesting for its metrical experiments, and had no effect on his reputation. Between his appointment as Poet Laureate and the publication of *The Testament of Beauty*, it may be estimated that this reputation suffered a gradual but steady decline. With the free verse movement of the 1920's, the vogue of the Imagists, and the greater influence of French Symbolist poetry in the late twenties and early thirties, Bridges seemed less and less a contemporary poet. His work was seldom attacked; more frequently it was not discussed at all. The present neglect of Bridges' poetry needs no documentation. In explaining why he does not discuss Bridges in his survey of modern poetry, F. R. Leavis, a minor acolyte in the critical temple of T. S. Eliot, gives a more or less representative opinion:

At this point it becomes necessary to mention a name that has been left out of the foregoing account — that of Bridges. . . . If one does not care for him one may say that he is so academic that there is no reason why he should come anywhere in particular. If one feels respectful one may compare him to Landor and say that he is aloof.[64]

Although Brett Young maintained that as a lyric poet Bridges "is more consistently fine than Keats," [65] by far the most faithful as well as the most vocal of his admirers has been an American critic, Yvor Winters:

It has long appeared to me that Bridges and Hardy must be regarded as the two most impressive writers of poetry in something like two centuries, perhaps since Milton; if Hardy is likely to appear the greater of the two on the first consideration, by virtue in part of the greater number of his highly successful lyrics, in part of the simpler, and thus more directly accessible richness of his feeling, Bridges may gain on more mature consideration, as a result of greater intellectual scope and of a wider diversity of artistic mastery. Bridges is certainly the more mature, complex, and, morally speaking, the more rich of the two men. Hardy at his best offers a kind of summation of folk wisdom: it is his power and his limitation. Bridges, though he may not be invariably the most sound of thinkers or of critics, is the heir of the universities, the descendant of Arnold and of Landor, of Herbert and of Milton; his subject-matter is the full experience of the civilized man.[66]

It is necessary, to complete this survey of Bridges' career as a lyric poet, to return to the seemingly inactive years following the publication of *New Poems*, and to the years immediately preceding that volume. The four parts of the *Yattendon Hymnal* were published between 1895 and 1899: these contained many translations, adaptations and original hymns. Besides essays on diverse subjects, there was a new version of *Milton's Prosody* (1901) and another Miltonic masque, *Demeter* (1904). Bridges' chief attention during these years, however, was devoted to experiments in classical prosody.

The time and effort involved in these experiments has never been fully appreciated. Mrs. Bridges believes that the first attempts to test William Johnstone Stone's theories of quantitative verse were made in 1898. The experiments were continued diligently until 1913. Mrs. Bridges says that when her husband first began to write in quantitative verse he would sometimes work all day without finishing to his satisfaction a single line. The primary difficulty was the necessity of learning to "*think* in quantities," [67] but the necessity of revising Stone's rules was a further obstacle to easy composition. The sixty-six pages of poems in classical prosody included in the one-volume *Poetical Works* probably represent the most rigorous poetical effort of Bridges' career.

These poems will be considered elsewhere. The important thing is that the effort changed Bridges' style. The difference between the lyrics of *New Poems* and *New Verse* is not merely the difference between accentual-syllabic and syllabic verse: in most of the poetry after *Poems in Classical Prosody* we may observe a tendency to "play with words." There is a much larger proportion of polysyllabic words, of archaisms and inventions. The difference in style, whether for better or worse, seems undeniably due to the effort required in finding words to fit classical quantities. Such poems as "Wintry Delights" created not only a new subject-matter but a new diction; it is the subject-matter and diction of *The Testament of Beauty*:

> Where the turrets and domes of pictured Tuscany slumber,
> Or the havoc'd splendours of Rome imperial, or where
> Glare the fretted minarets and mosks of trespassing Islam,
> And old Nilus, amid the mummied suzerainty of Egypt,
> Glideth, a godly presence, consciously regardless of all things,
> Save his unending toil and eternal recollections.

Even the shorter poems written in this prosody are philosophical rather than lyric in subject; the same emphasis appears in the next volume, *October*, which contains the first experiments in Neo-Miltonic syllabics. These experiments led to the last two years in which Bridges felt a strong impulse to write lyric poetry: 1913 and 1921. As we see by Bridges' note to the collection,[68] a new form (strictly syllabic verse) arrived at through the study of another poet was the primary source of inspiration. The following account of the composition of "The Flowering Tree" is of great interest:

One cannot originate a poem in an unknown metre, for it is familiarity with the frame-work which invites the words into their places, and in this dilemma I happily remembered that I had had for many years a poem in my head which had absolutely refused to take any metrical form. Whenever I had tried to put it into words the metre had ruined it. The whole poem was, so far as feeling and picturing went, complete in my imagination, and I set to work very readily on it, and with intense interest to see what would come. I was delighted to find that the old difficulty of mastering it had vanished, and it ran off quite spontaneously to its old title *The Flowering Tree*, which I dated in my book Nov. 7, 1913.

I had written it in sixes, that is in twelves with a caesural break: and it was no doubt the subject which led me to choose that form. Having exploited it as I thought successfully, and arrived at very rich and varied rhythms, it was after that single experiment a very definite form of marked effects and possibilities which I could use now at will; or, at least, it was ready within me to receive or reject anything that arose.[69]

A few paragraphs later Bridges tells of his last impulse to write lyric poetry, an impulse resulting not only in the Neo-Miltonic syllabics of *New Verse*, but also in his last accentual-syllabic poems.[70] One of these is the great lyric "Low Barometer." Bridges' abandonment of the accentual-syllabic prosody occurred at about the same as his relative abandonment of rhyme. Nearly all of Bridges' friends with whom I have spoken were impressed by his very strong distaste for rhyme in his later years, a distaste revealed not only in the poems, but in the "Letter to a Musician on English Prosody." [71]

Interesting as the last volumes are for their metrical experiments, they offered not more than a dozen important short poems. With the exception of these, Bridges' best lyrics were written before 1900, either in accentual or accentual-syllabic meters. The reason for Bridges' abandonment of the accentual-syllabic prosody is not far to seek: he had gone as far in that prosody as it was possible for him to go. The *Shorter Poems*, while very even in quality, reveal an exploitation of most of the resources and devices for variation possible within the given forms. We have seen that while Bridges developed his powers unusually late, so that his career as a poet may be said to have begun in 1872, he was in full possession of those powers by 1879. Much of the development which occurred during these seven years, much of the success of the period which followed, may be attributed to his sensitive study of earlier poets.

CHAPTER TWO

Heritage

Where couldst thou words of such a compass find?
Whence furnish such a vast expense of mind?
MARVELL, *On Mr. Milton's Paradise Lost*

The process which Wordsworth condemns as vicious, that
is, the loving discipleship from poet to poet, and the long
bond of influence and association uniting the oldest to the
newest, is the normal and healthy method for the progress
of poesy.

MURRAY, *The Classical Tradition in English Poetry*

T A TIME when the field of poetry seems divided between radical innovators and such dubious allies of traditionalism as T. S. Eliot and Ezra Pound, self-consciously in quest of the most esoteric literary allusions, a study of a naturally and unpretentiously traditional poet would seem to be of particular value. One of Bridges' best friends, curiously enough, was the most radical innovator of his day. Gerard Hopkins, who would have agreed with Edward Young that "illustrious examples *engross, prejudice* and *intimidate*,"[1] wrote to Bridges: "The effect of studying masterpieces is to make me admire and do otherwise. So it must be on every original artist to some degree, on me to a marked degree."[2] Bridges, on the other hand, knew that true and significant originality could be based only on inherited achievement: in the Dolben memoir he refers to "the classical authors of antiquity, whose masterpieces are

the grammar of literary art,"[3] and in "The Necessity of Poetry" he advocates "a long apprenticeship in studying the works of the great masters. Not that we are to be enslaved to those old models; but until we understand them we shall not understand either the limit of our faculties or the conditions of success."[4] Yet he was acutely aware of the dangers of slavish imitation and uncritical traditionalism: "No art," he wrote, "can flourish that is not alive and growing, and it can only grow by invention of new methods or by discovery of new material,"[5] and "In all fields of Art the imitators are far more numerous than the artists, and they will copy the externals, in poetry the Versification and the Diction, which in their hands become futile."[6]

The difference between critical and slavish traditionalism is commonly assumed, but only too frequently forgotten; and if the distinction is forgotten it is only too easy to classify Alfred Noyes and Austin Dobson with Yeats and Bridges as "traditional poets." The unimaginative traditionalist may always be pigeon-holed into a particular school, as Somerville, for instance, is pigeon-holed into the "school of Milton." Such poets as Yeats and Bridges, on the other hand, cannot be assigned to a particular school: through the study of a wide variety of poets they achieved a timeless aesthetic isolation, and defy easy classification. The truly traditional poet takes his traditionalism for granted, he is able to discriminate between the merits and faults of a given poet's work, and he understands not only the style of an earlier poet, but also the mental attitude which informed that style.

More than in any other poet of our time, we may see in Bridges the results of a truly catholic poetic education — though like every education his was at first fumbling and incomplete. In Bridges' study of Milton, for instance, we observe various stages of growth: direct but defective imitation, as in the earliest sonnets of *The Growth of Love*; successful direct imitation resulting in *pastiche*, as in the first lines of *Prometheus the Firegiver*, which are virtually interchangeable with the first lines of *Comus*; finally, the appearance of an individual style which retains much that has been learned, but which blends with it lessons learned from other poets, as in the sonnets which can be called neither Miltonic nor Shakespearean, yet which could not have been written without a sensitive knowledge of both Milton and Shakespeare.

Bridges' study of Heine reveals especially clearly the critical and selective quality of his imitation. Bridges admired the flawless stylist, but in his later poetry repudiated the cynical ironist: "Heine's file was as full of genius as his soul, so that, like Beethoven, the more he retouched his work the nearer it approached the perfect ease of spontaneity," [7] but "he is often contemptuous and infected with a cynicism — to use an old word in its modern sense — which is antagonistic to what is spiritual." [8] The type of poem in which Heine's influence appears usually defines a single mood in terms of external nature; in the last lines the human application of the melancholy scene is revealed. "I found today out walking" has no parallel in Heine's poems, but in every way — compactness, subject, and feeling — it sounds like a translation from the *Buch der Lieder*:

> There was no snake uncurling,
>   And no thorn wounded me;
> 'Twas my heart checked me, sighing
>   She is beyond the sea.

There are four other poems which in the same way show imitation not only of style but of feeling: "A poppy grows upon the shore," "A winter's night with the snow about," "My bed and pillow are cold" and "The evening darkens over." "In der Fremde" is an unusually fine translation of the first poem of a group of five by Heine similarly entitled. I quote the final lines from each:

> Doch weiter, weiter, sonder Rast,
> Du darfst nicht stille stehn;
> Was du so sehr geliebet hast,
> Sollst du nicht wiedersehn.

> Thy trembling is in vain
> as thy wand'ring shall be.
> What so well thou lovest
> thou nevermore shalt see.

Heine was very popular at the time Bridges began to write, and it was natural that he should have found in the German poet a literary model. He retained to the end a fondness for his old master, according to Mrs. Bridges, and his library contains several editions of the complete works. But while he was partly guided by Heine in formulating rules for the composition of accentual verse as late as 1921,[9] he quickly outgrew the German's romantic melancholy. He comments on Heine's influence in what was to be one of his last lyric poems written in accentual-syllabic meter, "Buch der Lieder":

> Be these the selfsame verses
> That once when I was young
> Charm'd me with dancing magic
> To love their foreign tongue,
>
> . . . .
>
> Alas, how now they are wither'd!
> And fallen from the skies
> In yellowy tawny crumple
> Their tender wreckage lies,
>
> And all their ravisht beauty
> Strewn 'neath my feet to-day
> Rustles as I go striding
> Upon my wintry way.

Gerard Hopkins, with his naive insistence on absolute originality, objected to the overtones of verbal reminiscence even more than to this very general kind of influence: "The echoes are a disease of education, literature is full of them; but they remain a disease, an evil."[10] Of such literary echoes Bridges wrote:

Shades of meaning more delicate than could ever be invented, intricate poetic allusion, with consequent command of emotion and adaptability to the most subtle varieties of feeling, glints of color from all climes and times — these are qualities which give distinction to much of the best of our modern literature. There is truly no kind of beauty more liable to mishandling, no artistic effect more uncertain and more fugitive, than that produced by these half-tones, as we may call them; yet to-day in Europe they are the legitimate and natural wealth of our inheritance, and it would be pedantry to depreciate it.[11]

Though his practice varies from poem to poem, Bridges frequently enriches his lyrics by the deliberate use of such half-tones. The great elegy, "The Summer House on the Mound," yields an unusually full harvest of literary allusion and reminiscence, and likewise illustrates the fashion in which Bridges draws, in a single poem, from several sources. The poem may have been suggested by the reading of Tennyson's "Maud" and "To the Rev. F. D. Maurice." In 1854 the forty-five year old Tennyson and the ten-year old Bridges were watching the expanse of water which divided the Isle of Wight from Walmer, in Kent, where Bridges lived as a boy. It was on that expanse of water that they watched Napier's fleet sail to the Baltic:

> . . . I saw the dreary phantom arise and fly
> Far into the North, and battle, and seas of death.
> — "Maud"

> Where, if below the milky steep
> Some ship of battle slowly creep,
> And on thro' zones of light and shadow
> Glimmer away to the lonely deep.
> — "To the Rev. F. D. Maurice"

> One noon in March upon that anchoring ground
> Came Napier's fleet unto the Baltic bound:
> Cloudless the sky and calm and blue the sea,
> As round Saint Margaret's cliff mysteriously,
> Those murderous queens walking in Sabbath sleep
> Glided in line upon the windless deep. . . .
> — "The Summer House on the Mound"

Undoubtedly the sight of the ships sailing to war was never forgotten by Bridges, but he may never have considered its possibilities for poetry until he read Tennyson's two poems. This reading may have revivified the scene, and provoked as well the feeling that Tennyson had missed a great poetic opportunity by introducing the ships so casually into his two poems. To be sure this is a matter for conjecture (even though Bridges quotes the lines from "To the Rev. F. D. Maurice" in his anthology, *The Chilswell Book of English Poetry*); the lines I have quoted show no direct borrowing. There are, however, instances of real conveyance from Milton and Shakespeare as well as from Tennyson. The reference to *Macbeth* gives great impact to the line,

> Those murderous queens walking in Sabbath sleep,

while Bridges'

> Fairer than dream of sleep, than Hope more fair
> Leading to dreamless sleep her sister Care,

seems an ingenious, if perhaps unconscious, reworking of lines from Tennyson's "Ode to Memory":

> In sweet dreams softer than unbroken rest
> Thou leddest by the hand thine infant Hope.

There are three unmistakable echoes of Milton, and they are drawn from three different poems:

> The Roman wolf, scratches with privy paw

comes from the famous line in "Lycidas":

> Besides what the grim wolf with privy paw,

while

> Or some immense three-decker of the line,
> Romantic as the tale of Troy divine,

surely owes something to "Il Penseroso":

> Presenting Thebes, or Pelops line
> Or the tale of Troy divine.

Less conscious, perhaps, is the clear indebtedness of

> Prone on the deck to lie outstretch'd at length,
> Sunk in renewal of their wearied strength,

to "L'Allegro":

> And, stretched out all the chimney's length,
> Basks at the fire his hairy strength.

In slightly over a hundred lines we have five unmistakable conveyances from five works by three different poets!

These do not, of course, exhaust the types of overtone found
in Bridges' poetry. Occasionally a line is taken directly from an
earlier work to indicate a more general indebtedness. Thus in
Eros and Psyche the line

> So now in steadfast love and happy state,[12]

serves as a gracious admission of the obvious Spenserian influence
on the poem's diction and stanza form. In *The Testament of
Beauty*, particularly, we shall find instances of paraphrase, as in
this passage deriving from St. Francis' "Canticle of the Sun":

> *Praisèd be thou, my Lord, for my sister, Mother Earth,
> who doth sustain and govern us and bringeth forth
> all manner of fruit and herb and flowers of myriad hue.*[13]

In "To Robert Burns . . . An Epistle on Instinct" we observe
still another way in which Bridges' reading acted on his imagination. Here Bridges uses the stanza-form which Wordsworth used
in "At the Grave of Burns" and "To the Sons of Burns":

> Through twilight shades of good and ill
> Ye now are panting up life's hill,
> And more than common strength and skill
>   Must ye display;
> If ye would give the better will
>   Its lawful sway.
>
> > — "To the Sons of Burns"

The feelings soft, the spirits gay
Entice on such a flowery way,
And sovran youth in high heyday
Hath such a fashion
To glorify the bragging sway
Of sensual passion.
— "To Robert Burns . . . An Epistle on Instinct"

The same kind of indirect literary allusion is found in "A Vignette," where a stanza which is almost a translation of part of Caedmon's hymn enforces the resemblance by the use of a similar verse-structure:

To them for canopy
The vault of heaven,
The flowery earth
for carpet is given.

Diction may result in even more obvious overtones, as in the following lines:

Francis Jammes, so grippeth him Nature in her caresses, . . .[14]

And drave them to the fold like sheep. . . .[15]

By soaring thought detained to tread full low. . . .[16]

No reader will miss the intentional reminders of Chaucer, the King James Version, and Milton.

The way in which Bridges' reading fed his imagination and the relationship of imitation to original creation may be observed most distinctly in poems admittedly based on earlier work. A brief study of *Eros and Psyche* should therefore be of interest. While Spenser's was the greatest stylistic influence on the poem, the basic source was the *Metamorphoses*. *Eros and Psyche* appeared in the same year as *Marius the Epicurean* and at a time when *The Earthly Paradise* was already well known, but Bridges read neither Pater's nor Morris' version of the story.[17] In sequence

of event and dramatic workmanship Bridges follows Apuleius
exactly.[18]

Bridges wrote of his substitution of "Hellenism for Latin vulgarity" as though he had been forced to change many passages,
but, as Professor Bush remarks, "The Hellenizing of the story
hardly goes beyond the substitution of Greek names for Latin
ones."[19] Aphrodite does not call Psyche a harlot, and three examples of Apuleius' realism are excised. Psyche "simplicissima,"
for instance, is allowed to count "to herself the months and
days,"[20] but is not permitted the second part of Apuleius' sentence: "crescentes dies et menses exeuntes numerat, et sarcinae
nesciae rudimento miratur de brevi punetulo tantum incrementu-
lum locupletis uteri."[21] In one case at least the sacrifice of earthi-
ness to respectability seems to involve a real loss. The second sister,
envious of Psyche's royal household, says:

Ego vero maritum articulari etiam morbo complicatum curiatumque,
ac per hoc rarissimo Venerem meam recolentem sustineo, plerumque
detortos et duratos in lapidem digitos eius perfricans, formentis olidis
et pannis sordidis et faetidis cataplasmatibus maun tam delicitas istas
adurens, nec uxoris officiosam faciem sed medicae laboriosam personam
sustinens.[22]

Bridges reduces this to

> 'Ay,' said the other, 'to a gouty loon
> Am I not wedded? . . .'

Bridges embellishes his original in three ways: he inserts allusions to classical mythology not found in Apuleius, as in the list
of Nereids in March 28 or in the splendid description of Talos,
"the metal giant," in April 13 and 14; he uses more description
and imagery, frequently making a detachable lyric poem out of
some bare prose statement, and he has his characters reflect about
their actions and feelings at greater length.

The thirteen stanzas April 18–30, expanded from fifteen lines
of prose,[23] are typical of the greater diffuseness of Bridges' treat-

ment, but the diffuseness seems justified by many stanzas of fine lyricism:

> And now the sun was sunk; only the peak
> Flash'd like a jewel in the deepening blue:
> And from the shade beneath none dared to speak,
> But all look't up, where glorified anew
> Psyche sat islanded in living day.
> Breathless they watcht her till the last red ray
> Fled from her lifted arm that waved adieu.

Usually Bridges' profits by Apuleius' felicities. There are a few exceptions. The lines of July 17,

> Eros, 'twas Eros' self, her lover, he,
> The God of love, reveal'd in deathless bloom,

seem a poor substitute for Apuleius' admirable touch — "she saw the meekest and sweetest of all beasts" —

videt omnium ferarum mitissimam dulcissimaque bestiam, ipsum illum lupidenem formosum deum formose cubantem, cuius aspectu lucernae quoque lumen hilaratum increbruit et acuminis sacrilegi novaculam paenitebat.[24]

Bridges must have considered the razor turning its edge not "good sense."

More often, however, he not only takes full advantage of Apuleius' best lines, but finds the germ for excellent poetry in a casual word or phrase. In comparing July 28 with its original we see the poet's creative imagination at work. From the barren material — "Nec deus amator humi iacentem deserens, involavit proximiam cupressum deque eius alte cacumine sic eam graviter commotus affatur"[25] — comes the magnificent stanza:

> ... but he, upon the roof
> Staying his feet, awhile his flight delay'd:
> And turning to her as he stood aloof
> Beside a cypress, whose profoundest shade

Drank the reflections of the dreamy night
In its stiff pinnacle, the nimble light
Of million stars upon his body played.

Another interesting development of a phrase in Apuleius is seen in October 16. In *Metamorphoses* VI, 5 (which would be chronologically equivalent to the end of 'October') we find, "Isto quoque fortunae naufragio Psyche porterrita," but the fruit of this seed appears fourteen stanzas earlier than we might have expected:

Then Psyche's hope founder'd; as when a ship,
The morrow of the gale can hardly ride
The swollen seas, fetching a deeper dip
At every wave, and through her gaping side
And o'er her shattered bulwark ever drinks,
Till plunging in the watery wild she sinks,
To scoop her grave beneath the crushing tide. . . .

Perhaps the most felicitous embellishment of all, for which the only basis is "Tunc indignata Venus exclamavit,"[26] occurs in September 15 and 16. Once again we find the complete visualization, the full reliving of the tale:

Then said the snowy gull, 'O heavenly queen,
What is my knowledge, who am but a bird?
Yet is she only mortal, as I ween,
And namèd Psyche, if I rightly heard.' —
But Aphrodite's look daunted his cheer,
Ascare he flew away, screaming in fear,
To see what wrath his simple tale had stirr'd.

He flasht his pens, and sweeping widely round
Tower'd to air; so swift in all his way,
That whence he dived he there again was found
As soon as if he had but dipt for prey:
And now, o'er ere he join'd his wailful flock,
Once more he stood upon the Sirens' rock,
And preen'd his ruffl'd quills for fresh display.

Sometimes Bridges gains humorous effects by deliberate anachronism. In November 10 he is apparently trying to find a substitute for Apuleius' realism:

> All which he took his silver stile to write
> In letters large upon a waxèd board;
> Her age and name, her colour, face and height,
> Her home, and parentage, and the reward. . . .

The most audacious anachronism puts Newton several millennia before his time:

> But as a dead stone, from a height let fall,
> Silent and straight is gather'd by the force
> Of earth's vast mass upon its weight so small,
> In speed increasing as it nears its source
> Of motion — by which law all things soe'er
> Are clutch'd and dragg'd and held — so fell she there,
> Like a dead stone, down in her headlong course.

The lucidity and ease of statement so characteristic of Bridges' style are revealed even more in his translations than in his adaptations. The last lyric in the third book of *Shorter Poems* reveals in an interesting way the mutations of a poem passing through several hands. The original is from the *Alciphron* affixed to Thomas Moore's *The Epicurean*; this was translated by Gautier, and Bridges' poem is a translation of Gautier's rendering.[27] I quote the last two stanzas from the three poems:

> If danger and pain
>   And death you despise —
> On — for again
>   Into light you may rise, —
>
> Rise into light
>   With that secret Divine
> Now shrouded from sight
>   By the veils of the Shrine.[28]

Si, méprisant la mort,
Votre foi reste entière,
En avant! — le cœur fort
Reverra la lumière.

Et lira sur l'autel
Le mot du grand mystère
Qu'au profane mortel
Dérobe un voile austère.[29]

If thou canst Death defy,
If thy faith is entire,
Press onward, for thine eye
Shall see thy heart's desire.

Beauty and love are nigh,
And with their deathless quire
Soon shall thine eager cry
Be numbered and expire.

Readers interested in the possibilities of poetic translation should compare the translations by Bridges and George Santayana of Michelangelo's madrigal, "Gli occhi miei vaghi delle cose belle," and Bridges' adaptation of a nona rime stanza found in Trucchi's *Poesie italiane inedite*. The original texts, with the translations and adaptations, will be found in the Appendix on Sources and Analogues.

I do not wish to burden the perhaps already impatient reader with a lengthy catalogue of poetic allusions and conveyances; I have therefore relegated the citation of many parallel passages to a special Appendix, where those who wish to annotate their own copies of Bridges' poems or who are curious concerning the specific ways a poet uses his reading may find it. Literary influence, indeed, is a far more complex matter than may be solved by the mere comparison of texts. A very marked poetic influence, such as that of George Herbert on Bridges, may result in few instances of actual borrowing, few unmistakable overtones. In various ways Bridges' rhythms and diction, his rich simplicity and masterful control of material, his ability to reduce a complex emotional experience to clear and compressed statement, go back to Herbert. Their subject-matter is often the same, and its treatment in both poets involves a refined series of rejections. In both poets, we find a desire to put aside the claims of the world (though their religious views were different), together with a willingness to meet and a power to master human problems. The intricacies of Bridges' prosody, firmly bent on catching the varied rhythms of the human voice, owe much to a study of Herbert. Yet for all this considerable influence the number of verbal conveyances, some of which are noted in a later chapter,[30] is very small.

It should therefore suffice at this point to pass in brief and rapid review a few of the more obvious and general influences observable in Bridges' poetry. While Bridges' literary treatment of human love is Florentine rather than Elizabethan, and no less than four of his lyrics are modelled on madrigals of Michelangelo,[31] his *amoretti* owe even more in style and attitude to Spenser and other Elizabethan poets. This is particularly true of the purely "literary" lyrics which show no serious Florentine idealization of love. "My lady pleases me and I please her," for instance, derives its logical and argumentative form from Sidney's "The Bargain," which begins,

> My true Love hath my heart, and I have his,

while "Dear Lady, when thou frownest" seems to owe a great deal to Carew's "I'll gaze no more on her bewitching face." This poem, which is typical of Bridges' "literary" love-poetry, bears an even stronger resemblance to an anonymous madrigal quoted by Bridges in *The Chilswell Book of English Poetry*.[32]

The Christian Platonism and refined Puritanism which Bridges shares with Spenser is undoubtedly a matter of resemblance rather than influence. In style, however, Spenser left a very strong mark. Although *Eros and Psyche* is written in a variation of rhyme-royal (ababccb), even the stanza seems Spenserian, the use of many monosyllabic words in the final lines approximating the effect of twelve syllable lines. The second stanza of the poem illustrates the Spenserian tone of the poem, which is due to the use of particular constructions as well as to a fondness for archaic forms. Too often, as in *The Faerie Queene*, grammatical inversion is at the service of the rhymes:

> Three daughters had this King, of whom my tale
> Time hath preserved, that loveth to despise
> The wealth which men misdeem of much avail,
> Their glories for themselves that they devise;
> For clerkly is he, old hard-featured Time,
> And poets' fabl'd song and lovers' rhyme
> He storeth on his shelves to please his eyes.

Spenser's "Epithalamion" clearly inspired one of Bridges' finest poems of the 1873 volume, "On a Lady Whom Grief for the Death of her Betrothed Killed." This "Epitaph for an Epiphilamy" owes something both to *The Faerie Queene* stanza and to the rhyme-scheme of "Epithalamion," while many of the properties — the speaker's orders for the ceremony, the music and the flowers — seem directly borrowed:[33]

> Sound flute and tabor, that the bridal be
> Not without music, nor with these alone;
> But let the viol lead the melody,
> With lesser intervals, and plaintive moan
>   Of sinking semitone;
>   And, all in choir, the virgin voices
>   Rest not from singing in skilled harmony
> The song that aye the bridegroom's ear rejoices.

More important, however, than such direct resemblances are those which indicate, through syntax, similar imaginative processes. In the following lines, taken from Bridges' "Indolence" and from *The Faerie Queene* respectively, there is no question of conveyance, yet the passages are virtually interchangeable:

> But turned his wondering eyes from shore to shore;
> And our trim boat let her swift motion die,
> Between the dim reflections floating by.
>
> .   .   .   .   .   .
>
> To laugh at shaking of the leaves light
> Or to behold the water worke and play
> About her little frigot, therin making way.[34]

Shakespearean influence is most evident in the plays, which will be considered later, and in *The Growth of Love*. The opening lines of many of the sonnets are distinctly Shakespearean or at least Petrarchan–Elizabethan:

> In thee my spring of life hath bid the while
> A rose unfold beyond the summer's best,

but more often we find lines, such as "By precedent of terror past" or "A wreck of fairer fields to mourn," which have the pure Shakespearean accent without actual conveyance. The number of purely verbal echoes, such as

> But think not I can stain
> My heaven with discontent,[35]

is surprisingly small.

There is perhaps a closer affinity between the artistic aims of Milton and Bridges than between those of any other English poets. Both regarded lyric poetry as an art rather than as a vehicle for the expression of personality, and both were consequently stylists in the best sense. The same individualism and imaginative autonomy combines in both poets with a traditionalism seeking its inspiration in very diverse and apparently irreconcilable sources. Both knew classical literature, and wrote poems in Latin; both were keen students of music and wrote on music. Unlike Keats, Bridges never tried to escape Miltonic influence, for he knew Milton to be at the very center of English poetry: the centripetal force which drew together the various strands of English poetry from Chaucer to his own day, the centrifugal force which made that early poetry accessible to later poets.[36] Yet Bridges was conscious of one dangerous aspect of Milton's influence, and his "Neo-Miltonic syllabics" represent an effort to open new fields for experiment, to rebuild the bridges Milton had burned behind him by the absolute, and in a sense devastating, perfection of his style: " . . . Milton's blank verse practically ended as an original form with Milton."[37]

Milton's marked influence on Bridges' prosody and on the style of the masques *Prometheus the Firegiver* and *Demeter* will be considered in later chapters.[38] His influence on the lyric poetry is seen primarily in *The Growth of Love*. There is no sonnet in which some Miltonic characteristic, such as grammatical inversion or suspension of narrative verb, does not occur. Some of Bridges' inversions recall particular lines in Milton, as in

> Until at length your feeble steps and slow,

but the full extent of Milton's influence can be observed only through more ample quotation. The sonnet "To the President of Magdalen College, Oxford," for instance, only too patently announces its parentage in Milton's sonnet "To Mr. Lawrence":

> Since now from woodland mist and flooded clay
> I am fled beside the deep Devonian shore,
> Nor stand for welcome at your gothic door,
> 'Neath the fair tower of Magdalen and May,
> Such tribute, Warren, as fond poets pay
> For generous esteem, I write, not more
> Enhearten'd than my need is, reckoning o'er
> My life-long wanderings on the heavenly way. . . .

The closest emotional affinities are with the Milton of the earliest
period, the Milton of "Arcades" as well as "Il Penseroso." In both
poets a joy in nature alternates with a placid and not uncherished
literary melancholy. Bridges' two Spring Odes owe their structure to "L'Allegro" and "Il Penseroso," while the diction of "On
a Lady Whom Grief for the Death of her Betrothed Killed,"
though Spenserian on the whole, shows the influence of the
Nativity Ode.[39] "May Morning" and other short poems by
Milton show the generalized treatment of nature found in Bridges'
poems, and achieve their verbal music by the same means. The first
stanza of "There is a hill beside the silver Thames," for instance,
has the very tone of Sabrina's song.

I have already mentioned the influence of George Herbert.
Only Thomas Gray, among eighteenth-century poets, left a dis-
tinguishable mark on Bridges' language. Although the skepticism
of "Among the Tombs" as well as its six-line stanza (rhyming
ababcc) remind the reader of Arnold's "Grande Chartreuse,"the
diction of the poem is certainly imitative of Gray's elegy. The
first stanza illustrates the very strong resemblance:

> Sad, sombre place, beneath whose antique yews
> I come, unquiet sorrows to control;
> Amid thy silent mossgrown graves to muse
> With my neglected solitary soul;
> And to poetic sadness care confide,
> Trusting sweet Melancholy for my guide.

The enumeration of the "forgotten dead" in the sixth, seventh,
and eighth stanzas had its origin in Gray's poem, and while there
are a few lines, such as "Their pompous legends will no smile
awake" (compare "The boast of heraldry, the pomp of pow'r"),
which contain definite echoes, the closest stylistic resemblance
appears where there is no actual conveyance, as in

> Even the vainglorious title o'er the head
> Wins its pride pardon for its sorrow's sake.

Although Bridges was one of the most classical poets of his age, Keats and Shelley

> The masters young that first enthrallèd me,

remained among his favorite poets to the end, according to Mrs. Bridges, while Blake received unusually rich representation in the two anthologies. There are certain spiritual affinities between Bridges and Blake,

> Under even grief and pine
> Runs a joy with silky twine,

but the later poet was influenced to a much greater extent by Wordsworth, Keats and Shelley than by Blake. Wordsworth's influence on *The Testament of Beauty* was extensive; his influence on the lyrics was small. Between Shelley and Bridges as lyric poets, on the other hand, there are very strong affinities. Both writers mediated with unusual success between the Greek and Christian traditions, and both are poets of *joy*, of an ecstasy founded on a harmony of impulses. The stylistic likenesses appear chiefly in the nature-poetry, in the quality of the diction and the type of detail used, as well as in the delicate handling of muted accent. In Shelley's "The Question" and in Bridges' "Indolence" we see a similar and at times disturbing tendency to arrange the landscape into formal pictures; the poems seem to be about paintings of nature rather than about real living scenes. Again, the two poets sometimes show the same kind of intellectual imagination. Behind the two passages which follow, from Shelley's "The Recollection" [40] and Bridges' play *The First Part of Nero*, we may discern kindred ways of thinking in syntactical forms:

> . . . the silence there
> By such a chain was bound
> That even the busy woodpecker
> Made stiller by her sound
> The inviolable quietness. . . .

> None answered, and awhile
> Was such delay as makes the indivisible
> And smallest point of time various and broad.

Bridges' small book on Keats is essentially a statement of his own poetic beliefs. Many critics have accused Bridges (wrongly, I think) of what he in turn considers Keats' greatest fault: in his "devotion to natural beauty lies . . . one true reason for Keats' failure in the delineation of human character." [41] As we shall see in the next chapter, one of the finest characteristics of Bridges' nature poetry is its naturalness, its lack of artificial ornament and embellishment. Perhaps Bridges was conscious of his indebtedness when he wrote that Keats as a nature poet was "for ever drawing his imagery from common things, which are for the first time represented as beautiful." [42]

The audacious attempt to rival Keats in "Nightingales" fortunately resulted in one of Bridges' best poems. The feeling of the poem, the longing of the birds in the second and third stanzas, is that of Arnold's "Philomela," and thus in a sense contradicts Keats' longing, yet the style was obviously inspired by Keats' ode. The overtones range from actual echoes such as "Where are those starry woods?" ("Where are the songs of spring?") to similarity of feeling ("Whose pining visions dim, forbidden hopes profound") and to similarity of diction:

> From these sweet-springing meads and bursting boughs of May.

Bridges' unreflective nature poems are like those of Keats in many ways. The first lines of "The Garden in September" announce their parentage in the "Ode to Autumn":

> Now thin mists temper the slow-ripening beams
> Of the September sun. . . .

The same heavy richness, the same ripeness which is almost over-ripeness, "swells and plumps" the rhythms of the two poems, a richness obtained by a skillful fusion of sense and sound and by

the use of heavy liquid vowels. In both poems the phrase dominates the line:

> While ever across the path mazily flit,
> Unpiloted in the sun,
> The dreamy butterflies
> With dazzling colours powdered and soft glooms,
> White, black and crimson stripes, and peacock eyes,
> Or on chance flowers sit,
> With idle effort plundering one by one
> The nectaries of deepest-throated blooms.

I have already recorded several echoes from Tennyson; instances
of further conveyance from his poetry, as well as from that of
Byron and Arnold, will be found in the Appendix on Sources.
There remains to be considered here only the very general and
on the whole indefinable influence of Gerard Manley Hopkins.
This influence was much less extensive than might have been expected in view of the two poets' intimate friendship. There was
an irreducible difference in their attitudes toward poetry, and this
difference prevented any real influence. Although we do not have
Bridges' letters, the one-sided correspondence conveys the impression of two minds struggling through barriers of isolation,
each more than willing to meet the other half way, and, though
never meeting, trying to preserve the necessary illusion of
understanding.

Much has been written about the influence of Hopkins' "sprung-
rhythm" on Bridges' lyrics. As we shall see in a later chapter, this
influence was in fact very small. Hopkins was never satisfied with
Bridges' use of his "invention"; inevitably he turned a frame-
work for violent excited rhythms into something chastened and
subdued, something nearer to the norm of English meter. Although his practice resembled Ben Jonson's use of sprung-rhythm
as much as it did Hopkins', Bridges probably studied his friend's
poems, particularly the long "Wreck of the Deutschland," before writing such experiments as "A Passer-By," "The Downs,"

and "London Snow." Hence we find a few unimportant echoes, such as the following:

> Since, tho' he is under the world's splendour and wonder. . . .[43]
> Look at the stars! look, look up at the skies. . . .[44]

> Or peering up from under the white-mossed wonder,
> 'O look at the trees!' they cried, 'O look at the trees!'
> — "London Snow"

Both poets had the same desire for artistic perfection, and though this does not appear to the casual reader of his poetry, Hopkins was even more relentless in its pursuit than Bridges. He suggested numerous emendations in Bridges' poems, many of which were adopted while a greater number were ignored. Hopkins' pertinacity in insisting upon a particular emendation is seen in his objection to the word "domeless" in the first line of *Prometheus the Firegiver*:

> From high Olympus and the domeless courts.

Hopkins objected to "domeless" in letters dated November 4, 1882; December 1, 1882; December 20, 1882; on October 31, 1886, he took "the opportunity of renewing my protest against the first line of *Prometheus*."[45] He finally carried the day, and the definitive edition of the play reads,

> From high Olympus and the aetherial courts.

The true value of Hopkins' influence can be felt only after a careful reading of his letters. The *minutiae* of echoes and emendations and even of minor prosodic influence disappear before the important fact of intimate friendship and sympathy. The two poets provided for each other that encouragement and understanding necessary to even the poet most indifferent to public acclaim. In October 1879, Bridges was evidently very discouraged: "You ask whether I really think there is any good in your going on writing poetry."[46] We shall never know the true influence of

Hopkins' reply, but it was enough to make any poet go on writing:

If I were not your friend, I shd. wish to be the friend of the man that wrote your poems. They shew the eye for pure beauty and they shew, my dearest, besides, the character which is much more rare and precious. . . . Since I must not flatter or exaggerate I do not claim that you have such a volume of imagery as Tennyson, Swinburne, or Morris, though the feeling for beauty you have seems to me pure and exquisite; but in point of character, of sincerity or earnestness, of manliness, of tenderness, of humour, melancholy, human feeling, you have what they have not and seem scarcely to think worth having. . . .[47]

CHAPTER THREE

Nature Poetry

My tale is but a fable of God's fair tapestry
the decorated room wherein my spirit hath dwelt
from infancy a nursling of great Nature's beauty
which keepeth fresh my wonder as when I was a child.
— "The Tapestry"

ORTY–FOUR of the ninety-eight lyrics finally selected to make up the canon of *Shorter Poems* are unreflective descriptions of nature, while many more use imagery drawn exclusively from nature. Although the majority of the Edwardian and Georgian critics who have commented on Bridges' work agree that it is as a poet of the English countryside that he will be read, if at all, by posterity, the large proportion of nature poems at once indicates his most serious limitation as a lyric poet and emphasizes his isolation from poetic trends of the last twenty years. Bridges maintained to the end that " . . . spiritual elation and response to Nature is Man's generic mark,"[1] but the attitude of most contemporary poets is rather that of Ronald Bottrall:

Nightingales, Anangke, a sunset or the meanest flower
Were formerly the potentialities of poetry,
But now what have they to do with one another
With Dionysius or with me?[2]

Of the four methods of treating nature which Arnold distinguished — the conventional, the faithful, the Greek, and the magical — there is a large preponderance in Bridges' poetry of the "faithful": there are few of the visions which Wordsworth knew. Occasionally Bridges mentions having such visions of a spirit far more deeply interfused, but he speaks reticently of them, and hardly conveys the ecstasy to which he lays claim. The temptation of *word-painting* was even more present to the Victorians than that of cloudy pantheism. Detailed description may have been the particular genius of the Victorian poets and novelists, but it was often an evil genius, as anyone may observe by removing bodily from Hardy's novels all the descriptive passages (and there are many) which do not contribute to the atmosphere of the scene.

Lessing's objection to the attempt to paint in words[3] remains unanswerable. Complete accuracy of observation and fidelity to the object seen are sometimes the making of Bridges' nature poems as well as of those of Wordsworth, but more often their undoing. The poet whose eye is on the object is likely not only to give a piecemeal enumeration of detail but also to make his poem seem the description of a map or a picture rather than of an actual living scene. Bridges has many lines which rival Wordsworth's "View from the Top of Black Comb":

> the narrow map of Crete
> Lay like a fleck in azure 'neath his eye. . . .[4]

> to view the plain he has left, and see'th it now. . .
> mapp'd at his feet. . . .[5]

The quality of particularization which T. S. Eliot misses in *L'Allegro*, "the feeling of being in a particular place at a particular time,"[6] sometimes leads Bridges into awkward obscurities:

> We lost our landscape wide, and slowly neared
> An ancient bridge, that like a blind wall lay
> Low on its buried vaults to block the way.

> Then soon the narrow tunnels broader showed,
> Where with its arches three it sucked the mass
> Of water, that in swirl thereunder flowed,
> Or stood piled at the piers waiting to pass.

It is evident here that Bridges had too clearly in mind a particular place at a particular time, and that the scene offered an ordered and detailed picture which he dared not violate.

In one further way Bridges tries to rival the painter: he emphasizes color as strongly as Tennyson emphasizes odor, and though a society which investigates the relationship of vowels to colors was flourishing recently within a hundred yards of the British Museum, the attempt to convey color in poetry seems as impractical as Des Esseinte's symphony of perfumes. In these fine lines from "The storm is over":

> In grassy pools of the flood they sink and drown,
> Green-golden, orange, vermilion, golden and brown,

the second line, by its tone and rhythm, strengthens the imitative harmony of the first, but it does not at a first reading convey the desired impression of varied color. Here at least sound has certainly triumphed over sense.

Bridges' frequent use of nature-mood symbolism probably derived from his study of Heine and other German romantic poets. This symbolism, like so many other literary conventions with a certain limited validity, has been discredited by more than a century of insensitive use. At its best it may achieve a kind of perfect, though minor, success:

> The evening darkens over
> After a day so bright
> The windcapt waves discover
> That wild will be the night.
> There's sound of distant thunder.
>
> The latest sea-birds hover
> Along the cliff's sheer height;
> As in the memory wander
> Last flutterings of delight,
> White wings lost on the white.

> There's not a ship in sight;
> And as the sun goes under
> Thick clouds conspire to cover
> The moon that should rise yonder.
> Thou art alone, fond lover.

It cannot be denied that the very general details succeed in creating the mood which is defined in the final line, a line which draws together and justifies the other fourteen. A great many of Bridges' short *vignettes* attain the same kind of success, but it is the success of A. E. Housman; that is to say, facile and obvious:

> The weeping Pleiads wester,
> And I lie down alone.

The number of nature poems is less disturbing than the repeated tendency to draw illustration for human feelings from nature. Bridges' range of feeling is fairly wide, but he reduces this range by considering very different material in the same terms. He maintained the power of discrimination, but not the ability to convey his discrimination, the same imagery being applied to important and unimportant things — to the plight of one's own feelings, let us say, and to the plight of a tree. The intensity of feeling developed in the lyric which follows (an intensity resulting from the conditions of the creative act, specifically the use of sprung-rhythm, rather than from the contemplation of the tree-fall) is equal to that developed in lyrics of a similar length which deal with problems of a wide human pertinence, and greater than that of all but a few of the love poems:

> The hill pines were sighing,
> O'ercast and chill was the day:
> A mist in the valley lying
> Blotted the pleasant May.
>
> But deep in the glen's bosom
> Summer slept in the fire
> Of the odorous gorse-blossom
> And the hot scent of the brier.

A ribald cuckoo clamoured,
And out of the copse the stroke
Of the iron axe that hammered
The iron heart of the oak.

Anon a sound appalling,
As a hundred years of pride
Crashed, in the silence falling:
And the shadowy pine-trees sighed.

A more radical example of this lack of discrimination may be
observed in the poems on what may be called the drama of
seasonal or atmospheric change. While "The storm is over" is
representative of one kind of Bridges' nature poetry at its best,
it displays a nervous excitement far in excess of that warranted by
the subject. The poem is nevertheless a great stylistic success in a
loose accentual meter which usually prohibits genuine variation.
I quote the third of four stanzas:

But ah! the leaves of summer that lie on the ground!
What havoc! The laughing timbrels of June,
That curtained the birds' cradles, and screened their song,
That sheltered the cooing doves at noon,
Of airy fans the delicate throng, —
Torn and scattered around:
Far out afield they lie,
In the watery furrows die,
In grassy pools of the flood they sink and drown,
Green-golden, orange, vermilion, golden and brown,
The high year's flaunting crown
Shattered and trampled down.

Though a few of the early nature poems are too particularized in
the sense that they try to convey an actual remembered scene,
many others succeed through a careful and selective use of detail.
Bridges had the botanist's eye of Lord de Tabley, yet only once
or twice descends to Whitman-like inventory. His careful ob-

servation is tempered by striking imagery and by an affectionate
use of the pathetic fallacy:

> The hazel hath put forth his tassels ruffed;
>   The willow's flossy tuft
>   Hath slipped him free:
> The rose amid her ransacked orange hips
>   Braggeth the tender tips
>   Of bowers to be.

Finally, there are other nature poems in the generalized classical
manner which succeed through rhetorical splendor. In a few of
these poems the sound predominates over the meaning, but in
the best of them there is a perfect fusion of sense and sound. The
second stanza of the justly famous "A Passer-By" shows an unusually skillful use of imitative harmony:[7]

> I there before thee, in the country that well thou knowest,
>   Already arrived am inhaling the odorous air:
> I watch thee enter unerringly where thou goest,
>   And anchor queen of the strange shipping there,
>   Thy sails for awnings spread, thy masts bare;
> Nor is aught from the foaming reef to the snow-capped grandest
>   Peak, that is over the feathery palms more fair
> Than thou, so upright, so stately, and still thou standest.

In the final lines we see Bridges' photographic vision put to proper
use: that is, he attains the effect of a moving picture (which, as
Lessing said, is impossible for the painter or sculptor) rather than
that of a fixed, dead landscape. The eye roves, with the rising and
falling meter, from the reef to the top of the mountains (the rise
being accentuated by the separation of *peak* from its epithets);
then down to the feathery palms on the shore; then up once more
(again with the kinetic enjambement) to the ship. And the upright appearance of the ship is conveyed by the use of the dental *t*:

> Than thou, so upright, so stately, and still thou standest.

It is more easy to find and isolate the flaws of Bridges' nature poetry than to describe its virtues. Certainly Bridges has written as much fine poetry of the English countryside as any other poet, but that poetry will live because of its stylistic success rather than because of its descriptive fidelity. And it is certainly of less importance than the poetry concerned with significant human emotions. Mrs. Bridges told me that her husband wrote all of his poetry outdoors, but he also read outdoors. The country near Chilswell is that of the "bold, majestic downs," but only a few miles away, within clear view, are the white and gray towers of Oxford.

CHAPTER FOUR

The Life of Reason

Poetry, if pursued either by the poet or the reader . . .
should offer a means of enriching one's awareness of human
experience and of so rendering greater the possibility of
intelligence in the course of future action; and it should
offer likewise a means of inducing certain more or less constant habits of feeling, which should render greater the
possibility of one's acting, in a future situation, in accord-
ance with the findings of one's improved intelligence. It
should, in other words, increase the intelligence and
strengthen the moral temper. . . .

YVOR WINTERS, *Primitivism and Decadence*

Poetry has, naturally enough, not yet attempted the salvation of souls or the enlightenment of the understanding. . . .

C. S. LEWIS, *The Personal Heresy*

LTHOUGH MR. LEWIS would be more
correct if he were to say that poetry is today,
for one of the first times in its history,
making no conscious effort to enlighten the
understanding, the opinion that poetry is
essentially amoral has achieved such nearly
universal currency that a critic who intends to speak of the "moral
value" of a given poet is forced, in a sense, to defend his quixotic
and antediluvian bias. In the severity of its reaction against Victorian didacticism and more specifically against the Neo-Humanist
excesses of our own time, contemporary criticism has either

severed any connection between art and the realm of human values, or, with I. A. Richards, has attributed to poetry a moral value because it aids in the satisfaction of the greatest possible complex of impulses. The completeness as well as the severity of this reaction make it necessary for me to justify the subsequent discussion of Bridges' attitude toward some of the central problems of human experience and of his position in the history of modern ideas, and to establish that this discussion is not wholly irrelevant to a consideration of his merit as a poet.

It is a sad commentary on the criticism of the last century that it should still be necessary to reaffirm the distinction between *moral* and *didactic* poetry; between poetry that illumines or enriches human experience and poetry that "teaches a lesson," espouses a cause or offers a noble example. Had the earliest translators of Aristotle and the first opponents of Puritan censorship substituted the word *human* for the word *moral*, they would have forestalled three centuries of critical confusion and they would have come closer to the meaning of their Greek master as well. Literature is moral if it has genuine human pertinence, and if it is realistic — that is to say, if its interpretations are based on a sound conception of human nature and if its record of how people feel and behave is accurate. If not immediately, at least ultimately, the great writer is concerned with making his readers see something of significance that they have not already seen. He may even wish to make us see something of that "sub-human and subrational" chaos with which Irving Babbitt felt the great writer should not be concerned: he may wish to make us see the private world of the criminal or the lunatic, or the unfathomable depths of the unconscious. For this reason, and to a certain degree regardless of whether the attitude of these authors is one of acceptance, rejection or indifference, the works of William Faulkner, James Joyce, John O'Hara, Ernest Hemingway and D. H. Lawrence (to mention only a few contemporary novelists who are often accused of being "immoral") are of moral value: they have added something to what we already knew about the workings of man's mind.

All this may seem pitifully obvious to the enlightened critic; but the number of enlightened critics is few, and their opinions have small weight in the recording of literary history. Restoration comedy is still condemned and dismissed as immoral, even by those critics and scholars who insist that moral concerns should have no place in literary criticism. Yet it is fairly obvious that Restoration comedy, with its cynical awareness that egotism, greed and sexual desire are strong motives for conduct, was based on a far sounder conception of human nature than the sentimental comedy which followed it. The writers of Restoration comedy observed how men behaved and made some shrewd surmises as to why they behaved so; the writers of sentimental comedy not only ignored contemporary life but rejected any reasonable psychology. For this reason Restoration comedy has considerable moral value, and sentimental comedy has none. For the same reason Racine, with his portraits of unbridled passion, has greater moral value than Corneille, in whose plays the triumph of will over passion is reduced to scarcely more than a mechanical formula.

I do not mean, by this brief defence of liberty to explore all levels of human experience, to imply that the attitude which an author takes toward his subject is of no moral significance: poetry especially is the expression of attitudes toward experience. If it were necessary to weigh the exact relative moral value of dramatists, we would have to place the angry and outraged Wycherley higher in our moral Pantheon than the gentle and complacent Etherege; but the really important fact is that both were, in the truest sense, realists, and that both therefore have real moral pertinence.

I hope I have dissociated myself, in the preceding paragraphs, from some of the narrower Neo-Humanist attitudes. There remains, however, the peculiar inability of the Neo-Humanists in general, and of Irving Babbitt in particular, to understand lyric poetry. Babbitt was a great moral philosopher, one of the few great moral philosophers this country has produced, but his concern with firm and well-defined ethical attitudes blinded him to the fact that a poem, because of its formal structure, can mean more or less than it literally says. There is certainly more to be observed about the "Ode to the West Wind" than that it pushes "the reciprocity between man and nature to a point where the landscape is not only a state of the soul but the soul is a state of the landscape,"[1] and only a critic insensitive to the nature of poetic perception could call Tennyson's grandiloquent line on Virgil,

Thou majestic in thy sadness at the doubtful doom of human kind,

"one of the finest in nineteenth century English poetry."[2] It is clear that in these two instances, at least, Babbitt failed to distinguish between the moral and the didactic, and failed to understand the true nature of poetic communication.

A great poem enriches the experience and understanding of its reader, but only seldom through what it literally says, and almost never through the precepts it offers. It deals with a significant human experience; it can hardly fail to take an attitude toward that experience. The more significant the experience and the more reasonable and consistent the attitude, the better the poem. But above all we must remember that poetic perception is the act of willing, seeing or understanding something, and that it is different from a normal everyday act of willing, seeing and understanding only because it involves a richer act of contemplation and rewards us with a fuller success. Here I am glad to join hands with G. Rostrevor Hamilton, elsewhere a leader in the attack on the moral function of poetry: "Poetry has value, both directly and indirectly, for the ordering of the mind: directly, since the poetic experience is itself marked by fine order; indirectly, since it promotes a contemplative habit of mind,"[3] and particularly with I. A. Richards, who regards poetry as "the unique linguistic instrument by which our minds have ordered their thoughts, emotions, desires. . . ."[4]

It should be evident from the foregoing that I do not propose to judge Bridges as a poet merely on the basis of his acceptance or rejection of a particular philosophy. His attitude toward emotional naturalism, which I shall discuss in the present chapter, certainly contributes to his moral stature as a poet. But it probably contributes less than the complex technique of contemplation which I shall examine more fully in the fifth chapter.

The great number of nature poems suggests affiliations with the early nineteenth century romantics, but Bridges' poetry as a whole is classical in feeling and style. Bridges' attitude toward romantic emotional naturalism is defined in the two spring odes: "Invitation to the Country" and "Reply." Their affinities are not with the Rousseauistic Wordsworth, but with the Wordsworth of the "Ode to Duty." In the "Invitation" one stanza summarizes the Rousseauistic ideal:

> Far sooner would I choose
> The life of brutes that bask,
> Than set myself a task,
> Which inborn powers refuse:
> And rather far enjoy
> The body, than invent
> A duty, to destroy
> The ease which nature sent. . . .

The "Reply" is explicit not only in its distrust of emotional naturalism, but of the romantic melancholy convention:

> One long in city pent
> Forgets or must complain:
> But think not I can stain
> My heaven with discontent;
> Nor wallow with that sad,
> Backsliding herd, who cry
> That Truth must make man bad,
> And pleasure is a lie.

Rather while Reason lives
To mark me from the beast,
I'll teach her serve at least
To heal the wound she gives:
Nor need she strain her powers
Beyond a common flight,
To make the passing hours
Happy from morn till night.

The number of poems dealing with the rejection of melancholy
or skepticism indicates that Bridges was troubled by these feelings during the years when he was beginning to write, and that
he recognized the need of solving the inner conflict which resulted from them. "The wood is bare" probably owes its immature and sickly melancholy to the poverty of its models, but there
are other poems in which the despair or skepticism is more than
literary. This skepticism is of various kinds — distrust of self, of
nature, of reason, of God. "O weary pilgrims, chanting of your
woe," for instance, though it uses a religious image, describes the
poet's failure in his Platonic pilgrimage toward Absolute Beauty.
"If I could but forget and not recall" is the first of a series of eight
"dark sonnets" which reveal various kinds of dissatisfaction. Like
sonnets 42 and 39, it is a conventional lament for the lost innocence and faith of childhood. Sonnets 43 and 44 consider the
futility of hopeless desire and the evanescence of joy; 45 faces a
feeling of disintegration. In 46, as the result of lost love, the poet
holds "all mortal things at strife," and 48, a great stylistic success,
is a Shelleyan invocation to sleep: "O shew and shadow of my
death." Sonnet 47 expresses doubt of immortality:

What is man's privilege, his hoarding knack
Of memory with foreboding so combined,
Whereby he comes to dream he hath of kind
The perpetuity which all things lack?

Which but to hope is doubtful joy, to have
Being a continuance of what, alas,
We mourn, and scarcely bear with to the grave;

> Or something so unknown that it o'erpass
> The thought of comfort, and the sense that gave
> Cannot consider it thro' any glass.

These eight sonnets form a connected series, and define a pessimistic skeptical attitude which was more or less the attitude of the age. This attitude is considered objectively in "The spirit's eager sense for sad and gay," the next sonnet, and repudiated in those which follow. While the obstacles and feelings of doubt in the "dark sonnets" were apparently created for the last poems to knock down or reject, they seem, in their own right, thoroughly genuine.

In "Among the Tombs" we may observe the poet's mind at the moment when he has realized that his skepticism is an incomplete and immature attitude, but has not yet been able to conquer that skepticism. He has arrived at the point of Gray's "Elegy Written in a Country Churchyard" or of Arnold's "Grande Chartreuse," and realizes the necessity of going beyond it. His attempt to do so is not successful. Although Bridges' elegy is polished and skillful in execution, and although the skepticism of the ninth stanza is partly qualified by the three succeeding stanzas, the feeling of the poem is on the whole self-indulgent. The apparent development of the theme is unexceptionable: the poet comes to the graveyard "unquiet sorrows to control" and largely succeeds in doing so, but the underlying quality of feeling — emphasized by echoes from the stereotyped diction of the eighteenth century Graveyard school — is one of abandonment to a kind of diseased melancholy:

> With my neglected solitary soul;
> And to poetic sadness care confide,
> Trusting sweet Melancholy for my guide.

The poem which follows "Among the Tombs," "Dejection," is one of a very large group of poems rejecting this mood. It is a brief and compact poem of great distinction:

Wherefore to-night so full of care,
My soul, revolving hopeless strife,
Pointing at hindrance, and the bare
Painful escapes of fitful life?

Shaping the doom that may befall
By precedent of terror past:
By love dishonoured, and the call
Of friendship slighted at the last?

By treasured names, the little store
That memory out of wreck could save
Of loving hearts, that gone before
Call their old comrade to the grave?

O soul, be patient: thou shalt find
A little matter mend all this;
Some strain of music to thy mind,
Some praise of skill not spent amiss.

Again shall pleasure overflow
Thy cup with sweetness, thou shalt taste
Nothing but sweetness, and shalt grow
Half sad for sweetness run to waste.

O happy life! I hear thee sing,
O rare delight of mortal stuff!
I praise my days for all they bring,
Yet are they only not enough.

The great compression and the pure simplicity of statement
testify, even more than the reversal of the last three stanzas, to the
poet's mastery of his own confused and immature feelings. Bridges
was not always so successful when depending, as in this poem, on
abstract rhetoric, but the richness of the first three stanzas, the
quiet and bitter irony of the fourth, and the convincing feeling
of the last two, demonstrate the possibility of success in this
manner.

In several poems thus rejecting pessimism Bridges explains that the mood is a characteristically youthful one, and that the mature man should overcome it. The first of the two quotations which follow may have been a conscious *apologia* for his refusal to take the tragic view of life which so many poets and critics consider necessary to the creation of great poetry:

> Ye thrilled me once, ye mournful strains,
>   Ye anthems of plaintive woe,
> My spirit was sad when I was young,
>   Ah sorrowful long-ago!
> But since I have found the beauty of joy
>   I have done with proud dismay:
> For howso'er man hug his care
>   The best of his art is gay.
>
> .   .   .   .   .   .
>
> For Fancy cannot live on real food:
> In youth she will despise familiar joy
> To dwell in mournful shades; as they grow real,
> Then buildeth she of joy her fair ideal.

The second passage should be compared with Wordsworth's "Ode to Lycoris":

> In youth we love the darksome lawn
> Brushed by the owlet's wing.
>
> .   .   .   .   .   .
>
> Still, as we nearer draw to life's dark goal,
> Be hopeful Spring the favourite of the soul.

The recurrence of the word "joy" in Bridges' poetry invites the reader to examine the longest poem on this subject: "Joy, sweetest lifeborn joy," a poem marred only by the stereotyped diction and monotonous rhythm into which Bridges fell whenever he used the seven-line stanza. In the early stanzas the romantic conception of poetic sensibility is assumed: the poet, though he builds the "towers fair and strong" of Joy, is also more susceptible

to mental pain than the common mortal — a favorite idea of
Chateaubriand and Byron:

> Sense is so tender, O and hope so high,
> That common pleasures mock their hope and sense;
> And swifter than doth lightning from the sky
> The ecstasy they pine for flashes hence,
> Leaving the darkness and the woe immense. . . .

This kind of feeling is varied through six stanzas, the fourth being
another statement of skepticism:

> And heaven and all the stable elements
> That guard God's purpose mock us, though the mind
> Be spent in searching: for his old intents
> We see were never for our joy designed:
> They shine as doth the bright sun on the blind,
> Or like his pensioned stars, that hymn above
> His praise, but not toward us, that God is love.

The last three stanzas bring the familiar reversal: "Then comes
the happy moment":

> not a stir
> In any tree, no portent in the sky:
> The morn doth neither hasten nor defer,
> The morrow hath no name to call it by,
> But life and joy are one, — we know not why, —
> As though our very blood long breathless lain
> Had tasted of the breath of God again.

Usually such reversals in Bridges' poetry seem not so much in-
sincere as too obvious. But in this poem, in spite of the fine compression of the third and fourth lines in the fifth stanza, the last
three stanzas are the best: the poet's supersensuous experience is
made real in such various ways as the use of Biblical overtones
("Divinity hath surely touched my heart"); of overtones from
the great mystics, perhaps Herbert in particular ("And having
tasted it I speak of it") and from the lines in *Macbeth* which best

summarize Shakespeare's skepticism (the same metaphor being used with an opposite application):

> Urging to tell a tale which told would seem
> The witless fantasy of them that dream.

The difference between Bridges' account of poetic sensibility and that of the romantics is revealed through a comparison with the "Ode to Melancholy":

> Ay, in the very temple of delight
> Veil'd melancholy has her sovran shrine,
>   Though seen of none save him whose strenuous tongue
> Can burst Joy's grape against his palate fine.

Keats says that only those who have felt joy can experience the "pleasures of melancholy"; Bridges, that the poet who is able to taste "of the breath of God" must, unfortunately, also suffer pain. "Joy, sweetest lifeborn joy" is typical of many poems by Bridges, including "Ah heavenly joy! But who hath ever heard," " 'Twas on the very day winter took leave," "The sea keeps not the Sabbath day," "Riding adown the country lanes," "Recollections of Solitude," "One grief of thine," "Melancholia," "Christmas Eve, 1917," and "The Great Elm." The list is a long one, yet includes only those poems which show the same change from feelings of despair to those of joy. There are many other "joyful" lyrics without this dualism of feeling. Usually the word "joy" connotes a feeling of physical and mental well-being, a full harmony of impulses. The supersensuous, almost supernatural character of this feeling is therefore founded on a basis which is largely natural. This relationship of the supersensuous to the sensuous is also characteristic of Bridges' aesthetic philosophy: his "religion of love." The failure of other religions of love during the past century, when unsupported by literal belief, makes it necessary to examine this aspect of Bridges' thought with some care.

"The Affliction of Richard," which Yvor Winters considers one of the "greatest short lyrics to be found in English," deals with "the experience of the intellectual who has progressed beyond the disillusionment of 'Dover Beach,' but has not forgotten his skepticism or its bitterness." [5] The poem is a good illustration of my assertion that it is easy to recognize Bridges' indebtedness to Herbert, but difficult to define that indebtedness in other than the most general terms.

> Love not too much. But how,
> When thou hast made me such,
> And dost thy gifts bestow,
> How can I love too much?
> Though I must fear to lose,
> And drown my joy in care,
> With all its thorns I choose
> The path of love and prayer.
>
> Though thou, I know not why
> Didst kill my childish trust,
> That breach with toil did I
> Repair, because I must:
> And spite of frighting schemes,
> With which the fiends of Hell
> Blaspheme thee in my dreams,
> So far I have hoped well.
>
> But what the heavenly key,
> What marvel in me wrought
> Shall quite exculpate thee
> I have no shadow of thought.
> What am I that complain?
> The love, from which began
> My question sad and vain,
> Justifies thee to man.

The compression of thought and simplicity of rhetoric, which makes the soul seem in intimate conversation with God, give this poem the seriousness and authenticity of a poem from *The Temple*. It is possible to find echoes from various poems by Herbert:

> how shall I grieve for Thee,
> Who in all grief preventest me? [6]

> Who can endear
> Thy praise too much? [7]

> Thou that hast given so much to me,
> Give one thing more, — a grateful heart. [8]

The desire to master skepticism is the theme of Herbert's "The Reprisal," which ends:

> Though I can do nought
> Against Thee, in Thee I will overcome
> The man who once against Thee fought,

and the argument is similar to that of "Love," the final poem in *The Temple*:

> Love took my hand, and smiling, did reply,
> "Who made the eyes but I?"

The slight verbal resemblances are in themselves of no importance, but the similarity of style and feeling is significant. "Among the Tombs" deals with the same kind of experience as "Church Monuments," but deals with it incompletely; and "Joy, sweetest lifeborn joy," which may derive its first line from Herbert's "Peace," is inferior to that poem more or less in proportion to its greater length and diffuseness. In "The Affliction of Richard," the imitation of Herbert is very successful.

The religious attitude of Bridges was, however, in some ways very different from that of Herbert. The first stanza of "The Affliction of Richard" reveals the point at which the poet has arrived. The fifth line means: though I may not attain the perfection or ideal at which I aim, I shall continue my effort. The first half of the second stanza may refer to the period of bitterness observed in the "dark sonnets" of *The Growth of Love*; the second half, to the orthodox theology which Bridges attacks throughout *The Testament of Beauty* and elsewhere. The first part of the last stanza admits the continued existence of dualism in nature and man, but the final lines give the same answer as that given in *The Testament of Beauty*: how can Love question Love, how can a thing judge itself?

A few lyrics, and many passages from *The Testament of Beauty*, if not read in the context of all of Bridges' poetry, would suggest an orthodox and literal belief. But in all the poetry God means the "Essence" or Platonic Idea of Love:

> God is seen as the very self-essence of love,
> Creator and mover of all as activ Lover of all,
> self-express'd in not-self, without which no self were
> In thought whereof is neither beginning nor end
> nor space nor time; nor any fault nor gap therein
> 'twixt self and not-self, mind and body, mother and child,
> 'twixt lover and loved, God and man; but ONE ETERNAL
> in the love of Beauty and in the selfhood of Love.[9]

The "frighting schemes" in "The Affliction of Richard" refer particularly to the Old Testament conceptions of God and damnation. The following passage from "Wintry Delights," with its explicit denial of original sin, is typical of Bridges' attacks on orthodox theology:

> . . . Science has pierced man's cloudy commonsense,
> Dow'r'd his homely vision with more expansive an embrace,
> And the rotten foundation of old superstition exposed.
> That trouble of Pascal, those vain paradoxes of Austin,
> Those Semitic parables of Paul, those tomes of Aquinas,
> All are thrown to the limbo of antediluvian idols,
> Only because we learn mankind's true history, and know
> That not at all from a high perfection sinfully man fell,
> But from baseness arose. . . .

However unorthodox may be his "religion of love," Bridges was of course one of the most Christian of poets, and he believed, as we have seen, that modern poetry should effect a compromise between the "Greek attainment and the Christian ideal." The insufficiency of the Greek ideal of love is the subject of one of his finest short poems, "Eros":

Why hast thou nothing in thy face?
Thou idol of the human race,
Thou tyrant of the human heart,
The flower of lovely youth that art;
Yea, and that standest in thy youth
An image of eternal Truth,
With thy exuberant flesh so fair,
That only Pheidias might compare,
Ere from his chaste marmoreal form
Time had decayed the colours warm;
Like to his gods in thy proud dress,
Thy starry sheen of nakedness.

Surely thy body is thy mind,
For in thy face is nought to find,
Only thy soft unchristen'd smile,
That shadows neither love nor guile,
But shameless will and power immense,
In secret sensuous innocence.

O king of joy, what is thy thought?
I dream thou knowest it is nought,
And wouldst in darkness come, but thou
Makest the light where'er thou go:
Ah yet no victim of thy grace,
None who e'er long'd for thy embrace,
Hath cared to look upon thy face.

Only the sixth line, in view of the last two stanzas, might require elucidation. Though unspiritualized and of "shameless will," Eros is an image or exemplar of physical beauty, which is an imperishable Idea or "Essence." Though ideally we should transcend this merely physical beauty, it is something "good" in itself:

> But think not Aphrodite therefor disesteem'd
> for rout of her worshippers, nor sensuous Beauty
> torn from her royal throne, who is herself mother
> of heavenly Love (so far as in human aspect
> eternal essence can have mortal parentage). . . .[10]

Very briefly, Bridges' religion as expressed in poetry earlier than *The Testament of Beauty* appears to be based on a love spiritualized in the Platonic fashion, as we have seen in *The Growth of Love*, but spiritualized also by Christian feeling. Thus it is compact both of love for an abstract idea and love for one's fellows, yet is not supported by any of the traditional literal beliefs. This, in its main outlines, is the religion of Shelley as well, and has so far proved an incomplete basis for conduct. Perhaps the greatest reason for its failure is a certain complacency that obscures particular issues — such as one's own character and judgments — by the intensity of an expansive emotion:

> Of painting, sculpture, and rapt Poesy,
> And arts, tho' unimagined, yet to be.
> The wandering voices and the shadows these
> Of all that man becomes, the mediators
> Of that best worship, Love, — by him and us
> Given and returned; swift shapes and sounds, which grow
> More fair and soft as man grows wise and kind,
> And, veil by veil, evil and error fall.[11]

Bridges has one passage which may stand beside this one of Shelley as an example of flatulent thinking; its only justification is that it was written to a musical score, and was perhaps not intended to be taken too seriously:

> All mankind by Love shall be banded
> To combat Evil, the many-handed:
> For the spirit of man on beauty feedeth,
> The airy fancy he heedeth.

. . . . . .

And out of his heart there falleth
A melody-making river
Of passion, that runneth ever
To the ends of the earth and crieth,
That yearneth and calleth;
And Love from the heart of man
To the heart of man replieth:
    On the wings of desire
    Love cometh to Love.

Just what the melody-making river of passion could achieve in the face of a particular problem is not mentioned: as Paul Elmer More says, "whenever sentiment comes into open conflict with the innate will to power, sentiment simply shrivels up as a motive of conduct." [12] But the passage is not at all representative. The "Love" of which Bridges speaks so often is not an expansive humanitarian feeling (as it appears to be in the last passage quoted) but a spiritual discipline for the individual in his progress toward perfection. *The Growth of Love* is concerned almost entirely with the individual soul. Bridges was very nearly unique in qualifying his aesthetic philosophy by an Aristotelian emphasis on self-control, though Wordsworth also perceived, in the "Ode to Duty," the insufficiency of love unsupported by the sense of duty:

Serene will be our days and bright,
And happy will our nature be
When love is an unerring light,
And joy its own security.
And they a blissful course may hold
Ev'n now, who, not unwisely bold,
Live in the spirit of this creed;
Yet seek thy firm support, according to their need.[13]

The humanistic side of Bridges' philosophy appears in his earliest complete poem, "Beatus Ille," though in the crudest possible form:

For it is not fit that the will should suffer
The mind to stray without rein or measure,
That the soul forsake her sphere, and offer
Her strength to the charm of a brutish pleasure.[14]

Most aesthetic philosophies have the same basis as Rousseauistic
naturalism: the idea that feeling is the highest human faculty.
In these philosophies impulse is itself sanctified, and restraint considered degrading, yet Bridges, who professes an aesthetic theory
of life, shows everywhere a grave and humanistic distrust of mere
feeling, of primary impulse and primary sensuous experience:

Thy love and wide benevolence
Full often lead thee
Where feeling is its own defence.

That feeling *is* its own defence is an important doctrine not only
of Rousseauistic naturalism (in which feeling and conscience are
identified) but of the aesthetic philosophy of Pater and others:
"For our one chance lies . . . in getting as many pulsations as
possible into the given time."[15] Bridges thus addresses Burns:

It seems but chance that all our race
Trod not the path of thy disgrace,
And, living freely to embrace
The moment's pleasure,
Snatch'd not a kiss of nature's face
For all her treasure.

There are many passages in *The Growth of Love* which reveal
the same distrust of unbridled impulse. The thirty-seventh sonnet
is a perfect illustration of what Irving Babbitt variously called
the "frein vital," the "inner check," and "work according to the
human law":[16]

At times with hurried hoofs and scattering dust
I race by field and highway, and my horse
Spare not, but urge direct in headlong course
Unto some fair far hill that gain I must:

> But near arrived the vision soon mistrust,
> Rein in, and stand as one who sees the source
> Of strong illusion, shaming thought to force
> From off his mind the soil of passion's gust. . . .

The desire for self-control could scarcely be stated more explic-itly; if anything, the statement is too easy and too explicit. The passage seems to be a commentary on the idea of self-control, rather than a vivification of the idea. A comparison of this sonnet with "Low Barometer," dealing with a more complex experience of a similar kind, will demonstrate the difference, and illustrate the moral value of Bridges' poetry at its best:

> The south-wind strengthens to a gale,
> Across the moon the clouds fly fast
> The house is smitten as with a flail,
> The chimney shudders to the blast.
>
> On such a night, when Air has loosed
> Its guardian grasp on blood and brain,
> Old terrors then of god or ghost
> Creep from their caves to life again;
>
> And reason kens he herits in
> A haunted house. Tenants unknown
> Assert their squalid lease of sin
> With earlier title than his own.
>
> Unbodied presences, the pack'd
> Pollution and remorse of Time,
> Slipp'd from oblivion reënact
> The horrors of unhouseld crime.
>
> Some men would quell the thing with prayer
> Whose sightless footsteps pad the floor,
> Whose fearful trespass mounts the stair
> Or bursts the lock'd forbidden door.

Some have seen corpses long interr'd
Escape from hallowing control,
Pale charnel forms — nay ev'n have heard
The shrilling of a troubled soul,

That wanders till the dawn hath cross'd
The dolorous dark, or Earth hath wound
Closer her storm-spredd cloke, and thrust
The baleful phantoms underground.

The tone of the poem is established in the first lines. The sixth line defines its subject, the internecine warfare in the cave between reason and rebellious instinct; the relationship of subject and image is strengthened by the double meaning of *caves* in line eight, as well as more obviously in the ninth and tenth lines. The twelfth line, and the fourth stanza, indicate the primitive character of this instinct: it is not something of which Reason is normally and specifically aware, such as impulse recognized and restrained, but something "in the blood," and which has lain long dormant in the mind's cave. The victory of Reason over this rebellious instinct is accomplished in the last two stanzas. The primary subject thus barely outlined is not original, but it is the most important subject a poet can have: the poet has admitted the possibility of rebellious instinct, has described its rebellion, and has won a rational victory over it.

The struggle of course is only partly conveyed by the poem's content thus paraphrased. The technical perfection of the poem is indissociable from the poet's intellectual mastery of his experience: "The spiritual control in a poem . . . is simply a manifestation of the spiritual control within the poet. . . ." [17] This technical or formal perfection cannot be completely analyzed: the unmistakable residuum which remains after analysis has been made is not a quality of feeling existing in a free state, but one so compact of all the analyzable elements of the poem interfused that the total eludes analysis. The extraordinary nervous experience of which the poem consists has two distinct yet related levels of feeling and idea, the first being the struggle I have mentioned, and the second being a perception of the close psychological kinship between fear and crime, a perception with very serious implications. Technically, the greatest merit of the poem is its masterly sequence or development of feeling. The first stanza consists of four unbroken lines, of a monotony which precludes any real personal feeling: the poem is laying claim to a quality of feeling which it does not convey. "On such a night" personalizes the poem, and explains the first stanza. The poem undergoes an increased nervous intensity as the prosody tightens and becomes more various: the placing of the word *then* is particularly effective. The temporary relaxation of the generalizing "And Reason kens" introduces a further deepening of feeling which comes with "Tenants unknown." Lines 10–16 show an exceptional harmony of diction and feeling: the consciousness of fear and sin is conveyed not only by the quality of the words but by the change in emphasis beginning with "Unbodied presences." This perfection of rhythm and sound is very noticeable in the fifteenth line. The casual "Some men" introduces a slight relaxation in the sixth stanza, but another climax is achieved with the break in the twenty-third line. The run-over lines in the last stanza, the literary overtones and languid rhythm of "dolorous dark," and the inverted first foot of the next to last line bring the poem to a natural "dying close": all passion spent.

The moral value of "Low Barometer" is greater than that of many lines of unimpeachable philosophizing, a moral value which consists in the perfect evaluation and control of a serious and complex experience. The evaluation is revealed by the reduction of that experience to simple general terms, by the great compression of feeling into a few lines; the control is seen in the formal excellence of the poem, its masterly distribution of emphases. Neither the form of the poem nor the feeling it expresses escape conscious control: every variation in rhythm, every image is deliberate and important.

Bridges' Aristotelian assertion that consciousness is the highest
human faculty — that the mind is more important than that
which it observes — recurs frequently not only in *The Testament of Beauty* (of which the main subject is the relationship of
"Reason," an imaginative Reason like that of Milton, to instinct
and primary sensuous experience), but throughout the earlier
lyric and philosophical poetry as well. In "Wintry Delights,"
Bridges says that if all art, beauty and love were taken away,

Yet would enough subsist in other concerns to suffice us,
And feed intelligence, and make life's justification.
What this is, if you should ask me, beyond or above the rejoicing
In vegetant or brute existence, answer is easy;
'Tis the reflective effort of mind, that, conscious of itself,
Fares forth exploring nature for principle and cause. . . .

The evolution of the human mind, the progressive evolution from
sensation to consciousness and thence to the creation of ideals,
the history of the Idea (a history which begins and ends in "Universal Mind"), is told in *The Testament of Beauty* in 4,374 lines;
it is told in "Narcissus" in 28. This poem is an exceptionally fine
example of compression in thought and of highly successful
allegory. It also explains the relationship between the apparently
diverse elements of Bridges' thought: his Aristotelian humanism,
his Lucretian or Spinozist naturalism, his Platonic idealism:

Almighty wondrous everlasting
Whether in a cradle of astral whirlfire
Or globed in a piercing star thou slumb'rest
    The impassive body of God:
Thou deep i' the core of earth — Almighty! —
From numbing stress and gloom profound
Madest escape in life desirous
    To embroider her thin-spun robe.

'Twas down in a wood — they tell —
In a running water thou sawest thyself
Or leaning over a pool: The sedges
    Were twinn'd at the mirror's brim

The sky was there and the trees — Almighty! —
A bird of a bird and white clouds floating
And seeing thou knewest thine own image
    To love it beyond all else.

Then wondering didst thou speak
Of beauty and wisdom of art and worship
Didst build the fanes of Zeus and Apollo
    The high cathedrals of Christ:
All that we love is thine — Almighty! —
Heart-felt music and lyric song
Language the eager grasp of knowledge
    All that we think is thine.

But whence? — Beauteous everlasting! —
Whence and whither? Hast thou mistaken?
Or dost forget? Look again! Thou seest
    A shadow and not thyself.

The poem may be paraphrased as follows: while man's thoughts (and hence his ideals) have arisen from "nature" and are developments of primitive instinct (lines 5–8), they are also emanations of "Universal Mind" and are eternal ideas or "Essences" (1–4). (It should be noted that the invocation seems to derive directly from Spenser's lines on the origin of the Idea of Beauty.)[18] The mind becomes conscious not only of external objects (so that there is a concept "bird" to correspond with the visible bird), but also of itself; and thus the mind comes to love itself (9–16). From this consciousness and love, the mind creates ideals and religions (17–24).[19] The final stanza is open to several plausible interpretations: it appears to me to be an assertion of the free and independent life of the Idea, which has no final embodiment before returning to "Universal Mind." This is what Bridges calls the "Ring of Being."[20] The poem might be paraphrased even more briefly by Santayana's famous dictum: "No ideal without a natural basis; nothing in nature without an ideal fulfillment."

From this theory of consciousness it is easy to understand the conceptual nature of Bridges' imagination. The quality of mind which transforms sensation into concepts and concepts into ideals is scarcely less evident in the lyric poetry (especially in *The Growth of Love*) than in *The Testament of Beauty*. It was as difficult for Bridges to confine himself to the level of primary sensuous experience as for Keats to transcend it. Bridges observes in all existence four stages, and "we must conceive these in gradation": "Atomic, Organic, Sensuous, Self-Conscient." [21] One of the sonnets defines Bridges' belief in the superiority of the "self-conscient" over the "sensuous" stage. Perhaps remembering Shelley's longing for the freedom of "a wave, a leaf, a cloud," [22] Bridges begins in the same vein, but in the sestet returns upon himself to assert that only consciousness and will make true freedom and pleasure possible:

> I would be a bird, and straight on wings I arise,
> And carry purpose up to the ends of the air;
> In calm and stormy my sails I feather, and where
> By freezing banks the unransom'd wreckage lies:
> Or, strutting on hot meridian banks, surprise
> The silence: over plains in the moonlight bare
> I chase my shadow, and perch where no bird dare
> In treetops torn by fiercest winds of the skies.
>
> Poor simple birds, foolish birds! then I cry,
> Ye pretty pictures of delight, unstir'd
> By the only joy of knowing that ye fly;
> Ye are not what ye are, but rather, sum'd in a word,
> The alphabet of a god's idea, and I
> Who master it, I am the only bird.

The implications of this Cartesian "Homo Sum" pride as it relates to Bridges' lyric poetry are various. Though guilty at times of lines which betray very careless thinking, at one time or another in his poetry Bridges denies each of the favorite fallacies of sentimental naturalism. In each instance we have a reassertion of the freedom and superiority of the human will: the superiority to "other creatures" not possessing the rational faculty and power to judge, as in "Wintry Delights"; the superiority of human art to natural beauty (same poem); the superiority of the intelligent man to the innocent child ("Pater Filio"); of the "thinking reed" to an impartial and mechanistic universe ("The sea keeps not the Sabbath day"); but above all, the superiority of the mind and will to the lower self of impulse, temperament, or rebellious instinct. In some of his poems, as in "I would be a bird," Bridges asserts the power of the mind to evaluate its own experience; in many others — nearly all of which have a serious human theme —he exemplifies the assertion.

In all these ways Bridges' intellectual imagination is of high moral pertinence, and gives to his poetry an ethical value seldom found in poetry of the last two centuries. Yet it is also the source of several defects in his early poetry. The plea for individualism in "Epistle to a Socialist" is vitiated by some inexcusable reasoning; socialism is condemned because it thwarts man's natural and primitive predilections for "Magnificence, Force, Bounty, Freedom." Finally, what has for one reason been praised must for another be gravely questioned — the arrogance of intellectual pride. The most serious defect in Bridges' early poetry, from the Christian or humanistic point of view, is the apparent absence of any genuine humility. Thus, though his poetry often has the tone of Herbert's, and though his skepticism has the same origin as that of Herbert, he did not go so far as Herbert: he did not realize the dangers of intellectual pride and individualism. This intellectual pride was an error of the age; even scientists are now less self-assured than thirty years ago. The error was to be acknowledged in the more mature thinking of The Testament of Beauty; it is even possible that Bridges went too far in the opposite direction, for intellectual pride is preferable at any time to the other extreme — Rousseauistic and Bergsonian contempt for the intellect.

The pride, then, is more or less a symbol of Bridges' individualism and isolation. It explains at once the greatness and the weakness of his lyric poetry. It contributed to that spiritual isolation which prevented him from fully understanding the everyday experience of other men, and thus imposed a certain limitation of range. On the other hand, it cannot be dissociated from his complete mastery of his own experience. His experience, compared with that of the greatest poets, was narrow, but his evaluation of that experience was at every point sound, lucid, complete.

CHAPTER FIVE

Expression of Emotion

. . . Love on buried ecstasy buildeth her tower.
— "The South Wind"

RIDGES' intellectual and spiritual individualism has nothing in common with the narrow subjective egotism which led such different writers as Rousseau, Chateaubriand and Byron to consider their every feeling of universal interest and importance. Critics have chiefly objected to Bridges' reticence, his austere reluctance to speak about himself. L. W. Miles writes, "What a difference between the vulgar yet splendid self-revelation of Byron's muse — that 'pageant of his bleeding heart' — and the proud elusiveness of the later singer."[1] One admits readily the difference, but questions the splendor of vulgarity — or of bad writing. It is true, as Winters says, that the "more personal lyrics of Bridges tend to become graceful and mild."[2] The weakness which Miles should have isolated was the mildness rather than the impersonality, a mildness caused partly by pride,

> 'Twere profanation of our joys
> To tell the laity of our loves,

and partly by a frequent indolence of mood, the indolence of "Clear and gentle stream," "Long are the hours the sun is above," "We left the city when the summer day," and many other poems. The early love poems, excluding those addressed to an ideal or "essence," are either addressed to an imaginary mistress, as in "Long

are the hours the sun is above," or are conventional *amoretti*, mere
literary exercises. The later love poems, with a few exceptions,
have the tone of presentation pieces ("An Anniversary," etc.):
they are the poems of happy married love rather than of love as
a dramatic literary theme. Even in his earliest poetry, Bridges
admires the quieter Florentine ideal:

> Passion with peace, . . . desire at rest, —
> A grace of silence by the Greek unguesst,
> That bloom'd to immortalize the Tuscan style.

A passage in "Wintry Delights" explains his unwillingness to
exploit his own love:

> Yea, put away all LOVE, the blessings and pieties of home,
> All delicate heart-bonds, vital tendernesses untold,
> Joys that fear to be named, feelings too holy to gaze on. . . .

It is hardly necessary to illustrate the impersonal character of most
of Bridges' lyrics. Many reasons could be advanced to explain
this distaste for self-revelation, of which the most important
would be his good taste, his individualistic pride, his ability to see
transient emotions *sub specie aeternitatis*,

> I can see
> Love's passing ecstasies endear'd
> In aspects of eternity,

and, not least, the quality of universal, rather than eccentric or
egocentric, imagination, which perceives that the feelings and
experiences which a poet shares with mankind at large are more
significant than those which are unique with himself, and therefore, in a measure, abnormal. This is a quality of imagination not
frequently found in recent poets.

To say that Bridges' lyric poetry is often mild and impersonal
does not mean that he did not enjoy what is loosely called "ecstasy." "Joy, sweetest lifeborn joy" is one of many poems dealing with such a feeling, and there is a related body of poetry

written in the "Tintern Abbey" vein, in the mood in which we seem "laid asleep in body, and become a living soul." *The Testament of Beauty* is framed by the familiar dream convention (only reversed), and there are many lines not only in this poem, but in the lyric poetry as well, which have the authentic Wordsworthian tone, if seldom the Wordsworthian faith:

> So nature in a frenzied hour,
> By day or night will show
> Dim indications of the power
> That doometh man to woe.

In several poems Bridges describes moments of "poetic vision," moments of intellectual or emotional excitement when conscious reason seems suspended, and the mind to have acquired an additional sense or faculty.

It is not surprising, considering the particular quality of Bridges' individualism, to find that his poetry has the greatest intensity and significance of emotion where it is least personal, or where, as in "Low Barometer," he has "depersonalized" his feelings by resorting to symbolic equivalents rather than to direct utterance. Many poems which on first examination appear, by reason of their subject, to have no personal application, reveal far more intense and genuine emotion than those most obviously autobiographical. A few poems of the first excellence which illustrate this assertion are "The fabled sea-snake, old Leviathan" (the description of a ship), "I heard great Hector sounding war's alarms," "On a Lady Whom Grief for the Death of Her Betrothed Killed," and the various nature poems dealing with the "drama of seasonal change." In addition to the poems already described treating the "internecine warfare in the cave" (and these are the most important), there are others, such as "Eros," "Democritus," and "Nightingales," [3] in which Bridges has selected impersonal subjects which might serve as symbolic contexts for his own ideas or feelings.

In one type of poetry, however, Bridges' idealism, isolation and pride contribute to intensity in the direct utterance of emotion. I refer to the poems in which this isolation is threatened, the idealism thwarted, the pride humbled. Where the danger is philosophical rather than psychological — that is to say, where the idealism rather than the pride is threatened — it may be considered with equanimity. Bridges' "All earthly beauty hath one cause and proof" has the almost indifferent, detached quality of the first lines of a sonnet of Spenser's which it echoes:

> Oft when my spirit doth spread her bolder wings,
>   In mind to mount up to the purest sky,
> It down is weighed with thought of earthly things
> And clogged with burden of mortality.[4]

But where Bridges fears, not the loss of an ideal, but the loss of personal identity, the immersion of his soul or mind in that of his mistress, his utterance is direct and impassioned:

> O my goddess divine sometimes I say: —
> Now let this word for ever and all suffice;
> Thou art insatiable, and yet not twice
> Can even thy lover give his soul away:
> And for my acts, that at thy feet I lay;
> For never any other, by device
> Of wisdom, love or beauty, could entice
> My homage to the measure of this day.
>
> I have no more to give thee: lo, I have sold
> My life, have emptied out my heart, and spent
> Whate'er I had; till like a beggar, bold
> With nought to lose, I laugh and am content.
> A beggar kisses thee; nay, love, behold,
> I fear not: thou too art in beggarment.

The intensity of this sonnet is not the result of a philosophical belief in pride or ideal love: it is purely psychological. In Thomist theology the evil of sexual intercourse lies not in carnal desire or pleasure, but in the submergence of the rational faculty.[5] It is this fear of the *ligamentum rationis*, as much as any more theoretical resemblance, which relates Bridges to Spenser:

> What warre so cruel, or what siege so sore,
> As that which strong affections do apply
> Against the forte of reason evermore
> To bring the sowle into captivity?[6]

And this is one of the reasons why Bridges is of value for us. If his spiritual isolation and his maintenance of rational control prevent him from penetrating far into the minds of men who did not share his lofty ideal, or prevent him from exploiting the dramatic possibilities of despair and self-abnegation, they also account not only for his unfailing control and evaluation of his material, but also for the vitality, the durability of his imagination:

> So 'tis with me; the time hath clear'd
> Not dull'd my loving; I can see
> Love's passing ecstasies endear'd
> In aspects of eternity:
> I am like a miser — I can say
> That having hoarded all my gold
> I must grow richer every day
> And die possess'd of wealth untold.

This soundness and emotional vitality is Bridges' substitute for the "spontaneous overflow of powerful emotion."

Bridges' skillful development of feeling in his lyric poetry is the essence of his greatness as a stylist: it is an aspect too often overlooked by his critics. The way in which he observes, evaluates and accepts or rejects his experience, rather than merely reflects that experience, is evident in all the poems: it is something which may be observed rather than described and measured, for it is present in his control of form and style rather than in the actual statements he makes. His emphasis is on the sequence and development of feeling rather than on feeling itself, the reduction of a varied or complex experience to an orderly pattern (indissociable from the mastery of a sound poetic form) being in itself a moral act.[7]

In the following pages I shall examine three poems which show different types of this sequence or development of feeling, of the relationship of the feeling of the poem to the poetic form in which it is embodied. The first poem, "The sea keeps not the Sabbath day," shows an effortless treatment of a complex and profound subject, and the method is a very simple one: progression by repetition:

> The sea keeps not the Sabbath day,
> His waves come rolling evermore;
> His noise grindeth the shore,
> And all the cliff is drencht with spray.
>
> Here as we sit, my love and I
> Under the pine upon the hill,
> The sadness of the clouded sky,
> The bitter wind, the gloomy roar,
> The seamew's melancholy cry
> With loving fancy suit but ill.
>
> We talk of moons and cooling suns,
> Of geologic time and tide,
> The eternal sluggards that abide
> While our fair love so swiftly runs,
>
> Of nature that doth half consent
> That man should guess her dreary scheme
> Lest he should live too well content
> In his fair house of mirth and dream:
>
> Whose labour irks his ageing heart,
> His heart that wearies of desire,
> Being so fugitive a part
> Of what so slowly must expire.

She in her agelong toil and care
Persistent, wearies not nor stays,
Mocking alike hope and despair.

— Ah, but she too can mock our praise,
Enchanted on her brighter days,

Days, that the thought of grief refuse,
Days that are one with human art,
Worthy of the Virgilian muse,
Fit for the gaiety of Mozart.

The poem has an unusual effect of authenticity, an effect which might be traced to its quiet tone, and to the apparently casual way in which the poem changes in scope and emphasis. The subject is that of much of Hardy's poetry — the dismay of an intelligent man in a mechanistic impersonal universe — but it is treated without Hardy's melodramatic struggle, and therefore more nearly approximates the experience of the average reader.

The first stanza introduces the feeling of melancholy in four unvaried and impersonal lines; the very first line states, in a fanciful way, the indifference of nature, but until the third stanza its function as something more than a verbal felicity is not apparent. The personal feeling of the second stanza becomes generalized in the third and wider in application in the fourth (with the word *man* and the Biblical overtone of the last line), and culminates in the extraordinary compression of the twenty-first and twenty-second lines. The sixth stanza, by shifting the emphasis from man to nature, depersonalizes the poem for a moment, but even in the statement of nature's indifference there remains something of the poet's own feeling. The reversal is skillfully managed by the play on "mocking" and the accelerated rhythm of the final stanza conveys the feeling of ecstasy and triumph. Bridges has many poems of an equally delusive simplicity embodying a similar mastery of a fairly complex experience: the lucid simplicity is the measure of the mastery.

The next two poems show directly opposite methods of developing feeling. In the first, "My spirit kisseth thine," the feeling which the poem conveys is, in the opening lines, less than the paraphrasable content would demand; in the second, the process is reversed:

> My spirit kisseth thine,
> My spirit embraceth thee:
> I feel thy being twine
> Her graces over me,
>
> In the life-kindling fold
> Of God's breath; where on high,
> In furthest space untold
> Like a lost world I lie.
>
> And o'er my dreaming plains
> Lightens, most pale and fair,
> A moon that never wanes,
> Or more, if I compare,
>
> Like what the shepherd sees
> On late mid-winter dawns,
> When thro' the branchèd trees,
> O'er the white-frosted lawns,
>
> The huge unclouded sun,
> Surprising the world whist,
> Is all uprisen thereon,
> Golden with melting mist.

In the first stanza Bridges makes the rhetorical statement that he is enjoying a supersensuous, ecstatic experience. But there is nothing in the poetry itself (in the rhythm, for instance) to convey such a feeling. In the second stanza the directness of the first and part of the second line, and the extraordinary simile of the fourth add some conviction, but the poem is still unequal to the statements it makes, to its paraphrasable content. The third stanza, with its rhythm mounting to a climax which does not come, also enriches the feeling, but the meaning — perhaps because of its audacity — is itself an obstacle. But the last two stanzas give a breathless rush which subsides only with the slow last line. The image immediately personalizes the poem: in other words diction and rhythm combine to achieve the feeling rhetorically announced in the first stanza. The climax of the feeling, for instance, is attained in the remarkable line,

Is all uprisen thereon,

a line revealing perfect fusion of sense and sound. This progressive development of feeling is of course intentional, and to my mind very effective.

The third poem, "The Summer-House on the Mound," shows a more difficult kind of mastery on a much wider scale. (Since this is a poem of more than a hundred lines, I do not quote it, but ask the reader to refer directly to the text.) It illustrates, as does Marvell's "To His Coy Mistress," extraordinary skill in the management of emphasis and climax through the studied use of *conventional language*,[8] or language in which an emotion unwarranted by the actual meaning of the words is conveyed. This emotion is conveyed by something which may loosely be called *tone*; that is, by sound, rhythm and other stylistic elements. As an example of such conventional language, the seventh and eighth lines of the poem,

Fairer than dream of sleep, than Hope more fair
Leading to dreamless sleep her sister Care,

convey a feeling of sadness which is not justified by the rational paraphrasable content of the lines. The sadness looks forward to something later in the poem; for the present, the poet intends that this sadness should remain a mystery.

The poem begins in a mood of happy recollection, which becomes, at the end of the introductory stanza, a kind of brooding melancholy. Then there is an immediate and at this point unaccountable deepening of tone: lines 9-16 are merely descriptive of a scene where the poet had played as a boy, but no one who reads the lines aloud will fail to observe the feeling of impending tragedy. The next eight lines show a relaxation of tension, a return to the half-playful mood of the beginning. The third stanza takes on a new gravity through a tightening of the style, though the words themselves merely describe the scene as it appeared to the child and the man.

Suddenly we are back forty years, looking with the child through the telescope, and there follow sixty-seven flawless lines, an achievement of sustained narrative style almost without equal in English poetry. The mood of the boy at the scene is substituted in this fourth section for that of the reflective man. Throughout this section further tension of feeling is created without adequate justification for that feeling in the matter. The fifth section begins almost jovially — but the child's joy is in watching the arrival of frigates, and once more the poem's gravity of tone returns, a gravity which is largely due to very strong rhymes and to powerful "masculine" lines given nervousness by the device of colliding accents. The section ends with a comparison between the frigates and the "heavy-hearted monsters of today."

Partly through this and other hints, but chiefly through the style, the suspense of latent unresolved feeling has become almost intolerable. And at this point comes the revelation, and the feeling or style of the poem finally coincides with the meaning at the splendid line:

Those murderous queens walking in sabbath sleep,

a line whose greatness is explained not only by the Shakespearean overtone or by its intrinsic excellences (such as the inversion of the third foot), but by the fact that it receives the impact of the feeling excited but not resolved in the seventy-four preceding lines. All of the intensity in the lines which precede looks forward to this line; most of the intensity in the rest of the poem looks back to it.

One of the "murderous queens" is the *Duke of Wellington*, and the poem goes back more years to the death of Wellington himself. The poem ends with a glimpse of decay. The final stanza is ostensibly a bit of old-fashioned Protestantism, but in reality conveys the feelings of irretrievable loss, of the impossibility of recovering the past. Even more this final stanza is a commentary on "envious and calumniating time," on historical decay.

It would be impossible to analyze fully the reasons why this is one of the most successful poems in the language. There is first of all the mastery of emphases and of the conventional which I have tried to show in my summary. The poet is in complete control of the relative intensity which he wishes to impose at any particular point; there is a potential seriousness of theme and implication of which the reader is aware at every moment, and from which all variations in theme or tone assume significance. Thus there is in nearly every line a struggle between the style and the material it expresses, a struggle which is not resolved until the seventy-fifth line. The intensity could partly be explained by the diction and versification; by the use of heavy monosyllables and a very marked rhythm from which each variation has some emotional significance. Lines 9–16 exemplify a gravity of tone not expected; the inversion of the last foot in the next to last line and of the third foot in the last line are examples of metrical substitutions whose emotional effect cannot be questioned. In addition there is the added association of feeling given by the echoes from Tennyson, Milton, and Shakespeare.[9] The poem appears to me to possess all the attributes of the greatest poetry: purity of diction, coherence and variety of meter, complete control over varied and complex feelings, and a moral pertinence which is partly due to the subject and partly due to this complete control. It should be observed that all these virtues are not incompatible with a very pronounced intellectual detachment.

One of the most popular of current theories — a theory supported particularly by T. S. Eliot — is that poetry should communicate rather than describe or transmute immediate sensation. This theory is traced by its modern proponents to the dramatic verse of Webster, and especially to Donne, who "strove to devise . . . a medium of expression that would correspond to the felt intricacy of his existence, that would suggest by sudden contrasts, by harsh dissonances as well as harmonies, the actual sensation of life as he had himself experienced it." [10] In his essay on "The Metaphysical Poets" T. S. Eliot made his now famous distinction between the intellectual poet, in whom we have "a direct sensuous apprehension of thought, or a re-creation of thought into feeling"; and the reflective poet, who has suffered a "dissociation of sensibility." [11] Professor Matthiessen, in commenting on this passage, makes a clearer distinction between dramatic poetry and reflective poetry, between

poetry that communicates emotion and poetry that talks about communicating it, a contrast that could be carried through other periods of English poetry, between such various poems as 'The Rape of the Lock' and 'The Castle of Indolence'; Blake's 'Echoing Green' and 'The Deserted Village'; the 'Ode to a Nightingale' and 'In Memoriam'; 'The Waste Land' and 'The Testament of Beauty.' [12]

One way in which the distinction may be applied is in the observation of the quality of a poet's language:

The dramatic quality is also wholly lost by the merely reflective poet who, instead of making a union of emotion and thought, instead of thinking in images and thus giving a living body to his ideas, tends to put his images aside and to fall back on abstract rhetoric when he comes to deliver his statements. [13]

Before considering the broader implications of the "dissociation of sensibility" we must examine the issue suggested by this last passage. The impossibility of reducing Professor Matthies-

sen's distinction to a law — a law which would require the poet
to avoid abstract language entirely and to think only in images
— seems apparent if we turn to such poems as Bridges' "The
Affliction of Richard" or Jonson's "Ode to Heaven." Jonson's
poem illustrates the possibilities of the lyric written almost wholly
in abstract language. It is one of the triumphs of English poetry,
and only a rigid a priori rationalist, noting the absence of images
and hence inferring a dissociation of sensibility, could fail to recognize it as such:

> Good and great God! can I not think of thee,
> But it must straight my melancholy be?
> Is it interpreted in me disease,
> That, laden with my sins, I seek for ease?
> O be thou witness, that the reins dost know
> And hearts of all, if I be sad for show;
> And judge me after, if I dare pretend
> To aught but grace, or aim at other end.
> As thou art all, so be thou all to me,
> First, midst, and last, converted One and Three!
> My faith, my hope, my love; and, in this state,
> My judge, my witness, and my advocate!
> Where have I been this while exiled from thee,
> And whither rapt, now thou but stoop'st to me?
> Dwell, dwell here still! Oh, being everywhere,
> How can I doubt to find thee ever here?
> I know my state, both full of shame and scorn,
> Conceived in sin, and unto labor born,
> Standing with fear, and must with horror fall,
> And destined unto judgment, after all.
> I feel my griefs too, and there scarce is ground
> Upon my flesh t'inflict another wound;
> Yet dare I not complain or wish for death
> With holy Paul, lest it be thought the breath
> Of discontent; or that these prayers be
> For weariness of life, not love of thee.

The qualities of this poem are such as should make it impressive to critics with very different attitudes towards poetry; in fact to any but the unregenerate romantic who demands vagueness and other typical forms of hysteria, or to the critic who rejects any poem with little imagery. For this poem is not only a precise and lucid definition of a complex and difficult emotional experience; it is also the product of an enriched sensibility; that is to say, it speaks to the heart and nerves as well as to the mind. It is a deeply moving poem, but it moves, if I may be permitted the play, as a result of its own movement. It appeals to the senses, but through its subject and structure rather than through borrowed and external sensuous experience (that is, rather than through analogy); it appeals to the senses through its capture of the living human voice, through its ordering and management of the subject, even through its very precision of abstract definition. Exactness of definition is possible through syntax or image or through a conjunction of both. Here the poet relies almost wholly on the more formal medium, yet no amount of imagery could increase the exactness of the definition and evaluation, which is already complete. And I doubt if it could increase the poem's intensity. By variety of cadence, by change of pace and tone, by pause and emphasis, and by compression and lucidity of statement, Jonson has made real what is frequently only a half-understood theological commonplace, the doctrine of original sin; he has elevated the doctrine from truism to immediately perceived truth without recourse to imagery. And, I repeat, it is truth immediately perceived not only by the head, but by the heart and nerves as well.

Instances of such complete reliance on abstract language are naturally rare. Nothing is easier to write than a generalization; nothing more difficult than to make an exact evaluation of an emotion in purely generalized language, and if many poets have deliberately excluded the resources of abstract language, few or none have deliberately excluded imagery. Yet it cannot be denied that some of the greatest English lyrics, from Raleigh's "The Lie" to Tennyson's "Ulysses," rely primarily on abstract language. This language is of course best suited to the *lieu commun*, to the expression of "universals," but it is also suited to the most personal and impassioned utterance, as we may see by referring to Samson's complaint on his blindness, beginning "O loss of sight, of thee I most complain" or to the octave of Gerard Hopkins' dark sonnet, "I wake and feel the fell of dark, not day." It is interesting to observe that four of the seven passages which Arnold selects as his touchstones for the judgment of poetry [14] are wholly devoid of imagery. From the time of Coleridge, Shakespeare has been commended as a poet for the richness of his imagery, for the concreteness of his language, yet many of the most memorable passages — the conclusion of King Henry's invective against the traitors in Southampton,[15] or Lear's "Pray, do not mock me: I am a very foolish fond old man," [16] or Cleopatra's "Give me my robe, put on my crown,"[17] for instance — are great precisely because of their exploitation of ordinary abstract language, and even in such a storehouse of good and bad imagery as the sonnets we find "The expense of spirit in a waste of shame," a sonnet written entirely in generalized abstract language.

Can we say, then, that thought unapprehended by the emotions results inevitably in abstract language, or that thought which has been modified by the sensibility necessarily produces images? The relationship of language to poetic perception can be reduced to no such simple formulae. It is easy enough to be glib in concrete images, as our neighbor's comments on a sunset or a painting only too patently assure us. Poetic perception (i.e., the personal act of willing, seeing or understanding something) may manifest itself in a hundred dark and inscrutable ways, of which the discovery of a new image is merely the commonest and easiest. Far more subtle, and to the sophisticated poet and reader sometimes far more rewarding, are the acts of perception expressed by the delicate disturbance of a cadence or the intricate management of logic (syntax). In Henry King's famous lines from "The Exequy"

> But hark! my pulse like a soft drum
> Beats my approach, tells thee I come,

the act of perception resides less in the striking simile than in the exquisite nervous control of the metrical line; without this control, the lines would have communicated an observation but not a perception. As in the best poetry, the two familiar vehicles for perception are here indissociable.

I have tried to show that a poem written in abstract language is not for that reason a failure. It is nevertheless true that reliance on barren expository statement often indicates that the poet has not explored his subject. (Obvious hackneyed imagery indicates precisely the same thing.) The distinction which Professor Matthiessen makes between dramatic and reflective poetry was made by Bridges himself in his essay on Keats, in which he compares "Keats' objective treatment and Wordsworth's philosophizing":[18]

> The coarser pleasures of my boyish days
> And their glad animal movements . . .

is contrasted with the last of Keats' images on human life:

> Stop and consider! Life is but a day;
> A fragile dew-drop on its perilous way
> From a tree's summit; a poor Indian's sleep
> While his boat hastens to the monstrous steep
> Of Montmorenci. Why so sad a moan?
> Life is the rose's hope while yet unblown;
> The reading of an everchanging tale;
> The light up-lifting of a maiden's veil;
> A pigeon tumbling in clear summer air;
> A laughing schoolboy without grief or care,
> Riding the springy branches of an elm.[19]

These, as Bridges says, are images of life "considered first as a dream on the brink of destruction, then as a budding hope, then as an intellectual distraction, then as an ecstatic glimpse of beauty, and lastly as an instinctive animal pleasure."[20] Where Bridges' own poetry, or Wordsworth's, approximates the paraphrase rather than the poem, its intrinsic weakness must be admitted. The intellectual observation must proceed to perception (by imagery *or by any of the other vehicles I have mentioned*) before it becomes poetic. (The late Irving Babbitt was inclined to consider a noble observation poetic by reason of its nobility; he did not demand that the observation be realized by an act of perception. It is here that my own position differs most radically from his.)

That the poet should not be satisfied with something similar to Bridges' intellectual paraphrase does not mean, however, that poetry should merely communicate sensation, or that it should sensualize thought completely. Nor does it mean that the poet's final act of perception should convey the feeling of life as he himself had experienced it. The "dream on the brink of destruction" would hardly be felt by Keats as a "poor Indian's sleep." The original source of the idea and the image might have been the memory of boyish dreams or carefree confidence, a memory now tinged with bitterness by a recurrence of his sore throat, and resulting in an ironic perception of one's frequent ignorance of impending disaster. The process which I assume, for the purpose of making my point, to have taken place (consciously or unconsciously) would be as follows: a vague feeling was analyzed and its general implications discovered. To present unaltered that vague feeling would obscure its general implications; to present those implications in a form not only purely intellectual but thoroughly banal would sacrifice the original or indeed any emotion. The feeling which had been refined into a generalization was therefore transmuted once more by an act of perception (in this case by the discovery of an image) which would evoke not only an idea but an appropriate feeling in the reader. In other words, an original feeling was examined for its general and universal importance; then re-created into a new feeling which would be more transferable than the original one, and which would comprehend as well the philosophical truth. The best poetry proceeds to this third stage.

As I understand it, the poetry of T. S. Eliot and his disciples proceeds from the first to the second stage, but then returns to something which tries to approximate the first rather than the third. Eliot tries to convey the original, and largely non-transferable first feeling, "the actual sensation of life as he had himself experienced it." The most serious implications of such a procedure for the poet is that it invites an uncritical acceptance of sensuous experience (broadly interpreted); the most serious for the reader, that the poem becomes obscure. This surrender of the poet to his subject matter (and the consequent obscurity) — this complete triumph of what Coleridge called organic form — seems to me the greatest weakness of modern poetry.

The two opposite views of a poet's relation to his experience are clearly defined in the following passages. Professor Matthiessen writes:

If, in the last analysis, the kind of poetry Eliot is writing gives evidence of social disintegration, he has expressed that fact precisely as the poet should, not by rhetorical proclamation, but by the very feeling of contemporary life which he has presented to the sensitive reader of his lines.[21]

The way in which Mr. Eliot gives this "very feeling of contemporary life" — its multiplicity, complexity, illogicality — is by writing verse which has these same qualities. Of his "Gerontion" Dr. Winters writes:

One has again, perhaps, the fallacy of imitative form; the attempt to express a state of uncertainty by uncertainty of expression; whereas the sound procedure would be to make a lucid and controlled statement regarding the condition of uncertainty, a procedure, however, which would require that the poet understand the nature of uncertainty, not that he be uncertain.[22]

The clearest modern expression of the "fallacy of imitative form" since Whitman appears in Eliot's essay on "The Metaphysical Poets":

it appears likely that poets in our civilization, as it exists at present, must be *difficult*. Our civilization comprehends great variety and complexity, and this variety and complexity, playing upon a refined sensibility, must produce various and complex results. The poet must become more and more comprehensive, more allusive, more indirect, in order to force, to dislocate if necessary, language into his meaning.[23]

These lines by Eliot are in one respect typical of much of his criticism: carefully worded, and with a skillful if unconscious use of sophistical reasoning, they seem to preclude the possibility of there being another side to the matter. As I see it, however, they may be paraphrased or interpreted thus: since society is loose, one must write loose poetry.

The superiority of the procedure recommended by Dr. Winters is that it does not permit looseness of thought or form; it demands that the poet discriminate in the moral sense. There is of course some discrimination involved in the illustrative details selected so carefully by Mr. Eliot, but in his desire to communicate directly sensation (even at the sacrifice of form or integrity of language) there is also involved a real intellectual surrender. It suggests as a primary aim the photographic recreation of experience rather than the intellectual control and understanding of that experience. And I venture to say that there is no subject matter so intractable that it cannot be made to submit, without loss, to the ordering of a great artist.

This intellectual control — the detachment of the mind from what it contemplates — is the quality of Bridges' poetry which most distinguishes it from much contemporary poetry; it is the ultimate quality of the best art. It should be remembered that Stendhal's "mirror dawdling down a lane" has, in common with all mirrors, no real power of discrimination, and this is true of the poet whose imagination or sensibility becomes in any sense a mirror, a highly sensitive machine for recording sensations and impressions. Such an imagination invariably loses its distinguishing human quality, autonomy and the power to discriminate. This autonomy is lost when thought is wholly submerged in feeling, and it would seem that the "unification of sensibility" which Mr. Eliot desires is the best way of losing such autonomy.

CHAPTER SIX

Form and Style

Language is a perpetual Orphic song,
Which rules with Daedal harmony a throng
Of thoughts and forms, which else senseless and shapeless were.
SHELLEY, *Prometheus Unbound*

EW TYPES OF CRITICISM are less rewarding than the minute analysis of a poet's style divorced from a consideration of the ideas and feelings which that style informs. The mechanics of versification, for instance, though far more important than many critics allow, are indeed merely mechanics unless their relationship to poetic perception is understood. Hence although I had little to say about meter or diction as such, my preceding chapter was essentially a discussion of Bridges' mastery of poetic form, of his complete control of the material with which he had to deal.

Formal experimentation, however, may often be profitably discussed in terms of sounds, syllables, accents and the like, and one of the prices which the truly experimental poet has to pay is the indignity of being subjected to such discussion. A highly conscious artist, Bridges was, from the beginning of his career to its end, one of the most unobtrusive and therefore one of the most valuable poetical experimenters of his time. The quietness and unobtrusiveness of his innovations must always be kept in mind: at no time was he willing to make a sharp break with the past.

Bridges' versatility and eager desire to face and conquer new obstacles is revealed in a matter so humble as his use of seventy-one

different stanzaic forms in the ninety-eight poems which constitute the final selection of *Shorter Poems*. But the firm yet cautious nature of his experiments in meter, in which the tentative
and untried new always rests securely on the "firm bedrock" of
the old, is of much greater interest. This caution is nowhere more
clearly revealed than in his use of the *sprung-rhythm* which Gerard
Hopkins claimed to have invented. Sprung-meter, or "the juxtaposition of heavily and more or less equally accented syllables
by other means than normal metrical inversion,"[1] appeared in
English poetry as early as Wyatt and Barnabe Googe, and was
used with great skill by Ben Jonson in the Prologue to *Volpone*,
but its occurrence in later poetry (in Browning and Meredith, for
instance) was fitful and probably accidental. Hopkins, instead
of using it as a variation on normal accentual-syllabic meter,
adopted it as his basic measure with peculiar and violent results:

> Not, I'll not, carrion comfort, Despair, not feast on thee;
> Not untwist — slack they may be — these last strands of man
> In me ór, most weary, cry *I can no more*. I can;
> Can something, hope, wish day come, not choose not to be.

The greatness of this and other poems by Hopkins does not alter
the fact that no other poet has been able to make a similar use of
the medium, a medium which in this wrenched form is perhaps
suitable only to the peculiar type of religious excitement which
Hopkins enjoyed. For this reason Hopkins' influence as a metrical
experimenter has been, on the whole, very small.

Bridges, on the other hand, always used sprung-meter as an
additional type of variation on a traditional norm, and his experiments have therefore a rather equivocal character. Let us consider
a very well known poem, "The Passer-By," an early experiment
in accentual meter. Although based on an accentual norm (in
which only the accents are counted), it may be scanned as a
poem in iambic pentameter, with certain normal variations and
with a few examples of sprung-meter.[2] There is only one un-

questionable "sprung" foot in the poem, the fifth foot of the thirteenth line:

Thy sáils /for áwn /ings spréad, /thy másts /báre . . .

This is a clear example of the accentual variety of sprung-meter, in which an unaccented syllable is lost. The line thus retains only nine syllables. Lines 3, 7, 12, 22 and 23 might also be considered as containing sprung feet, but in each of these lines it is possible to give other reasons for the rhythmical disturbance. If "That fearest," in the third line, is either elided or considered a trisyllabic foot, *cloud* becomes a monosyllabic foot, since the feminine ending does not count in the versification:

That féarest /nor séa /rísing, /nor ský /clóud(ing) . . .

On the other hand, there is no syllabic loss if this elision is not made; the line could then be scanned, though very unnaturally, as regularly iambic. The four other instances of possible sprung-meter could be similarly explained away; in only one line in the poem does Bridges fail to compensate for the monosyllabic or sprung foot by an extra unaccented syllable. In the history of poetry, such extremely cautious experiment ends by accomplishing much more than intense radical innovation. By introducing one or more sprung-feet into every line, Hopkins evolved a violent, exciting and intense medium, but a medium which has proved as impervious to significant variation (though for the opposite reason) as the most regular pit-pat of the Victorian metronome.

Further technical discussion of Bridges' metrical experiments must be reserved for an Appendix on Prosody, whither those who are interested may follow it. It is here necessary only to add that Bridges' studies of Milton's prosody, and many of his own poems, were directed toward the liberation of speech-rhythm, toward finding a prosodic structure which would accommodate this rhythm and yet preserve the fixed underlying norm without which the musical counterpoint of poetry is impossible. The final solution was the "Neo-Miltonic syllabics" of *New Verse* and *The Testament of Beauty*, but freedom of speech-rhythm was, at the time of their first appearance, the distinguishing stylistic feature of the *Shorter Poems*. It is only by comparing the subtle music of these lyrics with the beat of Swinburne's anapestic triphammer that we realize its historical importance. Bridges was certainly not the first poet to utilize speech-rhythm, but if we except Arnold, whose practice was less varied, and Browning, whose accidental successes scarcely compensate for his many failures, he was the only poet of his age to do so with conspicuous reward. It is natural that he should have gone back not only to Keats, but to the great masters of the seventeenth century who had exhibited success in this manner, especially Herbert, for his stylistic models. Incidentally, it is interesting to observe that in only three of the *Shorter Poems* does Bridges resort to the easy device of allowing the phrase to dictate the length of the line. These poems may be described as loosely accentual in meter, but they are no looser than "Dover Beach."

The experiments in alliteration, assonance and rhyme reveal similar caution. Bridges used rhyme in all his earlier lyric poetry, but eventually he discarded it. As early as 1909 he recorded his impatience with its "cloying" effects and its "conspicuous artificiality";[3] this impatience was revealed even earlier in the elaborate stanzaic patterns which he evolved and in the occasional wide separation of rhyming words, as well as in the frequent use of imperfect rhyme. He works the accepted device of visual rhyme as far as it will go, and in one stanza even goes so far as to rhyme together *down, gone, one* and *lone.* Furthermore he is not wholly guiltless of the "barbarous rhymes" of which he accuses Hopkins: for instance, *can be, philosophy; whist, is't?* A fault of which he was conscious in poetry other than his own appears occasionally, the use of obvious or necessary rhymes. The worst offender is *fire* and *desire*, and this is the less defensible because *fire* is not an apt metaphor to use in illustration of the quintessential spiritual aspiration which Bridges calls *desire*. Yet over and over, when *desire* appears, it carries *fire* in tow.

Bridges' interesting use of inner-rhyme in "April, 1885" and in "Larks" requires no comment. In the "Ode to Music Written for the Bicentenary Commemoration of Henry Purcell" (1895) Bridges shows a growing impatience with rhyme: in addition to separating rhymes by many lines in several instances, he also makes use of Milton's device [4] of occasional unrhymed lines. In his note prefixed to *October*, explaining the new syllabic prosody, Bridges wrote: "In this sort of prosody rhyme is admitted, like alliteration, as an ornament at will; it is not needed." [5] Several of the poems in *New Verse* were written to discover the relation of the new prosody to rhyme.[6]

In studying Bridges' use of alliteration it is easy to find occasional faults, but difficult to do justice, other than in very general terms, to the numerous beauties. That very uneven performance, *Eros and Psyche*, occasionally suffers like its stylistic model from excessive alliteration:

> Fell to their *f*east the *g*reat *b*irds *b*ald and *g*aunt
> And *g*orged on her *f*air *f*lesh with *b*loody *b*eak.

But a far more serious fault is Bridges' tendency to begin noun and epithet with the same letter; this, considered in connection with the deadening practice of assigning to each noun a single epithet, is one of his few serious stylistic mannerisms. A few typical offenders are *soft shower, shuddering seas, soft south, splendid ship, straight stems, soaring spars, sullen sea* and *sunny sea*. This mannerism is largely avoided in the later volumes.

Bridges' use of assonance shows fewer defects: if we except such poets as Poe and Swinburne, who revelled in sound for its own sake, Milton and Keats are perhaps his only peers in the art of verbal harmony. Usually assonance is combined with alliteration and rhyme, as in the "Elegy on a Lady Whom Grief for the

Death of Her Betrothed Killed," one of the great masterpieces of
the artificial style. Each stanza has a basic sound pattern; the tonal
basis for the third stanza, for instance, is the *er* sound:

> Cloke h*er* in *er*mine, for the night is *c*old,
> And *w*rap h*er* *w*armly, for the night is long,
> In pious *h*ands the flaming torches *h*old,
> While h*er* attendants, chosen from among
> Her faithful *vir*gin throng,
> May *l*ay h*er* in h*er* ced*ar* *l*itter,
> Decking h*er* cov*er*let with sprigs of gold,
> Roses, and lilies white that *b*est *b*efit h*er*.

Though he wished to accommodate "speech-rhythms" in his
poetry, Bridges did not try to recapture the discords and hesita-
tions of ordinary or vulgar conversation. He wrote that since
"poetic language is essentially a rarity of expression of one sort
or another, it is unreasonable to forbid apt and desirable grammatical forms merely because they are not read in the newspapers
or heard at the dinner-table." [7] In various ways the language of
Bridges' poetry is a rarity of expression: in his use of rare or
archaic words, of conventional epithets, "literary properties"
and grammatical inversion, his practice differs from that of most
twentieth-century poets.

The temptation to rebel against any very marked poetic influence is strong, and Keats' rebellion against Milton in September 1819 (not unlike Milton's rebellion against Shakespeare in his
later poetry) is expressed today by T. S. Eliot [8] in almost the same
words that Keats used.[9] Bridges' essay on Keats contains a long
explanation of the logical basis of grammatical inversion: in
putting the object before the epithet, the poet is rectifying a mal-
position of ideas, and is offering them "as he wishes them to enter
the reader's mind." [10] Most readers will feel, however, that since
adjective and substantive usually enter the mind as a single word
or concept, the real problem is whether inversion adds to poetic
beauty.

One encounters successful grammatical inversion throughout Bridges' poetry; it is easier to isolate types of failure. It can cause needless obscurity, as in the lines,

> Across all down the right, an old brick *wall*,
> Above and o'er the channel *red* did lean. . . .

Here *red* would appear to have been removed from its logical position to come to the aid of the meter in the second line. The Miltonic division of epithets can nevertheless contribute great beauty, as these lines by Bridges show:

> In autumn moonlight when the white air wan. . . .

> 'Twas here we loved in sunnier days and greener. . . .

> Whose pining visions dim, forbidden hopes profound . . . .

A more subtle problem of word-order is the placing of key words where they will attain the greatest significance. This felicitous placing of important words is at once the highest manifestation of a poet's formal excellence and the aspect of his style which, if successful, escapes the notice of the reader not bent on dissecting his verse. The importance of the placing of words is seen in the rearrangement of the following lines from the opening of *Paradise Lost*, Book II, which, as Bridges says, removes the value of the word *far*, making it "flat and dull . . . if it be unaccented it is useless, and if accented it is foolish": [11]

> High on a Throne of Royal State, which far
> Outshone the wealth of Ormus and of Ind.

> High on a Throne of Royal State,
> Which far outshone the wealth of Ormus and of Ind.

The reader can apply this test for himself to Bridges' lyrics; he will find that nearly always the same impoverishment will result. For the present, two examples of felicitous word placing should suffice:

> Thy spirit, Democritus, orb'd in the eterne
> Illimitable galaxy of night. . . .

> They trim afresh the fair
> Few green and golden leaves withheld from the storm. . . .

Although the language of Bridges' poetry is naturally one of the chief sources of its beauty, even a brief study of the diction can hardly fail to be outrageously pedestrian. Once again one is forced to recognize the difficulty of presenting the beauties by other means than extensive quotation, and the ease of isolating a few common faults. It is, for instance, apparent to the student bent on making catalogues of epithets that Bridges' criticism of Keats' monotonous overfrequent use of a few epithets may be directed against himself with even greater severity. He calls the chief group in Keats "languid"[12] and this is also the largest class in his own poetry: to those which he observes in Keats — *quiet, sweet, fair, white, green, old, young, little, tender, easy, fresh, pleasant* — we may add the commonly recurring *idle, drowsy, dreamy, gliding, indolent, fond, merry, pretty, fair, jocund, slumbrous, faery* and *happy. Heavenly* and *divine* are certainly used without sufficient discrimination, and there are six other epithets, suggesting a literary indolent melancholy, which are badly overworked: *sad, mournful, plaintive, lonely, gloomy, melancholy.*

This list, without doing justice to Bridges' less conventional and therefore less frequent epithets, reëmphasizes the *indolent* quality of his mood and creative imagination. The indolent mood cannot be denied; there is further evidence, in the repeated recurrence of a few phrases, that, though he was certainly not careless or uncritical in composing, he experienced over and over the same mood and the same kind of impulse to write. Few poets do not echo earlier work of their own occasionally, and the appearance of such a phrase as *everlasting dawn* on three occasions is not surprising; on the other hand, the repeated appearance of a few words or images, usually drawn from nature, becomes monotonous to anyone who reads all the poetry.

Bridges' defence of archaisms[13] is similar to that prefixed to *The Shepheards Calender*: by using good archaic words the poet may restore them to currency. Though the essay "Word-Books" might indicate the contrary, it is evident from his own poetry that Bridges' primary concern is with purity of meaning, and only afterward with beauty of sound and historical association. I have tried to show elsewhere how Bridges enriched his poetry through the use of words given force and dignity by the felicitous usage of earlier poets. But the first and greatest virtue of Bridges' diction is its unfailing rightness, its masculine quality. The following lines reveal particularly strongly that stress "on the naked thew and sinew of the English language"[14] which Hopkins found in Dryden:

> The fabled sea-snake, old Leviathan,
> Or else what grisly beast of scaly chine
> That champ'd the ocean-wrack and swash'd the brine,
> Before the new and milder days of man,
> Had never rib nor bray nor swindging fan
> Like his iron swimmer of the Clyde or Tyne,
> Late-born of golden seed to breed a line
> Of offspring swifter and more huge of plan.

In *Eros and Psyche* we discover the same mixture of archaisms and rare but correct words. The Spenserian movement and the broken versification give an impression of greater archaism than a close scrutiny of the poem reveals. Excluding obsolete grammatical forms there are only twenty-four real archaisms in the poem's 2,157 lines. The five inventions — *nurseried, unsoul'd, unfellied, pens* (pennons) and *outban'd* — are of interest, but contribute less to the tone of the poem than such obsolete grammatical forms as *drave, holp, wot, withouten* and *ywiss.*

The proportion of obsolete forms or words is smaller in the *Shorter Poems*; the grammar is almost never archaic. There are only three apparent inventions: *crinching*, *dislustres* and *sunshot*. *New Poems* reveals great purity of diction, but very few obsolete words and no inventions. In *Later Poems*, we find three dialectal words of good lineage: *rakel*, *teen* and *inscience*. In this volume, too, *conscience* is used for the first time in the sense of *consciousness*. Hereafter the word is so used consistently, though commentators on *The Testament of Beauty* have been misled by it. The word stands for both meanings in French, and Bridges, in trying to avoid the homophone, uses *inwit* once. In *The Testament of Beauty* he was forced to use several words to convey the idea of moral conscience.

Mrs. Bridges believes William Johnstone Stone requested her husband to test his theories of classical prosody in 1896. He began to do so immediately, but the main body of his work in classical meters was done between 1900 and 1910. Anyone who has used the Oxford English Dictionary knows that many of the examples for rare words are drawn from classical translations. This is because of the difficulty for the translator of finding verbal equivalents, but particularly, if he tries to write in classical prosody, of finding English words to fit classical quantities. Since Bridges was interested in perfecting Stone's prosody it is obvious that the difficulties for him would be correspondingly greater. Mrs. Bridges recalled that when he was beginning to write in this prosody, Bridges would sometimes work all day without completing a single line to his satisfaction. The two thousand lines of the *Poems in Classical Prosody* represent, therefore, a severe and prolonged effort in the face of great technical obstacles.

The result of this effort was an entirely new vocabulary — a vocabulary with a far greater proportion of polysyllabic words and words of Latin derivation — which was to be the characteristic vocabulary of *New Verse* and *The Testament of Beauty*. Apart from a markedly new emphasis on scientific terms, these poems reveal many rare compounds, such as *dispirited, disquiet, predestiny, upgathering, goldwaving, famous'd, convincement, dispeopling,* etc. Two adjectival forms which are used regularly in *The Testament of Beauty* appear: *inexhaustive, superstructive; frustrate* (frustrated), *regenerate*. While "Wintry Delights" is interesting as a comprehensive and learned account of the development of science, its subject was probably chosen because of the type of vocabulary, so suited to a quantitative prosody, which it permitted Bridges to use. Success in this radically new manner is intermittent, and "Wintry Delights" contains some of the ugliest lines in English poetry:

> Examination of its contexture, conglomerated. . . .
>
> Her metamorphoses transmuting by correlation. . . .
>
> In the flat accretions of new sedimentary strata. . . .

The last two volumes of lyric poetry, *October* and *New Verse*, show the influence of the years of experiment in classical prosody in such rare or coined words as *diluvian, plenishing, upliving, unhouseld, mischanged* and *alweighty*, but there are many short lyrics which could have appeared in earlier volumes. The diction of "Come Se Quando," one of the first fully successful attempts to write the twelve-syllable line of *The Testament of Beauty*, contains many lines which would not be out of place in the later poem. It therefore represents the last stage in the development of Bridges' diction:

> Ev'n so in our mind's night burn far beacons of thought
> and the infinite architecture of our darkness . . . .

In this poem, too, we see the tendency to play with words which tempts any poet with a very large vocabulary:

> Why must this last best most miraculous flower of all
> be canker'd at the core, prey to the spawn and spawl
> of meanest motes? must stoop from its divine degree
> to learn the spire and spilth of every insensate filth
> that swarmeth in the chaos of obscenity?

The fusion of sense and sound, Bridges wrote, "is the magic of the greatest poetry."[14] It is in the effecting of this fusion that meter and diction work in the closest collaboration. We have already observed instances of metrical variation combining with particular words to establish a mood or convey a change in feeling; in many of these instances the fusion was unobtrusive, imperceptible to the careless eye. The use of imitative harmony for what might be called a *trompe l'oreille* effect is naturally far more obvious. If nothing else, it testifies to a measure of technical skill. In "London Snow" the meter and diction combine to convey the actual impression of snow falling:

> When men were all asleep the snow came flying,
> In large white flakes falling on the city brown,
> Stealthily and perpetually settling and loosely lying,
>   Hushing the latest traffic of the drowsy town;
> Deadening, muffling, stifling its murmurs failing;
> Lazily and incessantly floating down and down. . . .

Hardy obtained a very similar effect in "Snow in the Suburbs":

> Some flakes have lost their way, and grope back upward, when
> Meeting those meandering down they turn and descend again.

A very successful use of imitative harmony is found in "The Downs," where the quality of the final lines in each of the stanzas reflects with remarkable fidelity the meaning:

> By delicate miniature dainty flowers adorned!

> They seem to be wearily pointing the way they would go.

> He masses his strength to recover the topmost crown.

The first line is brittle and "delicate" because of its dentals and very short syllables; the second "like a wounded snake drags its slow length along";[15] the third differs from the others in its strong rising rhythm obtained by long monosyllables and by the iambic last foot, which, following as it does on anapestic feet, gives the effect of finality.

Bridges isolated as the highest gift of all poetry "the power of concentrating all the far-reaching resources of language on one point, so that a single and apparently effortless expression rejoices the aesthetic imagination at the moment when it is most exacting and expectant, and at the same time astonishes the intellect with a new aspect of truth."[16] This effortlessness, the absence of strain, characterizes the most imaginative lines in Bridges' poetry: it is therefore difficult, and in the end unrewarding, to discuss particular phrases and images out of their context. A classification of types of imagery, such as is frequently made in discussions of metaphysical poetry, would tell us little that we do not already know. The successes possible to a highly intellectual but never straining imagination such as Bridges' may range from a perception of pure beauty, as when Aphrodite is described as

> Dappl'd with eye-rings in the sunlight blue,

to lines of purely rhetorical statement which summarize, so to speak, a whole philosophy, and which succeed in conveying a very marked feeling as well:

> Or rather doth the mind, that can behold
> The wondrous beauty of the works and days,
> Create the image that her thoughts unfold?

In the following passage the description of a promontory as a "furthest taper horn of land" is very striking, yet in its context completely natural:

> The southward stretching margin of a bay,
> Whose sandy curves she pass'd, and taking stand
> Upon its furthest taper horn of land,
> Lookt left and right to rise and set of day.

The particular intellectual quality of Bridges' imagination is perhaps best revealed in such passages as the following, in which perfect command of narrative through syntax gives the firmest possible frame to the imagery:

> . . . he stood aloof
> Beside a cypress, whose profoundest shade
> Drank the reflection of the dreamy night
> In its stiff pinnacle. . . .

> And 'neath the mock sun searching everywhere
> Rattles the crispèd leaves with shivering din:
> So that the birds are silent with despair
> Within the thickets; nor their armour thin
> Will gaudy flies adventure in the air,
> Nor any lizard sun his spotted skin.

In the last analysis it is impossible to dissociate the various elements which contribute to Bridges' success as a stylist: the intellectual imagination, with its firm control of feeling and tone; coherence and variety of rhythm; command of euphony; perfect exactness of phrasing. All of these are aspects of what we call style, and not the least important is the control of feeling and tone revealed in compression of statement and compactness of form.

PART TWO

Dramatic Poetry

CHAPTER SEVEN

The Rationale of Closet Drama

Nay, even of drama Aristotle held,
Though a good play must act well, that 'tis perfect
Without the stage: which shows that poetry
Stains not her excellence by being kind
To those encumbrances, which, in my judgment,
Are pushed to fetter fancy. . . .

The First Part of Nero, III, v

THE LARGEST BODY of Robert Bridges' poetry consists of ten plays and masques written between 1881 and 1904, amounting in all to 23,008 lines. Although these plays fill four and part of a fifth volume of the six-volume *Poetical Works*, they are almost completely unknown. Of the eight plays issued separately between 1885 and 1894, the first editions of five — *Palicio, The Christian Captives, The Humours of the Court, The Feast of Bacchus* and *Nero: Part II* — have not yet been exhausted. *The First Part of Nero* was sold out almost immediately because it was prescribed for certain history students at Oxford. There is no evidence that it reached a wider public. Only a few hundred copies of the beautifully printed six-volume *Poetical Works* in which these plays were reprinted have been sold. All of the plays except *The First Part of Nero* were intended for the stage,[1] but only *The Humours of the Court* and the masques *Prometheus the Firegiver* and *Demeter* achieved even amateur performance.[2]

Although *Demeter* was written in 1904, Bridges' dramatic activity was largely confined to the decade of 1880–90.[3] The eight plays (excluding the masques) received no critical notice on their first publication, but were reviewed only when included in the six-volume edition. They were accorded a certain amount of faint praise by the earliest reviewers, but thereafter were condemned in no uncertain terms. With a very few exceptions, notably Edward Dowden, critics who wrote general articles on Bridges' poetry dismissed his plays as unworthy of criticism. Such volleys of critical small shot as do exist, buried in the urbane pages of *The Athenaeum* and kindred publications, were obviously made with reference to a single criterion: the possibilities of stage production. A recent German critic offers a strictly representative epitaph:

All diesen Werken fehlt aber die richtige Bühnenfähigkeit, da sie meist in eine Reihe von Situationen zerfallen. Bridges ist zwar ein Verehrer, fast könnte man sagen Priester der Dichtkunst, aber es mangelt ihm, was sowohl Yeats als auch einige jüngere Vertreter des poetischen Dramas besitzen, Bühnenerfahrung.[4]

Much emphasis has been placed on the intricate construction of the plays; the most common accusation is that a mathematical interest in form, and lyricism for its own sake, have been encouraged at the expense of characterization and dramatic intensity. In most of the reviews the old familiar changes are rung with depressing regularity: the plays lack a "certain demonic energy" and "vital heat"; they have none of that "fury of the battle of life which is the stuff of drama"; their characters are "bookish." It would be futile to linger over these reviews. Only one critic, Dr. Winters, has described the plays as great drama. In a review of the poems of T. Sturge Moore he wrote:

The dramas of Mr Moore and of Robert Bridges have never to my knowledge been taken very seriously, yet it seems to me beyond all question that Bridges' two plays on *Nero* are the greatest tragedy since *The Cenci* and (if we except that furious and appalling composition, *Samson Agonistes*, which, though a tragedy, is no play) are quite possibly superior to any English tragedy outside of Shakespeare, that his *Christian Captives* is nearly as fine, and that his *Achilles in Scyros* is a performance as lovely as *Comus*, though doubtless less profound.[5]

It cannot be denied that Bridges' plays are, in the usual acceptation of the term, *closet drama*. Bridges' attitude toward stage convention is sufficiently explicit in the passage used as the epigraph for the present chapter. It is implicit in his essay, "The Influence of the Audience on Shakespeare's Drama," in which he accuses Shakespeare of playing false to his own artistic ideals in order to gratify his audience. He interprets Hamlet's speech to the players as an admission of truancy, and condemns Shakespeare where others praise or excuse him: for his brutality, his obscenity, his lack of consistency. Bridges nowhere reveals, in his few pages of dramatic criticism, any concern for *Bühnenfähigkeit*; he is more concerned with "dramatic qualities other than scenic,"[6] particularly with architectonic form and consistency of characterization. He refers in the essay on Keats to the "ugly and ill-shapen Elizabethan models," to the "imperfect delineation of the characters" in Keats' plays, and concludes that Keats lacked the "essential moral grasp" for drama.

Bridges' dramatic period roughly parallels that of Tennyson, and it is possible that the younger poet was led to make his own experiments as a result of the successful staging of Tennyson's historical poetic dramas. *The Cup* was produced in 1881, two years before the publication of *Prometheus the Firegiver*, and by 1888 Bridges had completed eight and perhaps nine of his plays. Yet neither poet was in accord with contemporary stage convention, for the vogue of Dion Boucicault was still strong, and it was during this same decade of 1880–90 that Pinero and Henry Arthur Jones made their bows to the stage with *The Magistrate* and *The Silver King*, while the early nineties were to bring not only Wilde's comedies, but the introduction of Ibsen's realistic problem drama into England. At the time that Bridges was writing his classical and Elizabethan plays in blank verse, the predominance of the realistic prose drama about contemporary life and problems was established.

The term *closet drama* is used more or less indiscriminately as a term of reproach in describing plays which do not act well, whether they were written to be acted, or merely to be read. The common assumption is that every play which will not act well on the contemporary stage is a closet drama, and that every closet drama is bad. With the growing influence in criticism of the man of the theater, for whom the chief criterion of a play's merit is its success on the popular stage, the importance of drama as an autonomous literary form has declined. The empirical approach has even gained foothold in academic criticism, in the books of Allardyce Nicoll for instance, so that it is now fashionable to maintain that the melodramas and water-farces of the early Victorian theater were better plays than the pseudo-Elizabethan tragedies written by nearly every important poet of the nineteenth century, because they were more in accord with contemporary stage convention, and similarly that the comedies of Noel Coward are better drama than the poetic plays of William Butler Yeats, because they attain a greater popular success on the stage.

Without considering the vital question as to whether a great and lasting prose drama is really possible, it seems necessary to make a distinction between dramatic and scenic qualities. For only rarely have the transitory precepts of "good theater" enhanced, rather than impeded, dramatic action. By dramatic action I mean the significant relationships between character and event which emphasize or illustrate important psychological or philosophical truths. The coming of Birnam Wood to Dunsinane is an example of dramatic action which suffers when transferred from the printed page to the stage; since the true drama is here purely subjective, the mere passing of a few twigs across the stage is less exciting to the spectator than to the reader, however well trained the former may be in a mature acceptance of dramatic symbolism. In other words, an unactable play may be more truly dramatic than a highly-stageable play, since it is free to dispose of such trammels as the *scène-à-faire* and other secondary exigencies. My point (and Charles Lamb's)[7] will perhaps be more clear if I suggest that Racine is a greater master of dramatic action than Molière, and often, in this respect, a greater master than Shakespeare.

There are at least five distinct types of closet drama, of varying legitimacy, so that an indiscriminate condemnatory application of the term seems unjustified. The most obvious and least defensible type of closet drama is the play intended for the stage only, but unpresentable because it is badly written or badly constructed. It observes contemporary stage conventions, but observes them unskillfully or incompletely. Innumerable unacted plays belong to this class.

A second type of closet drama is the dramatic poem intended only to be read. The dramatic form is simply a convenient accepted convention, a framework for the poetry similar in kind to a particular stanzaic form. Browning's *Paracelsus* is an example of this type.

A third common type is often known as the "poetic drama," another term frequently used ambiguously. Whether intended for the stage or for reading only, its emphasis is on the quality of the poetry rather than on characterization or action. The Elizabethan masque, however successful as an acted entertainment, belongs to this class: its success depended largely upon the loveliness of the poetry, or the splendor and lavishness of the production. Characterization and the moral which every masque was supposed to illustrate were really secondary. Most of the plays of Yeats belong to this class, as do Bridges' four plays or masques on classical subjects: *Achilles in Scyros*, *The Return of Ulysses*, *Prometheus the Firegiver* and *Demeter*.

A fourth type of closet drama involves the direct and absolute imitation of an obsolete dramatic convention or tradition. It endeavors to recreate an historical form without alteration or adaptation, dismissing the common theory that such a form was valid only in relation to the age and conditions out of which it arose. The most obvious example of this type is *Samson Agonistes*, with its faithful imitation of Greek tragedy. To this class belong many Elizabethan imitations of the nineteenth century, as well as four plays by Bridges: *Prometheus the Firegiver*, "A Mask in the Greek Manner" (which also belongs to the preceding class); *Palicio*, "A Romantic Drama in the Elizabethan Manner"; *The Feast of Bacchus*, an imitation of Menandrian comedy, and *The Humours of the Court*, an imitation of Shakespearean comedy.

A fifth and far more valid type of closet drama represents a fusion of the preceding types with the object of evolving a form which will make use of all good dramatic conventions, whether historical or contemporary, while eschewing all purely transitory stage conventions, conventions which may extend from the use of the Unities to the correct manner of bowing to an audience at the end of the play. The dramatist aims to restore the worthwhile elements of both the Elizabethan and the Greek stage, for instance, while ignoring the conventions of his Greek and Elizabethan predecessors which appear to have had a purely transitory significance. This ideal closet drama is more concerned with psychological and philosophical action than with the development of a story. This kind of drama is usually historical, and includes such plays as Racine's *Britannicus*, Shakespeare's *Troilus and Cressida* and Shelley's *The Cenci*. This mediation between various dramatic traditions appears in all of Bridges' plays, and three of them — *Achilles in Scyros*, *The Christian Captives*, and *The Return of Ulysses* — are described as in a "mixed manner."

At least three of his plays — *The First Part of Nero*, *Nero: Part II*, and *The Christian Captives* — seem to fulfill the ideal requirements of the *genre*. In these plays Bridges achieved not precisely a manner or idiom of his own, but one which might be called the common idiom of modern drama. His method may be described briefly thus: a timeless philosophical and aesthetic isolation results in the application of universal abstract moral principles or attitudes to time-determined *mores* or beliefs; thus we have a kind of universal vision, based upon the historical wisdom of the race, which lifts a mantle from the obscurations of history. And what is revealed is not our world, or any other particular world, but a strange world of aesthetic illusion, a world in which individualized puppets strut in the costumes of their own day, are bound by prejudices which are even more peculiarly their own, yet think and act in a manner common to all times. In these plays there are usually one or more characters acting as detached observers of the events; characters who serve, as it were, as interpreters of history. Dramatic form shares with the theme and moral attitude their universal, timeless quality: thus *The Christian Captives*, for instance, cannot be called Spanish, classical or Elizabethan, yet its diction is frequently Elizabethan, its plot and characters are partly borrowed from Spanish drama, and in form it makes use of a chorus and other classical conventions.

The principle which has militated against the acceptance of Bridges as a great lyric poet has proved an even more serious obstacle to the recognition of his plays — the principle that a writer should not only reflect the spirit of his age, but observe its literary forms. This enslavement by contemporaneity is even more serious in the drama than in lyric poetry, as the distance between the literary artist, whether he writes in poetry or prose, and those who have an intimate connection with the theater, grows daily wider. The voices of T. S. Eliot, Christopher Isherwood and W. H. Auden are voices in a wilderness. The majority of dramatic critics refuse to take into account the fact that stage conventions can be altered only through violation. Whatever attempts have been made to correct the banalities of present-day prose drama (such as the experimental theater in Russia and in America) have been misdirected because of the fallacy that literature must "progress";

that it is impossible to restore an obsolete form or convention, however great its absolute intrinsic merit may be.

On the basis of this theory that literature must "progress" reputable critics exalt the cheapest farce of a Planché above such a monumental work as *The Cenci*. Had a really competent master of Elizabethan style appeared in the nineteenth century — had Beddoes, for instance, fulfilled his early promise — his plays would be regarded with suspicion by critics who would praise the same plays had they been written in the sixteenth century. This prevalence of what Matthew Arnold called the "historical estimate" seems to me the greatest weakness of modern criticism. The value of a poem or a play is absolute in so far as anything is absolute, and not relative to the conditions of its creation. If, compared by a single standard, the plays of Robert Bridges are superior to those, let us say, of Philip Massinger, they deserve the same minute attention which the latter have received.

CHAPTER EIGHT

Historical Dramas

RIDGES' REPUTATION as a dramatist, as distinguished from his reputation as a dramatic poet, must rest on the four plays considered in the present chapter: *The First Part of Nero*, *Nero: Part II*, *The Christian Captives* and *Palicio*. All four plays are more or less Elizabethan in form, although the first three reveal that mediation between various dramatic traditions which I described in the preceding chapter. *Palicio*, probably the poorest of Bridges' plays, has all the defects of decadent Jacobean drama, and illustrates by contrast the firmness of construction and richness of characterization of the other three. Bridges' two plays on Nero have never received detailed study, but they seem to me to be in the first line of the poet's achievement — as important, in their way, as the *Shorter Poems* or *The Testament of Beauty* — and for this reason I propose to examine them at greater length than any of the other plays.

There is no more inviting field of exploration for the historical dramatist than the pages of Tacitus on the reign of Nero, and it is surprising that so few great writers have treated the subject.[1] The emperor, whether approached as the autocrat of Tacitus or the lunatic of Suetonius and Dion Cassius, offers much material for psychological speculation. According to J. S. Roberts "the downward progress of a self-indulgent maniac into criminal lunacy is a highly interesting theme, but not one well adapted to development on the stage."[2] This statement is clearly refuted by the living success of Racine's *Britannicus*, perhaps the most perfect of French classical tragedies. Racine's play deals with the hours preceding and immediately following the murder of Britannicus, and thus has the narrowest historical scope of any of the Nero plays, yet it succeeds, more than any of the others, in depicting the gradual disintegration and corruption of the emperor which is described but not adequately explained by Tacitus.

There are two alternatives open to the dramatizer of Tacitus: he may select, as did Racine, a single important portion of the reign, or he may give a "chronicle-history" treatment of an extended period. Most of the English dramatists have selected the second method. The author of the anonymous 1624 *Nero* tried, like Ben Jonson, to make use of everything which he found in his classical sources, while Matthew Gwynne, in the Latin *Nero* of 1603, gave an account of the entire reign, with no less than eighty-two actors. Lee's *The Tragedy of Nero* shows a cavalier disregard for historical fact, while Stephen Phillips' *Nero* (which was obviously inspired by Bridges' play)[3] gives us a distinctly *fin de siècle* and Wildean emperor.

Bridges' two plays illustrate the virtues and defects of the two methods: the first is a compact and highly selective historical drama, the second is loose in the Elizabethan "chronicle-history" manner. A brief summary of the two plays will clarify a more detailed analysis. *The First Part of Nero* begins with the events leading up to the murder of Britannicus, and concludes with the death of Agrippina. Nero's first appearance reveals him drunk with power, and eager to force "liberty" and joy upon a reluctant world. In the first scene of the play we find the roots of the entire tragedy: Agrippina's desire to rule her son, the difficult position of Britannicus, Nero's lust for power, and his first interest in Poppaea.

Agrippina, infuriated by Nero's growing neglect, tries to incite Britannicus to conspire against the usurper, and he, while unwilling to move in his own behalf, considers the conspiracy for the sake of Octavia. He puts the decision in Burrus' hands, but the reader learns he has misplaced his confidence: Burrus feels his first duty lies in his oath to Caesar. Domitia warns Nero of Agrippina's plot, but the Dowager Empress manages to remove his suspicions. Seneca warns Nero that either Britannicus or Agrippina must be exiled; the emperor thereupon decides to murder the prince, a murder which is finally accomplished at the end of the third act in a scene clearly reminiscent of the banquet scene in *The Cenci*. Domitia and Poppaea then conspire against Agrippina, and for some time Nero, weak and easily dominated, cannot decide between Poppaea and his mother. The play ends with the announcement of Agrippina's death. (There are interesting resemblances between *The First Part of Nero* and Gray's projected tragedy, *Agrippina*, which suggest that Bridges may have owed something to the summary printed by Mason. The scope of Bridges' play is much closer to that of Gray's planned tragedy than to that of any other play.[4])

Nero: Part II has the subtitle "From the Death of Burrus to the Death of Seneca Comprising the Conspiracy of Piso." Although it deals with the years A.D. 64–5, as against A.D. 54–9 for the first play, it offers a far less coherent record. Five years have elapsed since the conclusion of the preceding play:

> Since Burrus died, Nero hath broken loose: —
> Seneca's leading-string hath snapped in the midst
> Without a strain: — in greed of absolute power
> His will cast off restraint; in the possession
> His tottering reason doth the like.

A new conspiracy has been formed, this time on behalf of Seneca. He refuses the dangerous honor, however, and hopes that the general calamity — the fire which has just broken out — will turn attention from him.

In the second act it becomes clear that Tigellinus, Burrus' successor, is anxious to have Seneca overthrown. The third and fourth acts, and the first two scenes of the fifth act, give a discursive account of the organization and destruction of the conspiracy of Piso, and at the end of the play, the conspirators are tried, and Seneca, as the only remaining witness to the murders of Agrippina and Britannicus, is sent to his death.

Although the ambition of Poppaea, and the destinies of Britannicus and Agrippina, provide three distinct plot elements, *The First Part of Nero* is an historical drama rather than a chronicle-history play. There is a close organic relationship between the two murders; the machinations of Agrippina on Britannicus' behalf are directly responsible for his death, and the guilt of the first crime makes the second one necessary. The real subject of the play is the character of Nero. *Nero: Part II* is valuable chiefly for its characterizations of Seneca and Nero, but it is structurally weak.

The play (including both parts) is not a photographic description of Roman manners, but a picture of the spiritual degradation which produced Nero and his associates. Gerard Hopkins, who was "convinced it is one of the finest plays ever written,"[5] said it was "such a rich picture of life, indeed of our life as it would be without Christianity."[6] A speech by Nero in the second part indicates that this may have been Bridges' intention in writing the play, and reminds us of Renan's conception of Nero in *l'Antechrist*:

> The people might be masters; what they lack
> This Christ provides. Were I to prophesy,
> I'd say that should their cursed doctrines spread,
> They would one day drown all, learning and beauty,
> Wisdom and rule and art. For that I hate them,
> And love to destroy them. I AM THEIR ANTI-CHRIST.

Thrasea, Burrus, Britannicus and his sister Octavia, the fool Paris, and Otho, in the earlier play, variously illustrate by contrast the degeneracy of Nero, Agrippina, Poppaea, and, to a certain extent, Seneca. Thrasea and Burrus are honest men who illustrate the insufficiency of intellect unsupported by principle: both are willing to compromise with their moral judgments for the sake of civil order. Paris is a strange sensitive character not unlike Shakespeare's Feste: he too compromises, and joins the conspiracy against Agrippina in the hope of personal reward. Britannicus and Octavia are weak, negative peace-loving characters caught in the toils of circumstance.

Both plays are rich in subtly distinguished characters, each with a particular idiom of his own. The most vital character is perhaps Agrippina: the power of her tigerish personality is strengthened by the speeding tempo and violent rhetoric of her speeches. She is alive, indomitable, and wholly insensitive to the feelings of others, but she is also a static character, unchanging from beginning to end, and therefore less interesting than either Nero or Seneca. In serious drama the complexity and subtlety of a character, the amount of abstract philosophical and psychological observation which he may embody or occasion, is perhaps of greater importance than the illusion of living actuality which he may convey.

The character of Seneca, as revealed in the two plays, is a masterpiece of psychological observation. He represents an eternal type: the man of principle who tries to "swim with the tide." He represents as well, like Nero, an almost pathological weakness of personality, and a cowardice in judgment which leads him to rely, wherever possible, on the judgment of others. Throughout the first play he relies on Burrus; in the second play, on Thrasea. Agrippina, furious at his refusal to join Britannicus' conspiracy, takes his measure thus:

> Philosopher! come, teach me thy philosophy.
> Tell me how I may be a dauntless Stoic
> And a most pitiful ass. Show me thy method
> Of magnanimity and self-denial,
> Which makes of slaves the richest men in Rome.
> Philosopher! Ay, thou that teachest youth
> Dishonesty, and coinest honied speeches
> To gloss iniquity, sand without lime.

In the third act we actually see Seneca's casuistical reasoning at work. He has advised Nero to banish his mother, but this the emperor refuses to do. He plans to remove Britannicus instead. Seneca argues that it would be a greater evil to murder the innocent Britannicus rather than the guilty Agrippina; he does not try to dissuade Nero from murdering one of them. The emperor replies:

> This need is granted to all tyrannies,
> To slay pretenders, ay, and most of all
> Those of the family: but for a mother,
> The very Persian or the unrivalled Jew
> Would shrink from her dishonour.
>
> *Seneca (aside).*   What to say?
> Being out of kinship 'twere the lesser blot —
> Yet there's his innocence. Necessity
> Cannot suborn morality so far
> As such confusion, — nor the alternative
> May yet be shunned, — and when the best is wrong . . . .
>
> *Nero.* What thinkest thou?
> *Sen.*   Wait: it shall be my office
> To find some better means.
> *Nero.*   'Twill be thine office
> To show in such a speech as I may make
> After his death, that, howso'er he died, —
> 'Twas for the general good.
> *Sen.*   Be counselled, Nero.
> This is not my advice.
> *Nero.*   Thou offerest none
> Which can be taken.
> *Sen.*   See, I have brought your speech
> Touching the Parthian war.

In the fifth act, when Nero appears to have become reconciled with Agrippina, Seneca feels assured the emperor "must redeem the promise of his youth," that promise which had led him to support Nero's usurpation of the throne. But when the murder of Agrippina is accomplished, he refuses to take upon himself any portion of the blame. The speech is a fairly complete self-revelation:

> . . . he who deals with men, and seeks to mould
> A character to that high rule of right
> Which so few can attain, he works, I say,
> With different matter, nor can he be blamed
> By any measure of his ill success.
> His best endeavours are like little dams
> Built 'gainst the ocean, on a sinking shore.
> Nature asserts her force — and the wise man
> Blames not himself for his defeat. . . .
> I take unto myself no self-reproach,
> Nay, not a tittle of the part of mischief
> A vulgar mind might credit to my score.
> I have done my best, and that's the utmost good
> A man can do; and if a better man
> Had in my place done more, 'tis perverse Fortune
> That placed me ill. Thus far I agree with you,
> Who look on me askance, and think my heart
> Is tainted; as if I would in such case
> Do such a thing, as — poison my brother at table,
> Contrive to kill my mother. . . .

The characterization of Seneca in the second play involves fewer purely moral issues. The conspirators urge him to join them, emphasizing the atrocities of Nero's reign, but rather than be disturbed from his life of luxurious academic seclusion, he argues that things are not as bad as they seem. When he learns that Thrasea does not approve of the conspiracy, he definitely refuses to join it. His first reaction, upon hearing of the great fire, is that "A general calamity might turn attention from me." He resolves to renounce his wealth and leave Rome. But Tigellinus has poisoned Nero against his tutor, and Seneca meets death with dignity and courage.

The characterization of Seneca in the two plays seems to me one of the most profound in English dramatic literature. It is interesting as a plausible interpretation of an enigmatic historical figure; it is more important as a study of the relationship of principle to character and action. By his original error in condoning Nero's usurpation of the throne, Seneca was forced to excuse the emperor's crimes. Only thus could he justify his part in the first. Thus he was driven to a life of continual compromise and casuistry, and this had the effect of lessening his power of perception and judgment. Through an unwillingness to see Nero's crimes, he gradually became unable to see them. His recovery of courage at the end of the second play is neither unhistorical nor illogical: he had no decision to make, no moral choice to make. Thus his life ended in failure. In Seneca we have a complete portrait of the decay of the power of moral judgment through the casuistical corruption of principle.

In Nero we have a pendant study of the disintegration of personality through self-indulgence and surrender to impulse, and through lust for power. The characterization also illustrates, to a lesser degree, the loss of artistic sensibility. In the opening scene of *The First Part of Nero* we find Nero deluding himself into the belief that he is the benefactor of mankind:

> The curse of life is of our own devising,
> Born of man's ignorance and selfishness.
> He wounds his happiness against a cage
> Of his own make, and only waits the word
> For one to set his door open, — and look,
> Having his liberty is he not glad
> As heaven's birds are? — Now when fate's ordinance
> Sends him a liberator, ay, and one
> Not to cajole or preach, but will or nill,
> Who'll force him forth and crush up his old cage,
> With all who hang back and skulk therein,
> How shall he not be happy?

Nero's weakness of personality, on which the plot of the first play depends, is revealed in four great scenes (II, iv; IV, iv, v, vi). In these scenes we observe the most exciting kind of *dramatic action*, the visible weakening of a man's resolve before the force of a stronger personality. In each of these scenes Nero is at the mercy of his interlocutor, and is forced to abandon his original resolve. In the first one (II, iv) he has been informed by Domitia of Agrippina's plan to enthrone Britannicus, but in less than two hundred lines the dowager-empress convinces him of her innocence. She resorts to sentiment as well as to skillful reasoning, and at the end of the scene Nero is eating out of her hand. In the fourth scene of the fourth act his suspicions are renewed by Paris' announcement of Agrippina's alleged plot to marry Rubellius Plautus and make him emperor. Burrus is also accused of complicity. Nero is resolved on the immediate death of all the accused, but when left alone with Burrus he gradually loses his determination. At last he abandons rational argument, and begs the praetorian prefect to murder Agrippina. It takes Burrus only a few more words to make him give up the whole murderous project. In the following scene Agrippina not only removes all of Nero's suspicions, but gains such an ascendancy over him that she is able to dictate rewards for her friends and punishment for her accusers. (This brilliant scene derives from one brief sentence in Tacitus: "Thus instead of pleading her innocence, as though she lacked confidence, or her claims on him by way of reproach, she obtained vengeance on her accusers and rewards for her friends."[7]) In the ensuing scene, however, Nero is at the mercy of Poppaea, and is won back to his original resolve. By this time he is aware of his own weakness, and plans to have Agrippina murdered without taking Seneca or Burrus into his confidence. Thus, in terms of his own strange moral code, the second murder is a step down from the first; he regrets that he must stoop to concealed crime and subterfuge. His rationalization of the crime is interesting, showing as it does the fruits of his Senecan education.

Nero's degeneration since the death of Burrus is described by
Thrasea in the first scene of *Nero: Part II*:

> . . . in greed of absolute power
> His will cast off restraint; in the possession
> His tottering reason doth the like. His lust,
> His cruelty, his effeminate, blundering passion
> For art and brutal vice are but the brag
> Of a hideous nature, which will force the bounds
> Of human action, till the shames of Rome
> Shame shameless Rome to wipe away her shame.

The clearest indication of Nero's greater degeneracy is the changed
character of his associates: before he was at the mercy of Agrippina, Burrus and Seneca, and had for companions Otho, Petronius
and Lucan; now he is the plaything of dull-witted fools, and
Burrus' successor is the brutal Tigellinus. Nero's interest as a dramatic character is greatly enhanced by his ability to see himself,
as he thinks, objectively: he prides himself on his increased licen-
tiousness, and in the second act recommends the philosophy of
emotional naturalism. He has not entirely lost his illusion of himself as a benefactor:

> 'Tis the soundest principle
> To follow nature; and what nature is
> I well perceive: I judge all by myself:
> The appetites are universal gifts:
> Caesar will never stoop to flatter Caesar
> By such pretence of difference, nor withhold
> From others what himself loves. I believe
> That no man in the world worth calling man
> Is what philosophers term pure and good; —
> Nor woman either. All would gratify
> The strong desires of nature, and all shall,
> While I am emperor.

At the end of the second act, shortly after telling Poppaea
"There is no mischief, love, I am not a match for," Nero delivers

a long and interesting monologue. It appears at a first reading to be wholly inconsistent with the earlier characterization of Nero, and therefore a serious structural fault. Poppaea has just demanded that Actè, Nero's first mistress, be banished from the palace; while he speaks the great fire which destroys Rome is raging outside:

> 'Tis private pleasure that she seeks, nought else:
> And Seneca the same. That's the true fire,
> That burns unquenchable in all human hearts.
> Let it rage, and consume the rotten timbers
> Of old convention, the dry mouldering houses
> Of sad philosophy, that in their stead
> I may build up the free and ample structure
> Of modern wisdom. Ay, and let Rome burn.
> Blow, wind, and fan the flames till all's consumed;
> That out of full destruction may arise
> The perfect city of my reconstruction,
> Beautiful, incombustible, Neronic;
> Good of ill: or rather there's no ill:
> 'Tis good's condition, cradle; 'tis good itself.
>   But now for Actè, my Actè: poor little Actè.
> That bearest all so patiently; the insult
> And domineering scorn, which this fine lady,
> Whom for her beauty I have made my empress,
> Pours on thy head! Thou shalt have full protection:
> I cannot give it here, but I can send thee
> To those who hate thy rival, and for that
> Will cherish thee. Thy rival! rob me of thee!
> Why, there's no clown in my subservient world,
> No drudge of lot the vilest, but may smile
> Secure in tyranny of one fair province,
> Where young love first campaigned, the tender trust
> Of a devoted woman: and shall Caesar
> Throw up this allmen's joy? nay, here the heart rules;
> Who aims at thee wounds me.

The first part of the speech offers no difficulty, although Nero's early perception that gratification of animal impulse is the motive for his own conduct appears to have been lost; Nero's preservation of his youthful love for Actè, in view of his prolonged debauchery, is more questionable. But if it is observed that the emperor, ever more lonely, realizes that Actè is the only woman who loves him for himself, the speech falls in with the rest of his characterization as a supreme egotist. Yet the implication that the "heart" is not contaminated by evil and habitual surrender to animal instinct is dangerously Rousseauistic.

At the end of the play Nero reluctantly gives the order for Seneca's death, and in his final *apologia* we see that he has been self-deluded to the end:

> Yet by these flecks and flaws,
> Whate'er they be, 'tis fated that men fall:
> And thus may I, nay must; unless in time
> I heed good warning, for my fault is gross.
> I am over-generous; yes; ye say it; I know it.
> That is my flaw. It is because my schemes
> Are wider than his own, that Seneca hates me:
> Because the world hath tasted more of freedom
> Under my rule than under any Caesar
> Who went before. . . .

There is no conclusive evidence that Bridges read any of the earlier plays about Nero. Many resemblances between the various Nero plays may be attributed to the use of a common source.[8] The emphasis placed on Piso's conspiracy in *The Tragedy of Nero* (1624) may have suggested to Bridges its dramatic possibilities. The only evidence that Bridges read the play is the close resemblance between the meeting of the conspirators in both plays,[9] a meeting not recorded by any historian. There are a few interesting resemblances between Racine's *Britannicus* and *The First Part of Nero*, but none which conclusively prove influence. The most interesting of these is the conception of Nero's weakness of personality, his helplessness when faced by Agrippina or Burrus. Of his mother, in *Britannicus*, Nero says,

Mon génie étonné tremble devant le sien.[10]

Bridges' use of Tacitus is very illuminating. The *Annals* is a masterpiece of compression: the pages on Nero's reign are full of tantalizing hints, unmotivated actions, incomprehensible characters, unexplained crimes. What, for instance, is the explanation of the freedwoman Epicharis' participation in the conspiracy of Piso, and of her fortitude under torture "when freeborn men, Roman knights, and senators, yet unscathed by torture, betrayed every one, his dearest kinfolk"?[11] What share had Seneca and Burrus in the deaths of Agrippina and Britannicus? How did Seneca become involved in the conspiracy of Piso? Bridges' plays give conjectural answers to such questions as these. Briefly, he takes the results given by Tacitus, the recorded unexplained events, and, by studying the slightest hints, reconstructs possible causes. A comparison of Bridges' plays with Tacitus' account reveals with what curiosity and painstaking care the dramatist has explored his source material, weighing every event and every character. Such a comparison reveals, however, that Bridges' plays have a dramatic rather than a scholarly object, for the chronology is sometimes incorrect. For the sake of dramatic effectiveness Bridges has no scruples about compressing into a single day events which did not occur in close succession.[12]

Palicio, "A Romantic Drama in Five Acts in the Elizabethan Manner," is perhaps the poorest of Bridges' plays. It suffers from the faults of the three dramatic traditions which appear to have influenced it, Jacobean drama of the decadence, Spanish Renaissance drama, and the noble-brigand drama of the nineteenth century. These faults are structural looseness combined with inconsistency of characterization and inconsistency of ethical attitude. The subject of the play naturally reminds the reader of *Philaster*, but the skeleton of the plot was borrowed from Stendhal's "Vanina Vanini," an inferior tale of nineteenth-century *carbonari*.[13]

The plot centers in a rebellion of Sicilian patriots led by the brigand Giovanni Palicio. It is such a rebellion as had recurred, and was to recur, with disastrous frequency in that stormy land. Hugo, the Spanish Viceroy, is a stupid, head-strong tyrant. Manuel, who comes of the same stock as Palicio, is Chief Justiciary, betrothed to Constance, the daughter of Hugo. The heroine of the play, at times a very dubious heroine, is Margaret, the sister of Manuel. The Chief Justiciary is secretly in sympathy with the protests of the rebel poor, but he believes that most may be obtained for them by remaining friendly with Hugo. The Spaniard, in turn, knows that his own power is toppling, and he is glad to lean upon the popular Sicilian. Into this complex maze of persons and issues comes Duke Philip, a commissioner sent from Spain to investigate the rebellion. The play has more than these political antecedents to confuse and impede its progress: on a previous visit to the island, Philip had made love to Constance, and had deserted her. Upon his return to Sicily, he discovers that he still loves her, and his jealousy of Manuel creates most of the familiar difficulties of this kind of play. Behind and above the scenes of this dramatic nightmare is the apparently hopeless love of Margaret, the sister of the Chief Justiciary, and Palicio, the brigand. The story of their strange attachment constitutes the main plot, a plot too often submerged beneath the multifarious intrigues of minor characters.

Through four acts the tone of the play is that of tragedy, but by a shameless use of *deus ex machina*, a final reconciliation between all the main characters occurs, and of the play's many villains and heroes doomed to a certain death, only the Iago-like Blasco and one unidentified soldier suffer the expected reward. The happy ending of the play, as in many Spanish Renaissance dramas, is by no means logical or even to be hoped for. This structural weakness is the outward symbol of an even greater fault: an unjustifiable change in the author's critical attitude toward his subject-matter. In the early parts of the play, he makes an awkward effort to see the events through the eyes of those who are actively concerned in them, to assume their code of ethics; it is not until late in the play that he gives to the words of Manuel a ring unequivocally English and modern. The author of an historical play should either accept wholly, or criticize directly, the ethical attitude of his characters. To begin by accepting that ethical attitude, for the purpose of the fiction, only to introduce his own point of view late in the play, is a fundamental dramatic weakness.

The character of Palicio invites a direct examination of this principle. In the early acts we see him through the eyes of his enemies, who fear and respect him, and through those of Margaret, who loves him. Because she is first attracted to him by his unselfish patriotism — his willingness to sacrifice life and peace to a cause, whatever it may be — he achieves a stature and nobility in the light of standards totally at variance with the poet's own ideals of peace and brotherly love. Thus a convention of personality is established: we are transported, at the beginning of the play, into a world whose standards of conduct we may not respect, but which we accept for the purpose of the fiction. By these standards, Palicio is a noble man because he is a brave man of action.

The psychological plot — the real action of the play — consists in the salvation of Palicio's soul. He is torn between his love for Margaret and his *honor*, i.e., his faithfulness to the patriotic cause. In the end he relinquishes his own concept of honor (which Bridges rightly considers a mistaken one) in favor of his love for Margaret. The poet undoubtedly meant this transition to represent a kind of moral advance by which Palicio achieves breadth of vision and respect for law. But because the convention of the play, the original assumption of feeling, exalts blind patriotism, Palicio's change of mind seems to the reader a debasement, the embarrassed surrender of a weakened resolve.

The Christian Captives illustrates by contrast the defects of *Palicio*. Its formal structure is firm and the author's attitude toward his subject consistent. From the very beginning of the play all conduct is viewed in the light of a timeless morality more or less identical with that of liberal Christianity, yet transcending the ethics of any particular creed. The play might even be regarded as a plea for religious toleration. Although she is not converted until late in the play, Almeh represents far more than the Christian captives themselves the highest Christian ideals. Prince Enrique closes the play with much the same words of peace and brotherly love, of the power of intelligence over that of the sword, which were so incongruous at the end of *Palicio*. The play did not attract as much critical attention as some of the others, but it represents Bridges' nearest approach to stage drama, and lacks neither *Bühnenfähigkeit* nor imaginative fervor.

The plot is borrowed from Calderón's great tragedy of Christian patriotism, *El principe constante*,[14] but Bridges changes the theme from one of heroic martyrdom to a "tragedy of star-crossed lovers," since he is unable to share Calderón's passionate Catholic feeling. His attitude toward religious heroism is more detached than that of Calderón, and at times directly antithetical to it. Behind the personal tragedy of Almeh and Ferdinand, in Bridges' play, is the tragedy of religious war.

The Christian captives constitute the Chorus of the play, the use of which probably explains Bridges' description of the play as being "in a mixed manner." It is through the singing of the captives that Almeh is first attracted to Christianity. How amenable her mind would be to it is revealed at once:

> *Zapel.* They are unbelievers.
> *Almeh.*   True: yet that's no crime
> But what they might impute to you. Were we
> Fallen in their hands, thus cut off from our homes,
> 'Twere cruel to be tortured for the faith.
> *Zapel.* They are worthless dogs.

Almeh.   Alas! is all my teaching
           So cast away upon thy boorish soul?
           Pity makes brethren of our enemies.

Almeh is wooed by many noble lovers of her own race, but the
man with whom she falls in love is the Christian prince Ferdinand.
In the third act she admits to him that she has already found certain aspects of Christianity attractive: her real conversion had begun in the previous act when she had spoken to the Christian
captives. But she asks Ferdinand whether he is not, in his warlike
mission, trampling that "happy gospel, Peace on Earth." He replies in a passage characteristic of the splendid rhetoric of the entire play:

           Too late to ask. When conscience, like an angel,
           Stood in the way to bar my setting forth,
           Zeal and ambition blinded me; tho' yet
           Against the voice of them that urged me on
           There lacked not prodigies of heaven to stay me.
           For as we sailed from Lisbon, all the host
           That lined the shore with banners and gay music,
           Was changed before my eyes to funeral trains
           Of black and weeping mourners, who with wails
           And screams affrighted us. The sun in heaven
           Turned to blood-red, and doleful mists of grey
           Shut us in darkness, while the sucking ebb
           Dragged us to doom. And here now that I stand
           In the rebuke of judgment, I have no plea
           Save that I suffer; unless thou be found
           My unsought prize.[15]

The King, however, has destined her to be the prize of Tarudante, Prince of Morocco, so that his powerful support may be
assured for future battles with the Christian armies. Having discovered her pity for the prisoners, and her love for Ferdinand, the
King promises Almeh that on the day she marries the Moor, Ferdinand and the Christian captives will be freed. Ferdinand orders

her to give up the bargain in a scene which illustrates Bridges'
talent for lifting speech in common use from the trite and sentimental to a rhetoric of rare beauty and subtlety:

> *Ferd.*   Say, if thou canst, thou lov'st me: and if not,
> Thou shalt at least have heard, and I have told,
> My tale; how to Prince Ferdinand of Portugal
> Thou didst appear the only being on earth
> Worth his devotion; that for thy possessing
> He would have given all else, to live with thee
> As Christians use, in state of man and wife,
> Which God hath blessed.
>
> *Almeh.*   No more, I pray no more.
> The graveyard ghosts are not so waste and dead
> As is thy phantom picture.
>
> *Ferd.*   Dost thou love me?
>
> *Almeh.*   Why ask me? Yet be this an hour of truth,
> Tho' all time lie. I love thee, Ferdinand,
> Even as thou lovest me; would be thy wife,
> To live alone with thee as Christians use.

The King, with Tarudante and Sala, comes to the garden at this
moment, and finds Almeh in Ferdinand's arms. The proposed
royal marriage is immediately forgotten, and Tarudante deserts
the king, who is so enraged that he resolves that unless Ceuta is
ceded, Ferdinand will be starved to death: "Let not his life out-
drag three days."

The fine fourth act opens on the third and last day. Almeh, out
of sympathy for her lover, has herself refused to eat or sleep. The
King has intercepted a letter revealing that she has been baptized.
Simultaneously he has learned that Edward of Portugal is dead,
and that the regents are Prince Enrique, encamped a few miles
from Fez, and the imprisoned Ferdinand. The King is at first
tempted to kill Almeh, and thus remove the Christian stain from
his family, but in the end he relents. And now that Ferdinand holds
royal power, he is even reconciled to him, and sees in the hitherto

banned marriage a possible alliance of great advantage to himself. All obstacles to the happiness of the two lovers now appear to have been removed, and the King orders Ferdinand to be dressed in his finest clothes, and brought into the garden. But he is carried on the stage a dying man; his rich clothing mock the weakness of his body and mind, and the greatest scene of *King Lear* comes immediately to mind. The King points to a table covered with food, but Ferdinand refuses to eat. Even the news that he might rule does not stir him, nor does the letter from Prince Enrique promising to deliver him:

> For cometh he at even or at morn,
> Tomorrow or today, he cometh late.
> My eves and morns are passed, and my deliverance
> Is nearer than his coming: yet for that,
> Tho' I shall see him not when he doth come,
> Not the less will he come for so he saith.

King. Thou wilt not eat and live?
Ferd.   I thank thee, sire.

The King becomes more and more excited, as Ferdinand appears to be dying before his eyes. At last he offers the prince his daughter in marriage, and the prince, overjoyed, moves toward the food. But when he asks "And Ceuta?" the King cannot forbear striking a final bargain: "That is mine. Her price." Ferdinand wearily thrusts the food aside, and the King is filled with baffled anger. All his former hate returns with the memory of the ancient issue:

Ferd. It cheereth death to spend my last breath thus.
King. Sittest thou there balanced 'twixt death and life,
>   Of all that God could grant thee, life and love,
>   Wrung from me by my sorrow, to my shame
>   Preferrest the Christian hell? O Infidel
>   Apostatizing dog, lest now thy mouth
>   Should find the power to gasp one broken speech
>   Of triumph over me, die at my hand.
>   Death shall not rob me of thy blood that's left.

He stabs Ferdinand across the table:

> Thus let thy brother find thee, if I fail
> To send him also thither, where thou goest
> To thine idolatrous and thieving sires.

The Prince slumps forward, dead, and the King leaves the darkening stage. Presently a noise is heard, and creeping shadows appear. They are the Christian captives, trying to escape. They discover their dead Prince, and are stricken with grief. They carry the body away, hiding it in a bower at the back of the stage. As they go out, the "stage darkens quite." The King reënters the garden, and when he sees that Ferdinand's body is gone, he thinks that he has crept away to die. Sighing is heard, and, like that of Hamlet's father, it recurs in different parts of the garden. Finally the moon emerges from behind a cloud, and shows the ghost of Ferdinand, standing upright, "midway back" on the stage. The King lunges at the specter, which vanishes. When Sala enters, the King says "He lives," for so he believes. But presently the body is found, cold and dead.

The ghost of Ferdinand is a real ghost, and not a pathological hallucination, a figment of the King's mind. Sala says,

> The spirits of the dead have power to fix
> The image of their presence in the place
> Where life was robbed: there are a thousand stories
> Of such frail apparitions,

and presently a messenger reports "Prince Ferdinand's escape." —

> They tell me that he galloped thro' their company.
> They might have touched him. When they called his name
> He took no heed. Some fired their pieces at him:
> And some pursued: but he, as tho' his horse
> Were winged, held on, nor ever turned his head,
> And soon was out of reach.

In the fifth act Almeh comes upon the moonlit stage, and, discovering Ferdinand's body, dies of grief beside it. What remains to be said — full revelation and the final moral commentary — recalls the last scene of *Romeo and Juliet*. The Christian soldiers arrive, and the King of Fez is killed. The lovers are discovered, and Prince Enrique, "Henry the Navigator," decides that they shall be buried together in the sepulchre at Ceuta, which Sala, who has always loved Almeh, may visit whenever he wishes.

The last speeches of the play, delivered by Prince Enrique, explicitly state the moral of the play:

> For myself, I vow
> Never to draw sword again. I count all days
> That ever I spent in arms lost to my life.
> Man's foe is ignorance: and the true soldier
> May sit at home, and in retirement win
> Kingdoms of knowledge; or to travel forth
> And make discovery of earth's bounds, and learn
> What nations of his fellows God hath set
> In various countries; and by what safe roads
> They may knit peaceful commerce, — this is well,
> And this hath been my choice. To shed man's blood
> Brings but such ills on man as here ye see.
> To save my brother and these Christian captives
> I drew this sword, which thus I sheathe again
> For ever.

The Christian Captives is Bridges' only tragedy, if the Nero plays are defined as historical dramas. It lacks the profound psychological and philosophical observation of the latter, but, because of its greater simplicity of structure, would have a better chance of succeeding on the stage. Considered as a work of art, it suffers by comparison with *El principe constante*: Bridges lacked equally the narrow religious passion which made the subject one of intense immediacy to Calderón, and the fertile luxuriant imagination with which the Spanish poet could inform that passion. Compared with all but the masterpieces of Elizabethan tragedy, however, *The Christian Captives* excels in structural firmness, consistency of characterization and ethical attitude, and purified dignity of style.

CHAPTER NINE

Classical Masques and Dramas

BRIDGES' FOUR MASQUES or plays based on Greek mythology are even farther removed from the conventions of the late Victorian theater than the historical plays, and they are not dramatic even in the sense that the Nero plays are dramatic. For these very reasons they command greater respect from the casual reader, who does not apply to them the standards of acted drama. Although two of the four are largely allegorical, they have no great philosophical significance, and exist for the sake of the poetry they embody. Yet they are interesting as well as deliberate attempts to achieve that fusion of the Greek attainment and the Christian ideal which Bridges considered necessary to the highest art.[1]

"Believe me," Gerard Hopkins wrote to Bridges, "the Greek gods are a totally unworkable material; the merest frigidity, which must chill and kill every living work of art they are brought into."[2] Bridges agreed rather with Sturge Moore that "the Greek stories are of inexhaustible fertility" and that those "who confine themselves to either old or new must of necessity remain narrow and unreceptive."[3] Like Sturge Moore, he regarded these stories as splendid framework for symbolism and allegory. It is one of the astonishing facts of Bridges criticism that so few critics have perceived the real meaning of his two masques, *Prometheus the Firegiver* and *Demeter*.[4]

Prometheus the Firegiver, the earliest of Bridges' dramatic works, retells the transition of human worship from Zeus to Prometheus,

and symbolizes the substitution of the God of Love of the New
Testament for the angry God of the Old Testament; or, more generally, of modern Christianity for all less "human" religions.
The allegory should be obvious to any careful reader, certainly no
later than Prometheus' prediction of Christ's coming:

> . . . for there is whispered
> A word gone forth to scare the mighty Gods;
> How one must soon be born, and born of man,
> Who shall drive out their impious host from heaven,
> And from their skyey dwellings rule mankind
> In truth and love.

In the final lines of the ode which closes the play, the Chorus looks
forward hopefully to the fulfillment of the prophecy:

> For the god who shall rule mankind from the deathless skies
> By mercy and truth shall be known,
> In love and peace shall arise.
> For him, — if again I hear him thunder above,
> O then, if I crouch or start,
> I will press thy lovingkindness more to my heart,
> Remember the words of thy mouth rare and precious,
> Thy heart of hearts and gifts of divine love.

The resemblance between Bridges' attitude and that of Shelley
is thus, here as elsewhere, very clear. *Prometheus the Firegiver* is not
so thoroughly clogged with theory and allegory as *Prometheus Unbound*, but the main conceptions are the same. As in both plays
the "creeds outworn" [5] give way to a religion of love, so too there
is also substituted a worship of ideal beauty and of the spirit of
man. The chief difference is between Bridges' Prometheus and
Shelley's, who often speak in the lingo of the nineteenth century
humanitarian, or as the Voltairian antagonist of "thought-
executing ministers." [6] If occasionally Bridges' hero falls into
humanitarian jargon,

> O deem not a man's children are but those
> Out of his loins engendered,

he is usually much closer to the traditional character of Prometheus as the patron of knowledge: "in knowledge all my power." Bridges' play thus suffers less than Shelley's from a purely aesthetic aura.[7]

In his expository prologue Bridges' Prometheus has a distinctly Shelleyan character:

> Could I but win this world from Zeus for mine,
> . With not a god to vex my happy rule,
> I would inhabit here and leave high heaven:
> So much I love it and its race of men.

He is, in Shelley's words, the "type of the highest perfection of moral and intellectual nature, impelled by the purest and the truest motives to the best and noblest ends . . . he is susceptible of being described as exempt from the taints of ambition, envy, revenge, and a desire for personal aggrandizement."[8] Bridges, like Shelley, does not attempt to restore the lost play of Aeschylus. As the earlier poet says, "The moral interest of the fable . . . would be annihilated if we could conceive of him as unsaying his high language and quailing before his successful and perfidious adversary."[9] Yet on one occasion Bridges' Prometheus is guilty of unsaying his high language:

> Speak not of love. See, I am moved with hate. . . .
>
> Nay, were there now another deed to do,
> Which more could hurt our enemy than this,
> Which here I stand to venture, here would I leave thee
> Conspiring at his altar, and fly off
> To plunge the branding terror in his soul.

This speech is clearly inconsistent with the character of Prometheus as established in the opening lines of the masque, and it obscures the otherwise transparent allegory.

Once too, Bridges is drawn into his predecessor's most serious heresy: the advocacy of Rousseauistic primitivism:

> In vain was reason given, if man therewith
> Shame truth; and name it wisdom to cry down
> The unschooled promptings of his best desire.

Such lines as these cannot be justified. One can only point out that this primitivism is specifically contradicted in other parts of Bridges' work, as in the sonnet "At times with hurried hoofs or scattering dust," or in *Nero: Part II*, where, before proposing a public debauchery of the noblest Roman ladies, Nero says:

> 'Tis the soundest principle
> To follow nature; and what nature is
> I well perceive. I judge all by myself:
> The appetites are universal gifts. . . .

Prometheus and Nero are thus advocating the same philosophy. What Bridges fails to allow for is the possible coexistence, at any given moment, of both kinds of desire, and of the need of something above desire itself to discriminate between Inachus' and Prometheus' appetite for beauty and knowledge, and Nero's appetite for debauchery.

To say that Bridges' masque, in spite of its allegorical resemblances to *Prometheus Unbound*, was influenced even more by *Comus* and *Samson Agonistes*, is to say, among other things, that it is much nearer to the Greek spirit than is Shelley's play. The form of the masque is as strictly imitative of Greek drama as *Samson Agonistes*; the style is closer to the gentler Milton of *Comus*. Among the many conventions of Greek drama which appear are the Euripidean prologue (which also occurs in *Demeter*, *Achilles in Scyros*, and *The Return of Ulysses*), the use of *stychomythia* (as in lines 412 ff.) with its riddling one-line questions and answers, the story of Io's wanderings (1059 ff.) which takes on the aspect of the classical geography lesson, the dual function of the Chorus as actor and commentator, and the struggle between Argeia and Inachus as to whether Prometheus' gift should be accepted.

The opening lines of the masque clearly derive from the opening of *Comus*. This passage may be described, indeed, as the first perfect imitation of Miltonic blank verse in two hundred years of experiment:

> From high Olympus and the aetherial courts,
> Where Zeus our angry king confirms
> The Fates' decrees and bends the wills of the gods,
> I come: and on the earth step with glad foot.
>   This variegated ocean-floor of the air,
> The changeful circle of fair land, that lies
> Heaven's dial, sisterly mirror of night and day:
> The wide o'er-wandered plain, this nether world
> My truant haunt is, when from jealous eyes
> I steal, for hither 'tis I steal, and here
> Unseen repair my joy: yet not unseen
> Methinks, nor seen unguessed of him I seek.
> Rather by swath or furrow, or where the path
> Is walled with corn I am found, by trellised vine
> Or olive set in banks or orchard trim:
> I watch all toil and tilth, farm, field and fold,
> And taste the mortal joy; since not in heaven
> Among our easeful gods hath facile time
> A touch so keen, to wake such love of life
> As stirs the frail and careful being, who here,
> The king of sorrows, melancholy man,
> Bows at his labour, but in heart erect
> A god stands, nor for any gift of god
> World barter his immortal-hearted prime.

This is magnificent *pastiche*. In the first four lines alone, besides the obvious suspension of the narrative subject and verb until the last line, there is a typical Miltonic elision in the fourth foot of the first line, a Miltonic trisyllabic fifth foot in the third line, and a characteristic inversion of the fourth foot in the fourth line. The

whole passage might have come from Milton's pen, and to have
succeeded thus where the eighteenth century and even Keats
failed is in itself a great achievement. But if Bridges did not go
beyond Milton in these opening lines, he developed, later in the
same poem, a very distinct style of his own. A hundred lines after
the Miltonic opening we find, besides the lovely Vergilian lines,

> I see the cones
> And needles of the fir, which by the wind
> In melancholy places ceaselessly
> Sighing are strewn upon the tufted floor,

this very individual passage:

> Such are enough
> To burden the slow flight of labouring rooks,
> When on the leafless tree-tops in young March
> Their glossy herds assembling soothe the air
> With cries of solemn joy and cawings loud.

Demeter, written in a single month[10] at "the request of the ladies
of Somerville College,"[11] is less finished in execution than *Prometheus the Firegiver*. As in the earlier masque he relates the coming of Prometheus to the new religion of love, Bridges relates the
myth of Demeter to the Christian story of the resurrection, but
he does not ignore the original symbolism, the concealment and
return of the earth's reproductive powers in the winter and spring.
The dual aspect of the myth is suggested by Persephone in the
third act:

> Now Fate, that look'd contrary, hath fulfill'd
> My project with mysterious efficacy:
> And as a plant that yearly dieth down
> When summer is o'er, and hideth in the earth,
> Nor showeth promise in its wither'd leaves
> That it shall reawaken and put forth
> Its blossoms any more to deck the spring;

So I, the mutual symbol of my choice,
Shall die with winter, and with spring revive,
How without winter could I have my spring?
How come to resurrection without death?
Lo thus our joyful meeting of to-day,
Born of our separation, shall renew
Its annual ecstasy, by grief refresht:
And no more pall than doth the joy of spring
Yearly returning to the hearts of men.

Both Persephone and Demeter undergo radical changes of character: Persephone, by progressing from girlish innocence to wisdom, after an insight into human sorrow and the nature of absolute evil; Demeter, by partly overcoming grief for the loss of her daughter through her new love for mankind. Demeter's repentance of her resolution to threaten mankind with dearth is basically similar to that of Shelley's Prometheus.[12]

The play opens with a conversation between Athena and Demeter about the beauty and love of flowers. Persephone rebukes Athena for her "cold, essential wisdom" which encourages sorrow, rather than a carefree gaiety; she will love flowers for beauty, scent or hue alone. But she returns from Hades in the third act, grown from girl to woman. Demeter asks her what has reconciled her to her dark fate, and she relates what she has seen, and what has brought her wisdom, hinting that the "mysteries of evil" have been revealed to her. Demeter pleads that she tell of this revelation, and after some hesitation, Persephone describes a scene of absolute ugliness (III, 974 ff.), but admits that she cannot adequately describe the "mystery that is hid within." It is unfortunate that Bridges allowed Demeter to overcome Persephone's hesitancy, for a definition of evil in terms of physical ugliness is at best unsatisfactory.

Persephone then asks Demeter to imagine a temple where the initiated might see ideal beauty, and realize that before it evil is powerless and irrelevant. Demeter replies that she has inaugurated such a temple in Eleusis. Demeter then asks her what she saw in the Cave of Cacophysis, and Persephone replies:

> I saw
> The meaning and reason of all things,
> All at a glance, and in that glance perceiv'd
> The origin of all things to be evil,
> And the énd evil: that what seems as good
> Is as the bloom of gold that spread thereo'er
> May, by one stroke of the hand,
> Be brush'd away, and leave the ill beneath
> Solid and foul and black. . . .

Dem.   Now tell me, child,
> If Hades love thee, that he sent thee thither.

Per. He said it could not harm me, and I think
> It hath not.

Dem.   Nay it hath not, . . . and I know
> The power of evil is no power at all
> Against eternal good.

>   .   .   .   .

> But sure it is that Fate o'erruleth all
> For good or ill: and we (no more than men)
> Have power to oppose, nor any will nor choice
> Beyond such wisdom as the fisher hath
> Who driven by sudden gale far out to sea
> Handles his fragile boat safe thro' the waves,
> Making what harbour the wild storm allows.

This, then, is the philosophical core of the play, embodying three dubious and partly contradictory ideas: the identity of beauty and goodness; the superior force of goodness over evil, which is irrelevant; the assertion that man lacks freedom of will, and must therefore depend upon instinct for guidance. One feels that Persephone's education has been incomplete.

The story of Demeter's change is less confusing. She returns from her wanderings, during which, to assuage her grief, she mixed with mortals and nursed Demophöon. The following lines reveal how she (and hence the religious impulse in general) acquired pity and humanitarian feeling:

> Yea, ye shall hear how much I came to love him
> For in his small epitome I read
> The trouble of mankind; in him I saw
> The hero's helplessness, the countless perils
> In ambush of life's promise, the desire
> Blind and instinctive, and the will perverse.
> His petty needs were man's necessities;
> In him I nurst all mortal natur', embrac'd
> With whole affection to my breast, and lull'd
> Wailing humanity upon my knee.

Having observed that sorrow was man's "life companion," she sought a means of making "sorrow his friend," and asked King Keleos to build for her a temple in Eleusis.

It is evident that both masques were influenced by the then new science of ethnology, which showed that Christianity was but one manifestation of a human instinct responsible for the creation of all religions. By examining, symbolically, the moments of transition, on the one hand between the conception of God as unfriendly to man and the coming of a God of Love, and on the other hand, between a world of irresponsible gaiety, like that of Persephone among the flowers, or of barren sorrow, and a world in which sorrow had become, in a sense, man's friend, Bridges not only illustrates the ancient and pagan origin of Christianity, but expresses, more or less directly, the nature of his own religious beliefs. Such problems were of particular interest to late Victorian poets. In the "Hymn of Man" and "Hertha," Swinburne deifies the human race as the highest manifestation of nature, and in the latter poem he uses the Teutonic earth goddess as symbol for the natural basis of all life and thought. Meredith's "The Appeasement of Demeter" bears only a superficial resemblance to Bridges' masque, since it emphasizes the part of joy, rather than sorrow, in human life. But two poems by Thomas Hardy deal explicitly with the general theme of Bridges' two masques, the dissolution of outworn beliefs. "The Sick God" describes the gradual disappearance of the Angry God of the Old Testament, while "God's Funeral" symbolizes the surrender of belief as a result of the new science which showed God to be a creation of the idolatrous instinct. While accepting the findings of ethnology and anthropology, Bridges avoided with equal success the primitivistic pantheism of Swinburne and the pessimism of Hardy. That the Christian religion should have had a natural and pagan origin, and be in itself a myth, was no reason, in Bridges' mind, for rejecting it as a religion.

The blank verse of *Demeter* is less Miltonic than that of the early *Prometheus the Firegiver*, and in a few limping lines shows the effect of Bridges' prolonged experiments in classical prosody. The prologue is Miltonic, but the great body of the verse has a *differentia* of its own:

> The joy of Earth is in the breath of life
> And animal motions: nor are flowery sweets
> Dear as the scent of life. This petal'd cup,
> What is it by the wild fawn's liquid eye
> Eloquent as love music 'neath the moon?
> Nay, not a flower in all thy garden here,
> Nor wer't a thousand-thousand-fold enhanct
> In every charm, but thou wouldst turn from it
> To view the antler'd stag, that in the glade
> With the coy gaze of his majestic fear
> Faced thee a moment ere he turn'd to fly.[13]

Even Bridges' most captious critics have surrendered to the charm of *Achilles in Scyros*.[14] Though a formal five-act division was observed in the first edition, the play may be considered either as a masque or as a "poetic drama"; that is, as a play in which action and characterization are of no importance. The story follows closely the well-known tradition handed down by Apollodorus[15] of Achilles' concealment on the island of Scyros, and of his discovery by Ulysses. The story is refined by Bridges in a familiar manner. According to Apollodorus, "Achilles had an intrigue with Deidamia, daughter of Lycomedes, and a son Pyrrhus was born to him, who was afterward called Neoptolemus."[16] In Bridges' play Deidamia is innocent, and until Ulysses' coming believes that Pyrrha (or Achilles) is a girl; her maidenly shame at having allowed Pyrrha to kiss her so often (1443 ff.) is one of the few intrusions of modern sentiment. According to Apollodorus, Ulysses discovered Achilles by the blast of a trump, but Bridges follows the usual story:

that the crafty Ulysses spread out baskets and women's gear, mingled with arms, before the disguised Achilles and his girlish companions in Scyros; and that while the real girls pounced eagerly on the feminine gauds, Achilles betrayed his sex by snatching at the arms.[17]

Bridges' conception of the character of Achilles is Homeric rather than Shakespearean; he is the noblest of the Greeks. The conflict of the play is between love and honor, and between the craft of a sea-goddess and that of Ulysses, the wisest of mortals. Though characterization is not essential to the kind of poetic drama represented by *Achilles in Scyros*, there are a few brief and masterful strokes which personalize Ulysses, Diomede, Achilles, and Deidamia. The most modern character is Lycomedes, through whom Bridges expresses his own opinions. In at least three passages, Lycomedes' function as spokesman for the poet's ideas is obvious. In the first of these he suggests the imaginative and purely symbolical nature of religion:

> Where man is met
> The gods will come; or shall I say man's spirit
> Hath operative faculties to mix
> And make his gods at will?

His speech on the legitimacy of war and on the perfectibility of man is interesting.[18] Though Lycomedes is fairly explicit in his condemnation of war, the reader feels the same uncertainty which mars the passages in *The Testament of Beauty* on this subject. Finally, Lycomedes' defense of the quiet life may be interpreted as Bridges' *apologia* for his own life of retirement. The pleasures of Scyros are those of Yattendon and Chilswell:

> I'll tell thee what myself I have grown to think:
> That the best of life is oft inglorious.
> Since the perfecting of ourselves, which seems
> Our noblest task, may closelier be pursued
> Away from camps and cities and the mart
> Of men, where fame, as it is called, is won,
> By strife, ambition, competition, fashion,
> Ay, and the prattle of wit, the deadliest foe
> To sober holiness, which, as I think,
> Loves quiet homes, where nature laps us round
> With musical silence and the happy sights
> That never fret; and day by day the spirit
> Pastures in liberty, with a wide range
> Of peaceful meditation, undisturbed.

The treatment of the story, then, is not original; the characterization is slight, and the philosophical passages are either unsound or inconclusive. The indisputable greatness of the play lies rather in its poetry: the blank verse is of a quality unequalled for richness and variety of movement since Milton. The prologue spoken by Thetis is the most Miltonic passage in the play:

> The deep recesses of this rocky isle,
> That far from undersea riseth to crown
> Its flowery head above the circling waves,
> A home for men with groves and gardens green,
> I chose not ill to be the hiding-place
> Of my loved son. Alas, I could not take him
> To live in my blue caverns, where the nymphs
> Own me for queen: and hateful is the earth

To me, and all remembrance, since that morn
When, in the train of May wandering too far,
I trafficked with my shells and pearls to buy
Her fragrant roses and fresh lilies white.

There is a close resemblance in rhythm and diction between
Thetis' description of Achilles to Deidamia, and certain passages
in Bridges' late syllabic poetry:

But lo, I am come to give thee joy, to call
Thee daughter, and prepare thee for the sight
Of such a lover, as no lady yet
Hath sat to await in chamber or in bower
On any wallèd hill or isle of Greece;
Nor yet in Asian cities, whose dark queens
Look from the latticed casements over seas
Of hanging gardens; nor doth all the world
Hold a memorial; not where Ægypt mirrors
The great smile of her kings and sunsmit fanes
In timeless silence: none hath been like him;
And all the giant stones, which men have piled
Upon the illustrious dead, shall crumble and join
The desert dust, ere his high dirging Muse
Be dispossessèd of the throne of song.[19]

The greatest passage of the play happens to be the least Miltonic: the description of the Cretan ships spoken by Lycomedes,
part of which is based on Muley's well-known speech in *El
principe constante*. The passage extends to sixty-five lines, of which
the thirty-six quoted below challenge comparison with any descriptive poetry in the language:

The next day at dawn
I played the spy. Twas such a breathless morning
When all the sound and motion of the sea
Is short and sullen, like a dreaming beast:
Or as 'twere mixed of heavier elements
Than the bright water, that obeys the wind.

Hiring a fishing-boat we bade the sailors
Row us to Aulis; when midway the straits,
The morning mist lifted, and lo, a sight
Unpicturable. — High upon our left
Where we supposed was nothing, suddenly
A tall and shadowy figure loomed: then two,
And three, and four, and more towering above us:
But whether poised upon the leaden sea
They stood, or floated in the misty air,
That baffling our best vision held entangled
The silver of the half-awakened sun,
Or whether near or far, we could not tell,
Nor what: at first I thought them rocks, but ere
That error could be told, they were upon us
Bearing down swiftly athwart our course; and all
Saw 'twas a fleet of ships, not three or four
Now, but unnumber'd: like a floating city,
If such could be, with walls and battlements
Spread on the wondering water: and now the sun
Broke thro' the haze, and from the shields outhung
Blazed back his dazzling beams, and round their prows
On the divided water played; as still
They rode the tide in silence, all their oars
Stretched out aloft, as are the balanced wings
Of storm-fowl, which returned from battling flight
Across the sea, steady their aching plumes
And skim along the shuddering cliffs at ease:
So came they gliding on the sullen plain,
Out of the dark, in silent state, by force
Yet unexpended of their nightlong speed.[20]

An enumeration of the technical successes of this passage, such as the fine chiasma beginning "But whether poised," or the complete fusion of rhythm and sense without variation of outward form in the final lines, would require several pages. This is Bridges' style at its purest, and represents a distinct advance, in the direction of integrity of rhythm and freedom from mannerism, over the magnificent but pretentious prologues of *Prometheus the Firegiver* and *Demeter*. No one who has read this description of the Cretan ships can say that Bridges has merely reproduced the metrical pattern of Milton, though that would itself be a fine achievement. If it is less rich and daring than Milton's blank verse, it shows a greater directness and a greater freedom from strain.

Although *The Return of Ulysses* is incomparably the best dramatic version of the story in English,[21] it is of comparatively little interest. Written with the stage in mind,[22] its narrative progress is nevertheless often imperceptible, and there are few lyric passages of any distinction. Following the suggestion of Aristotle (as Stephen Phillips did not) Bridges confines his play to the closing books of the *Odyssey*. The first act comprises the dialogue between Athena and Ulysses, after he has awakened on the shore of Ithaca, and is taken from Book XIII (line 228–end). The second act, including Ulysses' conversation, while disguised, with Eumaeus, and his appearance in his true form before Telemachus, is taken from Books XIV, XV, and XVI. The third act, dealing with the wooers, is drawn from the last third of Book XVI and the first fourth of Book XVII. The fourth act, in which Ulysses appears disguised among the wooers and still in disguise talks with Penelope, and in which, with Telemachus, he makes plans for the slaying of the wooers, is taken from the second half of Book XVII and from Books XVIII and XIX. In the last act, his revenge is accomplished; the story is based on Books XX, XXI, and XXII. Very little is taken from Book XXIII, in which he makes himself known to Penelope and Laertes, and the final book, the quelling of the Ithacan rebellion (which is used by Rowe) is entirely disregarded.

The Return of Ulysses is a further illustration of the refinement of classical story which we found variously undertaken in *Eros and Psyche*, *Prometheus the Firegiver* and *Demeter*. Alfred Gilde observes and condemns the softening of Ulysses' character (it is only at Athena's command that he plans the slaying of the wooers): "Es wird damit dem Helden ein schöner, menschlicher, spezifisch christlicher Zug eingepflanzt, durch den auch Goethe seine Iphigenie adelte, aber Ulysses erscheint nun als ein willen-. loses Werkzeug der blutigen Göttin, welche in ihm Eifersuch wecken muss." [23]

Both Gilde and Gerard Hopkins accuse Bridges of unreality, but for precisely opposite reasons: Gilde because Bridges did not take the Homeric conceptions seriously and literally enough; Hopkins, because he took them too seriously. Hopkins wrote: "I hope other people will think otherwise, but the introduction in earnest of Athene gave me a distaste I could not recover from . . . in earnest, not allegorically, you bring in a goddess among the characters: it revolts me." [24] It is interesting to compare Hopkins' revulsion with the enthusiasm of William Butler Yeats. Yeats says of the coming of Athene helmed in "silver or electron" and of her transformation of Ulysses, that they are not "the climax of an excitement of nerves, but of that unearthly excitement which has wisdom for fruit, and is of like kind with the ecstasy of the seers, an altar flame, unshaken by the winds of the world, and burning every moment with purer and whiter brilliance." [25]

So far as that is possible, it would seem desirable to mediate between the pedantry of Gilde, the offended Catholicism of Hopkins, and the irresponsible mysticism of Yeats. Bridges' practice of treating the classical stories from a modern and Christian point of view seems defensible so long as it is consistent. I tried to show, in my introductory chapter on the plays, that a great deal of their value depends on the detached and critical attitude which the author assumes. Since I do not share Hopkins' intense religious fervor, I cannot see that Athena stands in any other relation to the modern spectator or reader than that of the various ghosts which pervade dramatic literature. Even less should the restoration of Eumaeus to his kingdom, to which Gilde objects because it does not appear in Homer,[26] and represents an incursion of modern pity, offend the reader.

If inconsistency be considered a major fault, however, the character of Athena is open to criticism. Bridges could have followed the theme begun with *Prometheus the Firegiver* and developed in *Demeter*, by setting in more obvious juxtaposition the wills of Athena and Ulysses. But to do this would have required that Ulysses' better desire be frustrated, or that he should triumph over the will of Athena, which would have been decidedly "unhomerisch." Instead of taking either of these alternatives, Bridges gives us a very changeable Athena, who is relentless in her demand for vengeance, yet says, in the Epilogue:

> . . . not less am I foe to faithlessness,
> Breaches of trust and of those modest laws,
> Which guard high thoughts and heavenly purity.

CHAPTER TEN

Comedies

THE FEAST OF BACCHUS, a free adaptation of Terence's *Heautontimorumenos*, and *The Humours of the Court*, a languid imitation of Shakespearean comedy, are the least interesting of Bridges' plays. Both plays are more suited to the stage than to the closet, but they are too slow and too involved to succeed on the stage, and contain little memorable poetry.

The Feast of Bacchus is "an attempt to give *Menander* on the English stage . . . based upon his 'Heautontimorumenos' as we know it through Terence."[1] Once again, in an attempt to attain a fusion of the Greek attainment and the Christian ideal, Bridges "softens" his original: he felt that the story of Antiphila's exposure would deprive Chremes of sympathy, and be unpresentable "to a Christian audience."[2] The chastening of the original is less radical than Bridges would have us believe. Brett Young writes that in "exercising a strict censorship over the original, Bridges has lost . . . something vigorous and satyric, the harshness of the violent wines of the south,"[3] but this something vigorous and satyric simply does not exist in Terence.

In Bridges' play, Chremes still possesses some of his Latin callousness. He says joyfully:

> I have had a daughter, who from her cradle
> Has never cost me a single penny, and the very hour
> She is thrown on my hands, she has offers of marriage.

Only the weakening of Chremes' resolve to banish his son, as a result of Antiphila's pleas, might have dissatisfied Terence's Rome or the Athens of the New Comedy:

Ant.   O father, do give in!
Chr. Now that's the first time, lass, you have called me father. I see
      I shall have to yield.

Bridges' interpretation of the story — the inconsiderateness of fathers toward their sons — is more Molièresque than Terentian: a Latin audience would blame Menedemus more for his ridiculous behavior (hence the title) than for his refusal to give his son greater freedom. But even Terence's play, like *Le Misanthrope*, may mean different things to different ages, and thus Bridges expresses a different attitude from that of Terence without substantially changing the plot or the main characters.[4] From the dramatic aspect, the substitution of a new scheming character, Philolaches, for the bickering Syrus and Dromo, does away with much of the prolixity of the original.

The suburban oracle Chremes is perhaps the most amusing character in the play. At one time or another, he is deluded by all the characters, including himself:

> Homo sum: humani nihil a me alienum puto,

is really a cloak for his prying curiosity, and his desire to help Menedemus is at least partly vain:

> I love to help a neighbour;
> 'Tis pleasure as well as duty: because it is a pleasure
> To be wiser than others, and even a friend's predicament
> Increases the satisfaction I feel when I think how well
> My own household is managed.

The most amusing parts of the play arise from Chremes' failure to manage his own household. Whereas Clinia loves Antiphila (Chremes' lost daughter, whose identity is revealed, in the true Latin manner, in the fourth act), Chremes' son Pamphilus is involved with the courtesan Gorgo. The two girls change names, so that Chremes, believing the vulgar Gorgo is Clinia's mistress, pays her a large sum (on Menedemus' behalf, but unknown to him) if she will agree to leave Clinia alone. Then Philolaches and Pamphilus arrive, dressed as Persians, and announce to Chremes (whose curiousity has caused him to impersonate Menedemus) that Clinia has been killed in Persia. They force him to give the customary gift to the messenger. In the end, Chremes repeats the fault of Menedemus, threatening to disinherit and drive out his son, and is dissuaded only at the last (by Menedemus in Terence; by Antiphila in Bridges).

The most that can be said for the comedy is that it makes good light reading. It is less involved than Terence's play, but contains no memorable poetry, and the theme was more or less exhausted in various plays by Molière. Chapman's *All Fooles* is a more successful adaptation of the *Heautontimorumenos*. The atmosphere of courtesans, exposed infants and rascally slaves is there modernized without the intrusion of modern sentiment. Chapman omits the self-torturing motive of the original, however, and emphasizes the strong contrast between fathers which he had found in the *Adelphi*.

The invertebrate meter of *The Feast of Bacchus*, based on a line of six speech stresses, is the least successful of Bridges' many metrical experiments.[5] There is a constant mixture of prose and verse rhythms, thoroughly confusing to anyone who tries to read the play aloud.

The Humours of the Court is a tedious comedy of 3,150 lines, including much prose, and many blank verse passages almost indistinguishable from prose. The play owes its plot to Calderón's *El secreto à voces*, though the first scene of the third act comes from the "Jornada Primera" of Lope de Vega's *El perro del hortelano*.[6] Calderón's comedy runs to 165 pages, and is perhaps responsible for the sprawling form and slow progress of Bridges' play, yet the original, because of the quality of the verse and the profusion of striking imagery, moves much more rapidly.

The idea of Bridges' play, however — the transformation of love in idleness into real love, as in *Twelfth Night* — is suggested by Lope's sub-title "Amar por ver Amar": love kindled by the sight of love. The influence of *Twelfth Night* cannot be ignored. There are interesting resemblances between Tristram, who pretends the Countess is in love with him, and Malvolio, who is really duped. Diana, like Orsino, takes "pleasures feverously and pines in plenty." And as Olivia finds in Sebastian another Cesario, Diana finds in Ricardo another Frederick. Much of the comic paraphernalia of Bridges' play is Shakespearean, and in one respect — in its mocking of euphuism and the courtly love convention — it is nearer to *Love's Labour's Lost* than to *Twelfth Night*.

Diana, in spite of her fits, is certainly the best character in the play. She believes that all men are dupes and fools; that love and social intercourse should be codified in every particular; that no feeling or speech should violate this rigid calendar of rules:

> Love is the one thing in the world which women
> Must guard from profanation; for by love
> They rule; and if they trifle with their power,
> They come to be men's chattels, not their queens.

There are several reasons for the more or less total failure of *The Humours of the Court*. It was obviously written for the stage rather than for reading, and thus a great deal depends upon conventional "stage business": the exchanging of gloves, the inability of the deaf major-domo to hear St. Nicholas' cries for help, and even the scene borrowed from Lope. The first condition of a successful imitation of Shakespearean comedy by a modern writer must be rapidity of movement. *The Humours of the Court* is slow, not because of a dearth of action, but because the verse is so languid. Comedy of this kind requires lively verse and conceited rhetoric. If Bridges cultivated a more conversational idiom in the interest of realism, he defeated his own object, for in a mad costumed world of disguised dukes and scheming lovers, everyday conversational tones are wholly unrealistic.

It is not easy to understand why the Oxford Dramatic Society in 1930 selected *The Humours of the Court* for production, and passed by the still-unacted *The First Part of Nero*, one of the few really great plays written in England in the last hundred years.

PART THREE

The Testament of Beauty

CHAPTER ELEVEN

The Testament of Beauty (I)

A S ROBERT HILLYER has said, "Not even Robert Bridges' admirers would have guessed that, to crown his many days, he would achieve one of the great philosophical poems of the world."[1] *The Testament of Beauty*, begun in 1925 or 1926 and completed by September 1929,[2] was published on Bridges' eighty-fifth birthday, October 24, 1929. We have seen that the greater part of his lyric and dramatic poetry was done before 1900. Labored experiments in classical meters and new editions of *Milton's Prosody*, collections of hymns and two anthologies, tracts for the Society for Pure English and letters to the *Times*, a few reviews and a few public lectures — all these were symptoms of a graceful literary old age. Certainly *October* and the last slim volume, *New Verse*, containing metrical experiments written in 1921, gave little indication that a philosophical poem of more than four thousand lines was yet to come.

The poem was in every way a surprise, and not least in its immediate and astonishing commercial success. It was the first of Bridges' works to achieve a large sale; while the plays have yet to reach their first thousand, over forty thousand copies of *The Testament of Beauty* have been sold. For the first time in his career, likewise, Bridges elicited from critics more than moderate and respectful praise. The chorus was appropriately initiated on the day of publication by the London *Times Literary Supplement*, whose reviewer described it as "the greatest poem he has written."[3] In America, Robert Hillyer wrote: "Critics have compared 'The Testament of Beauty' to Wordsworth's Prelude, but we must retire twenty centuries before that if we are to find a comparison that is not inept. . . . I believe that 'The Testament of Beauty' may well be the De Rerum Natura of our civilization."[4] Alan Porter described it as "the greatest English poem of our time,"[5] while according to Leonard Bacon it "stands by itself alone, a great didactic poem, something not to have been expected of the times."[6] John Finley, Jr. found "the apocalyptic force which is the quality of great works"[7] and Odell Shepard "the accent and timbre of a great voice."[8] Among the few dissenters were Herbert Read, who observed "something dry and Calvinistic throughout,"[9] Conrad Aiken, who complained of an "almost medieval simplicity and old-fashionedness,"[10] and Morton D. Zabel, who rang the old changes of "intellectual austerity" and "fastidious aloofness."[11]

It was in fact the absence of this austerity and aloofness which most surprised friendly as well as hostile readers of Bridges' earlier poetry. Accustomed to a fastidious art based on rejections rather than impulses of energy, an art which steadfastly refused to exploit the obvious rhythm or the "stock response," they were astonished to find a profusion of imagery and a Miltonic organ-roll on every page, long sections of impassioned tragic eloquence and uninhibited comic digression. For better or for worse the poem has much more romantic exuberance and imaginative fervor than any earlier work; it has, likewise, much greater freedom of form.

The casual reader of the *Shorter Poems* must have been surprised to find that Bridges had written a philosophical poem at all: at most he had seemed concerned with the moral and emotional choices facing a particular highly civilized individual. Yet we have seen that many of Bridges' lyrics and plays carry philosophical implications. We have observed a conscious Platonism in *The Growth of Love*; an evolutionary theory of the mind's growth in such poems as "Narcissus," in which the natural basis of ideals is affirmed; a repudiation of Rousseauistic primitivism in "Robert Burns, An Epistle on Instinct," and a reasoned aesthetic theory of life in *Prometheus the Firegiver* and *Demeter*. "La Gloire de Voltaire" contains in germ the idealism of *The Testament of Beauty*:

> . . . the least philosophy may find
> The truths are the ideas; the sole fact
> Is the long story of man's growing mind,

while several stanzas in "Robert Burns, An Epistle on Instinct" anticipate the naturalistic side of the later poem:

> But instinct in the beasts that live
> Is of three kinds; (Nature did give
> To man three shakings in her sieve) —
> The first is Racial,
> The second Self-preservative,
> The third is Social.

The refinement of these three instincts is considered in the last three books of *The Testament of Beauty*: "Selfhood" (Self-preservative), "Breed" (Racial), and "Ethick" (Social).

The first and second *Poems in Classical Prosody* are the most ambitious of Bridges' early philosophical poems. "Wintry Delights" considers many of the problems taken up more fully a quarter of a century later: the dualism of nature, the possibilities for good and evil of primitive instinct, the relationship of the mind and body, the achievements of science and the oppressions of traditional theology. The first seventy-five lines argue that man's consciousness is a sufficient justification for life. Even if the comforts and joys of ordinary life — art, the beauty of nature, love — were taken away, life would still be made worth living by

> . . . the reflective effort of mind that, conscious of itself,
> Fares forth exploring nature for principle and cause.[12]

The poem is primarily a learned survey of the progress and accomplishments of modern science, in which the latest theories of biology, geology, astronomy, anthropology, psychology and medicine are discussed. But most important of all is the "new science of MAN" — the proper study of Mankind is Man. The relationship of the mind and the body, examined at length in *The Testament of Beauty*, is dismissed in a few obscure lines. "Nature's essential object" is

> Self-matter, embodying substratum of ev'ry relation
> Both of Time and Space, at once the machinery and stuff
> Of those Ideas; carrier, giver, only receiver
> Of such perceptions as arise in sensible organs.[13]

The problem of cosmic dualism is considered at much greater length. Nature's indifference is stated in terms clearly reminiscent of Hardy:

> . . . Nature's superabundance,
> Her vast infinitude of waste variety untold,
> As her immense extent and inconceivable object,
> Squandering activities throughout eternity, dwarfeth
> Man's little aim and hour, his doubtful fancy: what are we? [14]

The answer to this problem is one of several developed in *The Testament of Beauty*:

> . . . I see man's discontent as witness asserting
> His moral ideal, that, born of Nature, is heir to
> Her children's titles, which nought may cancel or impugn. . . .[15]

The answer will be familiar to readers of Browning. Bridges' general attitude toward evil is, as Eaker says, "the idealistic one presented by Kant in his theory of the sublime. To Kant an attempt to reconcile evil with good in Nature shows a subjective purposiveness of our mind seeking its supersensible destination. . . ."[16]

Man's superiority to the rest of nature is determined by his human consciousness: "Judging other creatures he sets them wholly beneath him." Bridges dismisses traditional theology and the formal doctrine of original sin briefly:

Now 'tis away: Science has pierced man's cloudy common-sense,
Dow'rd his homely vision with more expansive an embrace,
And the rotten foundation of old superstition exposed.
That trouble of Pascal, those vain paradoxes of Austin,
Those Semitic parables of Paul, those tomes of Aquinas,
All are thrown to the limbo of antediluvian idols,
Only because we learn mankind's true history, and know
That not at all from a high perfection sinfully man fell,
But from baseness arose.[17]

Since "Wintry Delights" describes the progress of man as a result of the civilizing of primitive instinct, it is suprising to find that in "To a Socialist in London" Bridges objects to socialism chiefly because it restricts man's natural predilection for "Magnificence, Force, Freedom, Bounty." His second argument is that the prize men seek will disappear by subdivision, and his final point is that

Surely delight in goods is an ecstasy rather attendant
On their mental image, then on experienc'd operation.[18]

The socialist might well have answered that this is a fashionable delight, and that the poor cannot live on aspiration and on the mental image of the necessities of life.

In "Come Se Quando," the most important of the metrical exercises in New Verse, Bridges returns to the problem of cosmic dualism. "Come Se Quando" is a strange poem, in which the form of a transparent dream allegory is used. After a comparison has been made between the religion of awe and the religion of love, Nature's indifference to man is affirmed:

'What Providence is this that maketh sport with Chance
blindly staking against things of no ordinance?[19]

The birds are at the mercy of an "icy hail-gust"; the cities of men
at the mercy of a "shudder of earth's crust." After describing the
dualism of reason, its possibilities for crime and vulgarity as well
as for the creation of ideals, Bridges gives the negative conclusion
to man's search for a beneficent purpose in nature:

> 'Look to thy balance, THEMIS; Should thy scale descend
> bind up thine eyes again, I shall no more contend;
> for if the Final Cause vindicate Nature's laws
> her universal plan giveth no heed to man
> No place; for him Confusion is his Final Cause.' [20]

The refutation of this pessimistic philosophy is made by means
of allegory. The prophet who has thus maligned nature feels a
resurgence of natural piety; he recants his gospel of futility and
despair, and returns to convert a crowd of ordinary men. But
"the stong words of his chasten'd humanity" inflame the crowd,
which attacks him. He is rescued by a troop of angels; that is to
say, he is rescued from his doubts concerning nature by his faith.

One further poem, the sonnet "Democritus," brings some light
to bear on the problem of Bridges' philosophy prior to *The
Testament of Beauty*. Although it does not explain the relationship
of his naturalism to his idealism, it contains Bridges' most explicit
rejection of pure materialism:

> Joy of your opulent atoms! wouldst thou dare
> Say that Thought also of atoms self-became,
> Waving to soul as light had the eye in aim;
> And so with things of bodily sense compare
> Those native notions that the heavens declare,
> Space and Time, Beauty and God — Praise we his name! —
> Real ideas, that on tongues of flame
> From out mind's cooling paste leapt unaware?

The best things are as difficult as they are rare. The indolent
reader, opening *The Testament of Beauty* by chance, would probably not get beyond the seven-line invocation:

Mortal Prudence, handmaid of divine Providence,
hath inscrutable reckoning with Fate and Fortune:
We sail a changeful sea through halcyon days and storm,
and when the ship laboureth, our stedfast purpose
trembles like as the compass in a binnacle.
Our stability is but balance, and wisdom lies
in masterful administration of the unforseen.

Even if he were not puzzled by the meaning of this passage, disturbed by the spelling of "stedfast" or annoyed by the syntax of
the fifth line, the reader unprepared by the "Neo-Miltonic syllabics" of *New Verse* would find only one line, the third, with a
recognizable and satisfactory rhythm. The other lines would seem
a hopeless mixture of familiar rhythms with no fixed norm: the
number of accents would appear to vary from four to six, and the
number of syllables from twelve to fourteen.

The purely syllabic meter (the standard measure of French
poetry) is at once the greatest and the simplest of the poem's many
difficulties. Confusion has been worse confounded by Nowell
Charles Smith's patronizing but wholly inaccurate description
of the meter in his *Notes on The Testament of Beauty*: Smith describes the normal line as having twelve syllables and six stresses,
with some lines varying so far from this norm as to have sixteen
syllables and only four stresses.[21] The meter is in fact very simple:
except for a few indented lines (which have only ten syllables),
all lines have twelve syllables and a completely indeterminate
number of stresses or accents. The reader must simply eliminate
from his mind the concept of stress or accent, as he eliminates it
in reading Racine; the meter is identical with the French alexandrine, and as in the case of the French alexandrine the apparent
variation in the number of syllables is accounted for by elision.
Thus in the second and sixth lines of the invocation the second
syllable of "reckoning" and the last syllable of "stability" are
elided. The prosody, with its complex rules of elision (which,
incidentally, are optional), should not, however, be used as a

guide to reading: it is merely the formal background for elaborate variation. Although the seventh line contains two instances of elision, it should be read as though it had fourteen syllables. The reader should read the verse attending only to the sense of the words and the natural pauses. If he guards successfully against the temptation to read the poem in iambic or anapestic rhythms, he will soon discover and enjoy the meter's natural beauties. (For further analysis of the meter, see the Appendix on Prosody.)

The simplified phonetic spelling which Bridges uses in *The Testament of Beauty* presents no such real difficulty as does the elaborate system which he worked out and applied in his *Collected Essays*. There are a few inconsistencies of spelling, most of which may be explained by prosodic requirements.[22] The rules of punctuation are in general simplified. Commas are frequently omitted at the end of the line, or when no real pause is desired. Of the few obsolete constructions (such as "like as the compass") only those which are severely elliptical will give any real trouble:

was great felling of trees: for not Socrates knew. (iv, 773)

Most of these archaisms and innovations are harmless or are justified by their beauty; unfortunately, this cannot be said of the frequent obscurity in syntax.

In the end the reader will be far more disturbed by the general nature and structure of the poem than by any of these formal obstacles. *The Testament of Beauty* is a philosophical poem and the autobiography of a single well-stored mind rather than the geometric exposition of a system; a reasoned commentary on human experience rather than a footnote in the history of epistemology. The original title, *De Hominum Natura* (with its allusion to the *De Rerum Natura*), goes far towards explaining the poem's scope and method. Bridges agreed with Santayana that "it is the function of poetry to emotionalize philosophy,"[23] and like

Lucretius he recognized the need of beguiling his readers into studying his theories:

> Veluti pueris absinthia tetra medentes
> Cum dare conantur, prius oras pocula circum
> Contingunt mellis dulci flavoque liquore,
> Ut puerorum aetas improvida ludificitur
> Labrorum tenus, interea perpotet amarum
> Absinthi laticem, deceptaque non capratur,
> Sed potius tali pacto recreata valescat:
> Sic ego nunc . . . volui tibi suaviloquenti
> Carmine Pierio rationem exponere nostram
> Et quasi musaeo dulci contingere melle.[24]

The lyrical digressions of *The Testament of Beauty* are, however, far more than honeyed concessions to the indolent reader; they are, like Wordsworth's recollections in *The Prelude*, the very core of the poem:

> Beauty is the highest of all these occult influences,
> the quality of appearances that thru' the sense
> wakeneth spiritual emotion in the mind of man,   (ii, 842-4)

and beauty can be illustrated or exemplified, but never adequately described. The first long digression of the poem, for instance, a magnificent forty-line description of nature (i, 277-317), illustrates as no formal theorizing could that "spiritual elation and response to Nature/is Man's generic mark." The structure of the poem is deliberately loose and disorganized. Even more than *Paradise Lost*, its normal method of progression depends on the epic simile. An idea or theory is stated, and an illustration in support of this idea or theory offered. In the course of the illustration, a new idea, requiring a fresh illustration, is suggested. After this process has been repeated three or four times, some allusion brings the poet back to his original argument. The progression of the poem may be described in terms of a series of intersecting circles, the whole constituting an epicycloid.

Bridges' comment on Santayana's work shows that he recognized the dangers as well as the rewards of his method:

it has been said that George Santayana has imperilled the recognition of his philosophy by the fine robes in which he has consistently presented it; and that his readers have been distracted from the sincerity and depth of his purpose by the perpetual flow of his eloquence, his rich vocabulary, and the pleasant cadences of his sentences, with their abounding imagery, incisive epigrams, and jovial humor.[25]

The peril of a serious thinker who will sacrifice none of these fine robes and who expresses his philosophy in an unfamiliar poetical form is even greater. Yet it must not be forgotten that Bridges was a serious thinker, and that his poem is philosophy as well as poetry. This philosophy, drawn as it is from very diverse sources and argued in such a random manner, can hardly be understood after a single reading of the poem.

Bridges' philosophy, like that of Santayana and Meredith, is essentially an idealism based on natural foundations; the aim of this philosophy is attainment of the *life of reason*, "a name for that part of experience which perceives and pursues ideals — all conduct so controlled and all sense so interpreted as to perfect natural happiness." [26] Like Santayana and Meredith, and unlike Tennyson, Bridges believed that man's instincts are the basis for his intellectual and spiritual achievements; that these instincts are intrinsically good, though the material for vice as well as virtue; that happiness depends upon a harmony of impulses effected through the agency of reason, and that man's ideal aspirations, without which his life is meaningless, find their firmest support in physical beauty. Thus, although he did not share Meredith's materialistic belief that matter can *become* thought, Bridges accepted and used the evolutionary theory of Darwin, and remained undismayed by that struggle for existence which alarmed and repelled so many of the contemporaries of his youth.

The main problem which faced Bridges was that of vindicating human instincts and emotions without succumbing to the primitivism of Rousseau or the early Wordsworth, and without having to depend on an ethical system so unreliable as Shaftesbury's. He solved this problem at least in part by the primacy which he assigned to reason, the active agent which turns natural forces into ideal goods, and by an Aristotelian insistence on the importance of habit and the desirability of self-control. At the beginning of the second book of *The Testament of Beauty* we find Plato's famous image of the soul of man as a charioteer (reason) and two horses (spirit and appetite).[27] In Bridges' poem the charioteer is still reason, but the horses are Selfhood (the self-preservative and self-assertive instinct) and Breed (the sexual or racial instinct). Bridges furthermore breaks with Plato's dualism at the very outset: in the *Phaedrus* one horse is good and one bad, while in *The Testament of Beauty* both horses are intrinsically good, though needing the continual guidance and control of the charioteer.

How are natural forces turned into ideal goods? How does the self-preservative instinct become translated into the impulses of art and song? There is in fact no Cartesian division between the mind and nature, and in the thoughtless song of birds we may discern the root of that "urgence" which Bach and Mozart obeyed. Selfhood, Spinoza's *conatus sese preservandi*, is the deepest of all instincts, and the newborn child sucks and clutches like a plant for food. There are four stages in all existence — "Atomic, Organic, Sensuous and Selfconscient" — and as *conscience* (Bridges' word for *consciousness*) emerges it shapes and moulds the primitive impulses of which it has become aware. Reason may shape and mould the impulse of Selfhood until it finds expression in murder and war, but eventually it perceives its ideal function and directs primal energy into the channels of painting, sculpture and song. So too the impulse of Breed, directed by reason, deserts unreflective procreation and may ultimately attain the spiritual love of Dante for Beatrice.

But as Selfhood may be misdirected into war, so Breed may be guided into the most unnatural sexual perversions. What then is the authority of this reason, with its unaccountable divagations? Certainly formal reason, geometric reasoning, has sometimes absurdly explained the unknowable, or otherwise frustrated that life of reason which is essentially a habit of faith. Bridges answers this skepticism by reminding us that the good which reason accomplishes outweighs the bad, and, more sophistically, that a thing has no right to question its own authority, that only reason can question reason. The first argument is the more important one. That reason can seduce us into "the rioting joys that fringe the sad pathways of Hell" is no sufficient justification for sacrificing that spiritual art, love and religion which it alone makes possible.

Such, in brief, are the naturalistic and almost materialistic foundations of Bridges' philosophy. But Bridges does not acknowledge, with Laplace, that he had no need for God in his system, and he consequently erects a Spinozist cosmology capable of giving his thoroughgoing idealism a meaning and purpose. He calls his main conception the "Ring of Being," perhaps in allusion to Pope's very different "Chain of Being":

> From Universal Mind the first-born atoms draw
> their function, whose rich chemistry the plants transmute
> to make organic life, whereon animals feed
> to fashion sight and sense and give service to man,
> who sprung from them is conscient in his last degree
> of ministry unto God, the Universal Mind,
> whither all effect returneth whence it first began.   (iv, 116–22)

The movement of the "Ring of Being" requires an epistemological explanation, founded, as it happens, on Santayana's elusive theory of essence. There exist in the unconscious mind an infinite world of essences or influences (as they are sometimes called) which have emanated from Universal Mind. These essences, which exist apart from the human mind which intuits them, wander "at liberty to find their procreativ fellowship." Since every man, according to his disposition and experience, will intuit ("possess," as Bridges says) a different group of essences, all men are different, and nobility of the soul consists of a rich harmony of essences. It is the task of reason to further this harmony. When the mind has become conscious of sufficient essences it will conceive of the ideas of immortality and Universal Mind; it will become conscious, in fact, of the "Ring of Being." When a particular combination of essences has been achieved, and all finite concerns have been cast away, the human mind will return to that Universal Mind of which it is now worthy to become a part. It will have achieved that disinterested and ideal immortality described by various naturalistic philosophers from Lucretius to Santayana:

> The Ring in its repose is Unity and Being:
> Causation and Existence are the motion thereof.
> Thru'out all runneth Duty, and the conscience of it
> is thatt creativ faculty of animal mind
> that, wakening to self-conscience of all Essences,
> closeth the full circle, where the spirit of man
> escaping from the bondage of physical law
> re-entereth eternity by the vision of God.   (iv, 123–30)

The mind perishes with the body unless

> the personal co-ordination of its ideas
> hav won to Being higher than animal life. . . .   (iv, 1263–4)

The Ring is closed when God loves himself through our love of him: God, indeed, is "the very self-essence of love." Or, as Spinoza says, "love towards God is part of the infinite love with which God loves himself." [28]

At times, however, Bridges' God seems very different from the purely intellectual being of Spinoza and Aristotle, and many lines of *The Testament of Beauty* suggest not only a teleological interpretation of nature but also an orthodox Christian faith. In the final lines, God is defined as the active lover of all; in an earlier passage, Bridges rejects Aristotle's sternly intellectual God, and his belief that there can be no friendship between God and man because of their great disparity. Yet the "ultimate Reality" is variously referred to in the poem as "Natur," "Wisdom," "Universal Mind," "God" and "Goddes Love." In view of these terms, it is difficult to see any difference, other than the relative importance assigned to intellect and to emotion, between the God of Spinoza and the God of Bridges. In the majority of his passages on the subject, Bridges seems to mean by immortality the ideal and impersonal immortality of Spinoza and Santayana. Yet there are other passages testifying to a belief in the God and the personal salvation of traditional Christianity. In this connection, Bridges' review of Santayana's *Little Essays* is of great interest:

There is, perhaps, the same difficulty in Santayana as in Spinoza of reconciling the religious attitude with the metaphysical or philosophical tenets. In both of them Christ is the wisdom of God and also merely a supreme offering of human imagination: and for many a like notion the later philosopher seems to me to deserve from the Papal Curia no better treatment than Spinoza got from the Synagogue.[29]

The difficulty was equally great for Bridges, and only one thing appears certain: that he was less orthodox than a first reading of his poem, with its many Biblical allusions and its systematic use of Christian figures, would indicate. While he is Christian in the sense that Shelley is Christian, and is even perhaps inclined to overemphasize the place of Christianity as the greatest civilizing force in history, Bridges probably meant by God both the whole of nature and the concept of love, and by immortality or re-union with God, the attainment of individual perfection and of freedom from earthly and transitory concerns.

Bridges' ethical theory, which leans very heavily on that of Aristotle, contains few serious obscurities. A definition of duty as the law of necessity become conscious in man is followed by a not unfamiliar discussion of the relative importance of education and disposition. Bridges distinguishes, in somewhat Bergsonian terms, between a higher and a lower ethics; between the dynamic ethics of prophets and teachers and the lower ethics of a traditional and conventional morality. Curiously enough, he finds socialism, with its attempt to legislate virtue, a particularly pernicious expression of the lower ethics. Like Aristotle, Bridges ultimately places ethical responsibility on the individual, and insists on the primary importance of habit and self-control. Thus he corrects and qualifies his naturalism by a humanism which makes no submission to natural law.

Such, in brief, are the main elements of Bridges' philosophy as expressed in *The Testament of Beauty*. Whether or not, as Stevenson claims, Bridges "accomplished at last what the poets had been striving for during almost a century,"[30] by harmonizing the tenets of evolutionary theory with an idealistic and spiritual faith, the elements of his philosophy are not original. Indistinguishable at times from that of Santayana, this philosophy nevertheless represents an extraordinary compendium of western thought. Like many similar works, its final value may reside in its specific arguments and in the commentaries on human experience which these arguments provoke, rather than in a series of formulated conclusions. The detailed commentary in the following chapter will seek to elucidate some of these specific arguments and reflections, as well as to follow as closely as possible the main lines of the poem's reasoning.

CHAPTER TWELVE

The Testament of Beauty (II)

THE POEM is divided into four books: *Introduction, Selfhood, Breed,* and *Ethick.* Selfhood and Breed, substituted for Plato's spirit and appetite, are man's basic instincts, while Ethick is the science of the charioteer who guides these instincts to ideal ends. The first book is, as its title indicates, an introduction. It establishes the evolutionary naturalism which is to be the philosophical basis of the poem, and introduces some of the main ideas which are to be considered at length: the apparent dualism of reason and of nature, the real homogeneity of all nature and the essential continuity of mind and body, and the successes and failures of reason in history.

The second book, "Selfhood," outlines the evolution of the instinct of Selfhood from its manifestations in the lowest forms of plant and animal life to its fruition in human art and human warfare, an evolution aided by the sense of beauty and by reason or *conscience* (consciousness). Much of the second book is devoted to a refutation of Plato's *Republic* and of modern socialistic theories. The evolution of Selfhood should end in a Spinozist loss of self in God, but history records many instances of retrogression. The book ends with a stern and gloomy reflection on the first world war.

As the second book studied the growth of Selfhood from animal assertiveness to spiritual art, so the third book, "Breed," describes the growth of love from the origins of sex to the highest spiritual love. This book includes a difficult analysis of the nature of love. A refutation of the artificial divorce between spiritual love and the sensuous beauty from which it grew involves an historical survey of the struggles which Christian marriage had to wage against puritanism and paganism.

The fourth book, "Ethick," describes the "life of reason," a reasoned harmony of all interests and impulses, which has as its ultimate object the habit of faith and the love of beauty. Duty is defined as "Necessity become conscient in man," and the evolution of duty from physical to moral ends is traced in the same manner as the evolution of Selfhood and Breed. Since reason should try to satisfy every valid impulse, morality should refine, rather than restrict or destroy man's instinctive aspirations. The relative importance of disposition and education is then considered. Each child is endowed with a "birthright of beauty," and hence is led unconsciously to imitate the more beautiful things. This observation leads to a discussion of the importance of imitation and habit.

Later in the fourth book, the poet plunges into the "darksome grove and secret penetralia of ethic lore." This study of the nature of the mind is influenced, in part, by modern theories of the "unconscious." The "Ring of Being" is discussed in this connection: this strictly Spinozist conception sees everything as emanating from Universal Mind, and ultimately returning thereto, and therefore furnishes the basis for belief in a disinterested and ideal immortality. In the final passages, Bridges suspects the old seducer, formal reason, and the traditional palinode ensues. The last lines of the poem define God as the "very self-essence of love."

The detailed commentary which follows is intended primarily as an elucidation of a very difficult poem. By quoting key passages and by explaining the significance of seemingly irrelevant digressions, the author hopes to serve as a guide to the reader who has only a limited time to give to the reading of the poem. The reader interested in the indebtedness of Bridges to other philosophers and poets should make constant reference to the notes. These notes also supply cross-references to other discussions in *The Testament of Beauty* of a particular idea.

BOOK I: INTRODUCTION

The first book has three major parts: the first (lines 1–336) considers the relationship of Reason and Beauty, and suggests the main problems with which the poem will be concerned; the second part (337–500) affirms the continuity of man's reason and the rest of nature; the third (501–790) reviews the successes and failures of reason in history.

The poem begins, after a conventional invocation, by describing a mood which came upon the poet late in his "long journey."[1] As with Wordsworth,[2]

> a glow of childlike wonder enthral'd me, as if my sense
> had come to a new birth purified, my mind enrapt
> re-awakening to a fresh initiation of life. . . .   (i, 10–12)

In such a mood,

> . . . nothing was new to me, only all was vivid
> and significant that had been dormant or dead. . . .[3]   (i, 39–40)

Feeling the domination "of nature's secret urge," Bridges also feels a kinship and sympathy with nature:

> . . . for in truth the mind
> is indissociable from what it contemplates,
> as thirst and generous wine are to a man that drinketh
> nor kenneth whether his pleasur is more in his desire
> or in the savor of the rich grape that allays it.   (i, 52–6)

This commentary on the relationship of subject and object serves to introduce Bridges "sensational" philosophy, in which he is indebted to Locke and his followers. "Man's Reason is in such deep insolvency to sense" that though it guides his spiritual aspirations, it can also

> . . . delicately and dangerously bedizen
> the rioting joys that fringe the sad pathways of Hell.[4] (i, 60–1)

Yet reason should not contemn sense, for only by alliance with the animal senses does reason have any "miracle"; without the sense of hearing, bird music would not exist for man: "sound would hav no report."[5] The love of music is one which man shares with birds, who not only enjoy their music, but "to their offspring teach it with care," so that the song of the nightingale will appeal to the fancy of men separated by many generations, awaking poetic eloquence "alike in Sophocles and in the sick heart of Keats."[6]

Thus it may be seen how deeply-rooted in natural instinct is the "urgence where to/Bach and Mozart obey'd. . . ." After a brief digression which compares the flight of birds to man's flight with airplanes, Bridges resumes the philosophical thread of the poem. A statement of the aesthetic justification for life is followed by a consideration of the dualism of nature:

> Man's happiness, his flaunting honey'd flower of soul,
> is his loving response to the wealth of Nature.
> Beauty is the prime motiv of all his excellence,
> his aim and peaceful purpose; whereby he himself
> becoming a creator hath often a thought to ask
> why Nature, being so inexhaustible of beauty,
> should not be all-beauteous; why from infinit resource,
> produce more ugliness than human artistry
> with any spiritual intention can allow?[7]   (i, 120–8)

But "Wisdom" will repudiate the philosopher who seeks to learn the origin and reason of things; his task is to learn "WHAT IS."[8] The spirit disheartened by the apparent indifference and dualism of nature should remember to suspect the human tendency to distinguish "moralities where never is none,"[9] and to observe that in questioning nature, the mind is questioning itself, which came from nature, "who by her own faculty in thee judgeth herself. . . ."[10] Reason is important, though so "small and tickle a thing."[11] The conscious is to the unconscious mind as "the habitable crust/is to the mass of the earth." (Schopenhauer used the same figure.[12]) This intellect, which distinguishes man from the rest of nature, "is nascent also in brutes." Since human sorrow derives from man's conscious thought, some men (Rousseau, for instance) have envied the carefree life of animals. But it should be remembered that man's pleasure as well as his sorrow is caused by reason, and above all that

> our hope is ever livelier than despair, our joy
> livelier and more abiding than our sorrows are. . . .[13]   (i, 198–9)

Furthermore, pleasure depends upon the spiritual significance which contemplation gives to "objects of sense."[14] If the Rousseauistic primitivist were granted his blind wish, he would not be able to enjoy "the human satisfaction of his release from care." Man's quarrel and dissatisfaction with nature is healthy, however, since it

> springeth of a vision which beareth assurance
> of the diviner principle implicit in life.[15]   (i, 224–5)

The mention of this vision — man's aspiration to perfection — introduces a long lyric digression on St. Francis (226–76). Even Francis could praise nature, and thus he wrote his *Canticle of the Sun*, which Bridges paraphrases. This digression is followed by a forty-line description of an English countryside, one of the great lyric passages in the poem. This description is not a further digression, but illustrates that

> . . . spiritual elation and response to Nature
> is Man's generic mark.   (i, 318–9)

Though animals sometimes appear to feel this spiritual elation, the "true intellectual wonder" is first found in children and savages, and among them we find the foundations of all our religion, science and art. Philosophy, for Bridges as for Plato, begins in wonder.

The second section opens by asking if there can be any will or purpose in nature, that external universe which seems only a "structur of blind atoms," or a mere figment of the mind, as the absolute idealists claim. But the division of man's mind from the rest of nature is a "stronger impertinence than Science can allow." This observation leads to one of the most succinct statements of Bridges' evolutionary naturalism:[16]

> Man's mind, Nature's entrusted gem, her own mirror
> cannot be isolated from her other works
> by self-abstraction of its unique fecundity
>   in the new realm of his transcendent life; —
> Not emotion or imagination ethic or art
> logic of science nor dialectic discourse,
> not even that supersensuous sublimation of thought,
> the euristic vision of mathematical trance,
> hath any other foundation than the common base
> of Nature's building. . . .   (i, 361–70)

Men cannot therefore be separated from the "impercipient," although there are so many types of men that it might seem as if "true Individuality within the species were peculiar to man":

> . . . one man how loveable
> another how hateful, alike man, brutal or divine.[17] (i, 380–2)

Among these many types of men the skeptic has an "honorable place":

> thatt old iconoclast who could destroy the gods
> soon as man made them, vain imagery and unworthy,
> low symbols of the Eternal that standeth unchanged.
> like some medicinal root in pharmacy, whose juice
> is wholesom for purgation, — so is he — [18] (i, 383–7)

Bridges returns in line 411 to the relationship of the mind and nature, reaffirming their continuity. Nothing can be unlike in cause and substance "to the thing it groweth on." *Conscience* (consciousness) is like a flower-bud on a vigorous plant; this bud

> is but a differentiation of the infertile leaf,
> which held all this miracle in intrinsic potence.   (i, 420–1)

These considerations give Bridges the occasion to ridicule those who marvel at the intelligence of animal behavior. To term such behavior "marvels of instinct" is foolish; man's reason is "the exception and marvel." It is obvious that as our life is animal, so our conduct is mainly instinctive, while "pure Reason"[19] relies on "axioms and essential principles," things far beyond her, and holding "her anchor in eternal Mind."

Such speculations lead to the conclusion that there is little or no accord among philosophers: thought is conditioned even more than the body by "time and clime": "what then and there was Reason, is here and now absurd."[20] This reflection on the disagreements of philosophers introduces a brief digression on St. Thomas Aquinas, which closes the section, and serves as a pendant to the earlier passage on St. Francis. Bridges cannot see how Thomas, "with all his honesty and keen thought," could have accepted "the myth of a divine fiasco" — the fall of man.

The poem then proceeds to an examination of the successes and failures of reason in history. This historical survey is divided more or less artificially at line 615. Eight lines on the swarming of the lemmings in Norway into the sea[21] permit Bridges to compare their mad instinctive rush to destruction with a human expedition, the second Crusade.[22] If reason, looking to find

> . . . the firstfruits of intelligence
> showing some provident correction of man's estate
> to'ard social order, a wise discriminat purpose
> in clear contrast against the blind habits of brutes,   (i, 524–7)

reviews the history of Europe since the birth of Christ it will find only a story of "irredeemable shame." From the three centuries of the Goths' invasion nothing remains "save the broken relic of one/good bishop, and the record of one noble king." [23] Otherwise the Goths have left no trace except for their share in the creation of Don Quixote. This unexpected allusion gives Bridges the opportunity to comment on irony, and to observe that

> . . . The wise will live by Faith,
> faith in the order of Nature and that her order is good.
> 'Twer skepticism in them to cherish make-believe,
> creeds and precise focusings of the unsearchable. . . .[24] (i, 562-5)

The reference to Don Quixote, and the reflections which it occasions, were suggested, perhaps by Santayana's comments on laughter.[25]

Although "desire of perfection is Nature's promise," we must not expect to find greater stability in reason than elsewhere "in the flux of life." Yet

> . . . 'tis mightily
> to the reproach of Reason that she cannot save
> nor guide the herd; that minds who else wer fit to rule
> must win to power by flattery and pretence, and so
> by spiritual dishonesty in their flurried reign
> confirm the disrepute of all authority —
> but only in sackcloth can the Muse speak of such things.[26]
> (i, 609-15)

The final section of the book begins with the first extended exposition of the "Ring of Being," a conception which is considered more fully in the fourth book. "Wisdom" replaces "Nature" or "Universal Mind" so that the Biblical allusion in the first line of the following passage [27] may be used without alteration:

> WISDOM HATH HEWED HER HOUSE: She that dwelleth alway
> with God in the Evermore, afore any world was,
> fashion'd the nascent Earth that the energy of its life
> might come to evolution in the becoming of Man,

who, as her subject, should subjéct all to her rule
and bring God's latest work to be a realm of delight.
So she herself, the essential Beauty of Holiness,
pass'd her creativ joy into the creature's heart,
to take back from his hand her Adoration robes
and royal crown of his Imagination and Love.[28]   (i, 616–25)

Bridges then examines some of these adoration robes, the arts
and philosophy. The ensuing one hundred and fifty line summary
of the arts prior to the coming of Christ is one of the most impressive passages in the poem, but it requires little elucidation. Although sixty centuries have brought no finer work than that of
the sculptors of the Sphinx, "Wisdom," in Egyptian art and
philosophy, was not yet "justified of her children." The success
of the Greeks, however, leads one to suspect that

. . . man's faculties
were gifted once for all and stand, 'twould seem, at stay. . . .
(i, 700–1)

The Greeks' harmony of instinct, reason and spirit, as we see it in
their literature and art, might make us fear that their grace, like
the grace of childhood, was lost in growth, and could not return.
But it would be vain to deplore this, since true "beauty of manhood" is greater than childish charm. After a digression, in which
he asks how beauty can thrive in our crowded democracy, Bridges
points out that we have far exceeded the Greeks in music and
mathematics.

Hellas, in her love of "fleshly power" overesteemed "the nobility of passion and of animal strength." This observation leads
to a brief account of the decline of the free city-states, and the
absorption of Hellenism "into the great stiffening alloy of Rome."
This hint at Graeco-Roman civilization as a *praeparatio evangelica*
in turn introduces the final passage of the first book, in which,
in language borrowed from the New Testament, Bridges tells
of the coming of Christ:

For He, wandering unarm'd save by the Spirit's flame,
in few years with few friends founded a world-empire
wider than Alexander's and more enduring;
since from his death it took its everlasting life.
HIS kingdom is God's kingdom, and his holy temple
not in Athens or Rome but in the heart of man.
They who understand not cannot forget, and they
who keep not his commandment call him Master and Lord.

But the great light shineth in great darkness, the seed
that fell by the wayside hath been trodden under foot,
that which fell on the Rock is nigh wither'd away;
While loud and louder thro' the dazed head of the SPHINX
the old lion's voice roareth o'er all the lands. (i, 775–82; 786–90)

BOOK II: SELFHOOD

The second book opens with the important allusion to Plato's famous image of the soul of man as a charioteer (reason) guiding two horses (spirit and appetite). In Bridges' version the charioteer is still reason, but the two horses, naturally good, are Selfhood (the self-preservative and self-assertive instinct) and Breed (the sexual instinct). The second, third and fourth books deal respectively with Selfhood, Breed and Ethick (the science of the charioteer). In general, the second book resumes the main themes of the poem: the relationship of instinct to reason and the evolution of ideals from natural sources. Specifically it describes the growth of Spinoza's *conatus sese preservandi* or Schopenhauer's "will to live" to self-assertiveness in war and self-expression in art.

Like Schopenhauer, Bridges traces Selfhood to the lowest forms of life.[30] He describes the first actions of a new-born child as kindred to the absolute Selfhood of plants and animals:

Look now upon a child of man when born to light,
how otherwise than a plant sucketh he and clutcheth?
how with his first life-breath he clarioneth for food! (ii, 67–9)

Bridges suggests that if such Selfhood prevails throughout organic life, it may be that even the "dumb activities" in atom and molecule are likewise expressions of "Selfhood in its first degree." Although we do not blame this "Autarchy of Selfhood" in lower forms of life, it is denounced as heartless by reason, and regarded as man's "original sin." Thus nature, repudiating the foundation on which everything was built, "again would seem at variance with herself." Yet

> correction awaited not the human charioteer;
> Selfhood had of itself begotten its own restraint — (ii, 93–4)

Even beasts of prey hunt in packs, thus learning submission to a controlling will, while pastoral animals herd together in self-defense, "congregating their young/within their midst for safety."

The parental instinct, though related to Breed, "was born of Selfhood," since the mammal "must feel her suckling a piece of herself." In a passage borrowed directly from La Fontaine,[31] Bridges shows that birds, inured by long brooding, will protect their "chickens heedfully," as may be seen in the ruse of the partridge to detract the attention of the hunter from her brood. This introduces one of the main contentions of the poem:

> In man this blind motherly attachment is the spring
> of his purest affection, and of all compassion, — (ii, 125–6)

Later in the second book "Reason" says:

> "Hav I not learn'd that Selfhood is fundamental
> "and universal in all individual Being;
> "and that thru' Motherhood it came in animals
> "to altruistic feeling, and thence-after in men
> "rose to spiritual affection?" (ii, 699–703)

In the "Ring of Being" God's love, coming to the child from the mother's embrace, brings to him his first spiritual ideas. There is a striking resemblance between this conception and the social psychology of Erasmus Darwin. In "The Temple of Nature,"

Storgè (parental love) is the "first chain of society." [32] Beach describes Darwin's system as follows:

... Darwin has a kind of social psychology, based in the physical relations of parenthood and sexual love, and in the perception of ideal beauty (arising from the sense of touch) and the impulse of imitation. Parental love (personified as Storgè) is the "first chain of society," giving rise to tender affections. The second chain of society is sexual love, personified by Cupid and Psyche. And the "great bond of society" is Christian morality, typified by the Seraph Symphony, derived from imitation.

This system of psychology is something unique in English poetry. The nearest approach to it is perhaps found in Bridges' "Testament of Love" [sic]. [33]

The resemblance is striking; yet Bridges' clear debt to Wordsworth is probably of greater significance. In the *Prelude* Wordsworth also describes the child as receiving from his mother's embrace God's love, which he will ultimately return to God. [34]

Since man's purest affection and his ideal aspirations come to him from God through the mother's embrace, it is necessary to ask how nature accomplished her ideal ends in forms of life from which she withheld motherhood, or whether she was able to accomplish them at all. This question introduces the long fable of the bees (183–447), inspired, perhaps, by Bernard de Mandeville. [35] Bridges describes the life of the bees to illustrate his contempt for socialism. [36] The main argument is that our "economical bee-minded men" do not know that

> ... the high goal of our great endeavour
> is spiritual attainment, individual worth,
> at all cost to be sought and at all cost pursued,
> to be won at all cost and at all cost assured;
> not such material ease as might be attain'd for all
> by cheap production and distribution of common needs,
> wer all life level'd down to where the lowest can reach. . . .
>
> (ii, 204–10)

In the course of his fable Bridges refutes Plato's sophistry in the
Republic, denying "family life to his republicans" [37] on the ground
that since the love of mothers is a source of such inestimable good,
it would be wise for law to "forbid privat property" in its benefits.

The fable of the bees is interrupted for a brief fanciful (and rather
Wordsworthian [38]) variation on the idea that consciousness is the
soul's remembrance of an earlier life. Bridges refers, of course, to
the child's inherited instincts, rather than to remembered ideas or
things, as in Plato:

> So 'tis with any Manchild born into the world,
> so wondereth he awhile at the stuff of his home,
> so, tho' slowly and unsconsciently, he remembereth. —
> The senses administrant on his apperception
> are predisposed to the terrestrial influences,
> adapted to the environment where they took shape. . . .[39]
>
> (ii, 314–9)

The child will meet with no older acquaintances than bees —
and thus Bridges gets back to his fable. In common with most
philosophers, he had an aristocratic ideal. He feared above all that
socialism would restrict the individual's artistic and spiritual aspirations. Here again his philosophy is in close accord with that
of Santayana. There could be no better summary of the moral
of Bridges' fable than Santayana's argument against collectivism:

To ambition; to the love of wealth and honor, to love of a liberty
which meant opportunity for experiment and adventure, we owe
whatever benefits we have derived from Greece and Rome, from Italy
and England. It is doubtful whether a society which offered no personal prizes would inspire effort; and it is still more doubtful whether
that effort, if actually stimulated by education, would be beneficent.
For an indoctrinated and collective virtue turns easily to fanaticism; it
imposes irrational sacrifices prompted by some abstract principle or
habit once, perhaps, useful; but that convention soon becomes super-
stitious and ceases to represent general human excellence.[40]

The second part of the second book closes with a reflection on the "dominant function" of Reason, and with an account of the growth of intelligence in the child. Spiritual ideas, but also spiritual pain, come through reason:

> Savagery hath the throes; and ah! in tender years
> the mind of childhood knoweth torments of terror
> fears incommunicable, unconsolable,
> vague shapes. . . .[41] (ii, 457–60)

Yet "for the gift of his virgin intelligence," a child is always our truest picture of happiness:

> and as he ever drinketh of the living waters
> his spirit is drawn into the stream and, as a drop
> commingled therewith, taketh of birthright therein
> as vast an heritage as his young body hath
> in the immemorial riches of mortality.[42] (ii, 472–6)

Then the child goes forth into the world "in the joyous travail of the everlasting dawn." Although there will be "blastings and blightings of hope and love," yet to the enamored soul "evil is irrelevant and will be brushed aside." Even if the chariot is already pointed heavenward,

> 'tis faith alone can keep the charioteer in heart —
> Nay, be he but irresolute the steads wil rebel,
> and if he looketh earthward they wil follow his gaze;
> and ever as to earth he neareth, and vision cleareth
> of all that he feareth, and the enemy appeareth
> waving triumphant banners on the strongholds of ill,
> his mirroring mind wil tarnish, and mortal despair
> possess his soul: then surely Nature hath no night
> dark as that black darkness that can be felt: no storm
> blind as the fury of Man's self-destructiv passions,
> no pestilence so poisonous as his hideous sins.[43] (ii, 510–20)

The second part of the second book concerns the relationship of Selfhood to War and Art. The contradictions of reason cause

Bridges to reconsider the basic development of spiritual emotion from instinctive Selfhood. The fact that his ideas concerning war were badly muddled makes his argument difficult to summarize. The Spartan general Brasidas, as recounted in Plutarch, freed a mouse which had bit him because he admired the mouse's courage, and saw the instinct of Selfhood in the mouse to be the same impulse which in himself was accounted virtue. Yet a "mystical horror" of bloodshed may make all killing seem to a "purist . . . mortal pollution of soul." But

> . . . fatherhood dispenseth with this vain taboo:
> the duty of mightiness is to protect the weak:
> and since slackness in duty is unto noble minds
> a greater shame and blame than any chance offence
> ensuing on right conduct, this hath my assent, —
> that where there is any savagery ther wil be war:
> the warrior therefore needeth no apology.   (ii, 561-7)

The argument continues with rather dangerous reasoning. Love of war is natural to man. Children will play at war, and read those parts of the Old Testament filled with bloodshed; since all empire had origin in bloody invasion, man naturally conceived his Gods as wrathful. The Biblical stories often exalted the foe of God, as in the case of Milton's devil, or Methuselah, who, since he outlived the Flood, was forced to swim from peak to peak for safety.[44]

Poetry, too, honors the steeds above the charioteer: the poetry of war would seem to belong to the vanished past, but in fact "nothing can wholly perish" and primitive instinct is part of our inheritance. At this point in his argument Bridges' attitude toward this natural heritage is very different from that of the primitivist:

> . . . ther is no birthright
> so noble or stock so clean, but it transmitteth dregs,
> contamination at core of old brutality;
> inchoate lobes, dumb shapes of ancient terror abide:
> tho' fading still in the oceanic deeps of mind

their eyeless sorrows haunt the unfathom'd density,
dulling the crystal lens of prophetic vision,
crippling the nerve that ministereth to trembling strength,
distorting the features of our nobility. . . .   (ii, 663–71)

This discussion of inheritance by the "unconscious" leads, however, to a rather primitivistic attack on intellectualism. The attempt to understand "those infinit dark happenings" is as futile
as the attempt of the astronomer, with his eye screwed here or
there at some "minutest angle-space" of the sky, to comprehend
the "illimitable worlds thronging eternity." [45] Therefore it is
necessary again to enquire of reason itself its authority. Bridges
again presents his familiar argument, that only reason can judge
reason.[46] Futhermore, the child is nearer to "the Omniscient"
than man's "unperfect Reason." The "unconscious mind" contains, potentially, everything. Each child has "a given quantum of
personality":

a treasure that can be to good fortune assured
by Reason, its determinant and inexplicable
coefficient, that varieth also in power and worth: (ii, 722–4)

Reason in art is barren unless the artist is rich in "spiritual
nativities" — how barren may be seen in the comments on art
of philosophers, unless they are "twin-gifted" like Plato. An allusion to the difficulties which Plato's doctrine of ideas gave to
Aristotle serves as an excuse for a defence of idealism:

and truly if all existence is expression of Mind,
ideas must themselves be truer existences
than whatever else, and in such thought their nearest name.

(ii, 771–3)

With this preliminary, Bridges begins the exposition of his doctrine of "Influences" or essences.
"Powers unseen and unknown are the fountains of life." An
animal knows that the sunlight is warm, and will shift his posture

as reasonably as will a man — but man makes a dial for it. Through science he is able to detect some of its physical properties, yet he knows that his analysis has not approached the secret of its living power. Reason therefore

> owneth to existences beyond its grasp, whereon
> its richer faculties depend, and that those powers
> are ever present influencing the unconscious mind
> in its native function to inspire the Will. . . . (ii, 805–8)

As the "waken'd mind" grew to intellect, the animal instincts developed to "spiritual sight"; man's trouble "came of their divergency." Man is disconcerted between the rival promises of intellect and sense; it is evident that

> . . . true wisdom were a reason'd harmony
> and correlation of these divergent faculties.[47] (ii, 818–9)

The living compact between spiritual emotion and sensuous form "maketh our Art," wherein "material appearances engage the soul's depth." The ear is "more aesthetic than the eye" because that sense was earlier endowed in animals. "So" — and the *so* is very gratuitous in view of the preceding argument:

> . . . if we, changing Plato's old difficult term,
> should rename his Ideas Influences, ther is none
> would miss his meaning nor, by nebulous logic,
> wish to refute his doctrin that indeed ther are
> eternal Essences that exist in themselves,
> supreme efficient causes of the thoughts of men. (ii, 834–9)

The doctrine of Influence is mentioned by Bridges at this point merely to announce a theory which will be argued more fully in the fourth book, and to introduce the definition of *beauty* which immediately ensues. Thus far, Bridges has merely affirmed that in art reason must make use of influences which she cannot herself create, and which come to her through the senses.

> *What is Beauty? saith my sufferings then*: — I answer
> the lover and poet in my loose alexandrines:

Beauty is the highest of all those occult influences,
the quality of appearances that thru' the sense
wakeneth spiritual emotion in the mind of man:
And art, as it createth new forms of beauty,
awakeneth new ideas that advance the spirit
in the life of Reason to the wisdom of God.[48] (ii, 840–7)

With this definition of beauty at hand, Bridges again questions the authority of reason, and is able to establish it at last, because reason's

> . . . discernment of spiritual things,
> the ideas of Beauty, is her conscience of instinct
> upgrown in her (as she unto conscience of all
> upgrew from lower to higher) to conscience of Beauty
> judging itself by its own beauteous judgment.[49] (ii, 864–8)

The authority of reason lies in its position as a necessary mediator between the natural and the ideal.

With the authority of reason established, Bridges returns to the old dilemma of war, and decides that war ranks with those things "that are like unto virtue, but not virtue itself." Judged by the ideal of spiritual beauty, war seems an evil, but it is "like unto virtue," since it encourages the virtues of heroism, self-sacrifice and discipline. And so long as men remain savage, love of war will seem a virtue to them.

An allusion to Milton — "All *virtue is in her shape so lovely*" [50] — brings another digression from the theme of war. While agreeing with Aristotle that "a good disposition is Goddes happiest gift," Bridges contemns his sternly intellectual God. A God whose Being lies "in the unbroken exercise of absolute intellect" cannot move his desire. Rather,

> I see the emotion of saints, lovers and poets all
> to be the kindling of some Personality
> by an eternizing passion; and that God's worshipper
> looking on any beauty falleth straightway in love;
> and thatt love is a fire in whose devouring flames
> all earthly ills are consumed, and at least flash of it,

be it only a faint radiancy, the freed soul glimpseth,
nay ev'n may think to hav felt, some initiat foretaste
of that mystic rapture, the consummation of which
is the absorption of Selfhood in the Being of God.[51] (ii, 918–27)

There could be no more succinct summary of Bridges' "religion
of love."

The closing paragraphs of the second book again revert to the
theme of war. Not only men impelled by hate, or ambitious and
disorderly men, approve of war. Honest men "who seek peace
and ensue it,"[52] seeing war as a field for exercise of spirit which
else might "fust unused,"[53] will embrace it. Yet war brings sorrows which no "glory can atone." Bridges feared younger generations than his own would forget the horrors of war, and he
ends the second book with a stern recollection:

> . . . nor men kenn'd as they fell,
> desperatly unrepentant to the "scourge of God,"
> how 'twas the crowded foulness of their own bodies
> punish'd them so: — alas then in what plight we are,
> knowing 'twas mankind's crowded uncleanness of soul
> that brought our plague! which yet we could not cure nor stay;
> for Reason had lost control of his hot-temper'd steed
> and taken himself infection of the wild brute's madness;
> so when its fire slacken'd and the fierce fight wore out,
> our fever'd pulse show'd no sober return of health.
> Amid the flimsy joy of the uproarious city
> my spirit on those first jubilant days of armistice
> was heavier within me, and felt a profounder fear
> than ever it knew in all the War's darkest dismay. (ii, 988–1001)

BOOK III: BREED

The third book, "Breed," is concerned with love in all its aspects, and was probably much influenced by the first chapter of
Santayana's *Reason in Society*.[54] Bridges describes the evolution of

love from its origins in sex and animal life to the spiritual love of
Dante for Beatrice in the same way that he described, in the second
book, the evolution of Selfhood from the *conatus sese preservandi*
to spiritual emotion in art. Once more reason and beauty are
all-important aids to this evolution. As Santayana says, "Love is
a brilliant illustration of a principle everywhere discoverable;
namely, that human reason lives by turning the friction of material
forces into the light of ideal goods." [55] Santayana affirms that no
philosopher can do justice to the subject of love unless he remem-
bers two things: "one, that love has an animal basis; the other,
that it has an ideal object." [56]

The third book is more unified than either of the preceding ones.
Except for a digression on pleasure in food (21–151) and an account of the struggles which Christian marriage had to wage
against paganism and asceticism (478–774), the poet stays close
to his main theme. The book begins with a reminder that the
image of the soul of man as a charioteer and two steeds is merely
an image. Like Santayana, who begins his analysis of love with
an account of the dual function of sex for reproduction and love, [57]
Bridges observes that "in Nature's economy the same impulse
may work to divers ends." Santayana's comparison of the relative
importance of nutrition and reproduction [58] may have suggested
to Bridges his humorous digression on "PLEASUR IN FOOD," which

> when once it findeth conscience in the Reason of man
> is posited by folly as an end-in-itself;
> till by sensuous refinement it usurpeth rank
> beside his intellectual and spiritual joys. (iii, 29–32)

While admitting that a reasonable pleasure in food and wine is
legitimate, Bridges rejects any philosophy based wholly on sensuous pleasure. Nevertheless, the epicure's gluttony

> . . .cometh of Self, as War doth; and hereby
> 'twer well to note how some would derive War from Breed,
> tho' sex is but the occasion, when jealousy of love
> provoketh Selfhood to anger. . . . (iii, 141–4)

Thus, in his familiar allusive manner, Bridges return to his main subject. Breed is to the race as Selfhood to the individual: the two primary instincts are independent of each other. Breed (here, *sex*) is necessary both to plants and animals, but the apparatus of sex in animals is of a more specialized kind:

> and since race-propagation might have been assured
> without differentiation of sex, we are left to guess
> nature's intention from its full effects in man. . . . (iii, 159–61)

Bridges' "dissension from Spinoza here" leads him to reflect on that philosopher's work in perfecting the microscope, and thence it is an easy transition to a discussion of Mendel's theory of particulate inheritance:

> a theory on such wide experiment upbuilt
> that the enrichment of species may be assumed to be
> the purpose of natur in the segregation of sex. (iii, 175–7)

This new knowledge throws no light on human mating by eugenic principles. Nevertheless, and although the origin of sex lies in the darkness of all origins, we can trace its development from plants to man, in whom all the more primitive elements contribute to the forming of

> . . . a constant conscient passion, by Reason transform'd
> to an altruistic emotion and spiritual love. (iii, 203–4)

Like Selfhood, Breed illustrates the fact that the animal instincts are the material for both virtue and vice, rather than for vice alone:

> for as Self grew thru' Reason from animal rage
> to vice of war and gluttony, but meanwhile uprose
> thru' motherly yearning to a profounder affection,
> so Breed, from like degrading brutality at heart,
> distilleth in the altruism of spiritual love
> to be the sublimest passion of humanity,
> with parallel corruption. . . . (iii, 206–12)

In "higher natures" who are in love, "sense is transfigured quite," as it was with Dante in that miracle of love at first sight "which is to many a man his only miracle." [59] So too Lucretius, seeking order in "Chance," encountered "some frenzy of beauty" and left "his atoms in the lurch" to worship Aphrodite:

> and waving the oriflamme of her divinity
> above the march of his slow-trooping argument,
> he attributeth to her the creation and being
> of all Beauty soe'er: NEC SINE TE QUICQUAM
> DIAS IN LUMINIS ORAS EXORITUR,
> NEQUE FIT LAETUM NEQUE: AMABILE QUICQUAM. [60]
>
> (iii, 249–54)

It is evident that "Beauty will be engaged in man's love." The attraction of beauty "bettereth the species"; without physical beauty, beauty of spirit could not have evolved. And this high beauty of spirit, when once it has been awakened,

> needeth no more support of the old animal lure,
> but absolute in its transmitted power and grace
> maketh a new beauty of its own appearances. [61] (iii, 285–7)

Since the lover is more in love with love itself than with any of its particular embodiments, the time comes, in his progress toward Absolute Love, when the qualities of those particular embodiments, such as beauty, will no longer be required to evoke his passion.

Love's true passion is of immortal happiness. The Greeks, whose later poets told of a heavenly Aphrodite, had some "dim prescience" of this before man really arrived "at thatt wisdom thru' Christ." Yet sensuous beauty is not discredited, since she is herself "mother of heavenly Love." As Santayana says, "there can be no philosophic interest in disguising the animal basis of love." [62]

Bridges proceeds to a comparison between men and women in passion and sexual attraction:

> The allure of bodily beauty is mutual in mankind
> as is the instinct of breed, which tho' it seem i' the male
> more activ, is i' the female more predominant,
> more deeply engaging life, grave and responsible.[63] (iii, 325-8)

The question of why physical beauty is deemed a feminine attribute introduces a brief digression, another description of a country scene. The poet then reaffirms woman's "deeper purpose" and "higher function and duty" in sex. It is curious that man is slow to recognize this higher purpose, since everything that his spirit has attained "came to him thru' motherhood of the nursling boy." Lesbianism, in view of the natural relationship of motherhood and sex, is "a backsliding and treason against nature":

> Nor can the ethic that here intrudeth be deny'd,
> since if man speak of morals 'tis of sex they think;
> for why the passion of it both transporteth their souls
> and troubleth daily life with problems of conduct. (iii, 474-7)

The ensuing two hundred and fifty lines are difficult to summarize. Having considered one perversion of Breed, lesbianism, Bridges turns to another: the hatred of sexual love. Christian marriage is the desirable mean between such extremes, but only

> . . . after tough battle against two mighty outbursts
> of Pagan Poetry coud marriage come in the end
> to its own, from being a tolerated discordancy
> to be an accepted harmony, and hallow'd as such
> within the Church, a sacrament. Of these two wars
> the story is long, and now 'tis here briefly to tell. (iii, 492-7)

These two wars Bridges fancifully calls the first and second wars of the Essenes. He uses the term Essene to mean ascetic, and does not refer to the actual Jewish sect in the time of the Manichees. The first war of the Essenes was with the poetry of Selfhood:

the pagan poetry dealing with the wars of the Huns, Goths and Vikings. When "Rome's mitred prelates" won the Gallic provinces to Christianity, the submissive pagans were driven in "flocks to th' font, but got little washing therein." The priests denounced the pagan poets, but, since their proscription was unavailing, encouraged these poets "to make like stirring balladry of the Bible tales." Bridges traces the lives of the saints, medieval religious drama, and the Arthurian legends to this priestly mitigation of pagan savagery.

The second war of the Essenes was with the "young poetry of BREED," the poetry of courtly love which appeared quite suddenly at the end of the eleventh century in Languedoc. Bridges makes no very serious effort to find an origin for the spirit of Provençal love poetry, a problem which scholars have not been able to clarify. He compares the appearance of the Troubadours to that of wading tribes of fowl who without warning rise from "their beauties' ambush in the reedy beds":

> Nor wer these Troubadours hucksters of song who tuned
> their pipes for fee: some far glimpse of the heav'nly Muse
> had reach'd and drawn the soul by the irresistible
> magnet of love: as when in the blockish marble
> the sculptor's thought of beauty loometh into shape
> neath his rude hammerstrokes, ere the true form is seen;
> so had the monks' rough-hewing of the old pagan tales
> discover'd virtue: — an Ideal of womanhood
> had striven into outline; which, tho' passion heeded not
> yet art had grasp'd, divining fresh motiv for skill. . . .[64]

(iii, 633–42)

Reflection on the carefree life of the Troubadours arouses in Bridges a nostalgic longing for Provence and other lands of sunshine, and he takes the opportunity to make a Miltonic catalogue of poetic names: Hawaii, Nairobi, Pasadena, Beziers, Castelnaudary, Carcassonne and others. He then returns to Provence, and describes the national and racial pluralism which flourished there. Jew and Gentile, Saracen and Christian, Catalan and Frank met in peace, and even the most "abominable, persecuted and defamed" of sects, the Manichees,[65] was harbored safely in the court of Raymond of Toulouse.

Bridges describes the creed of the Manichees, who, "seeing in natur a power maleficent to man, estopp'd his growth in love." Their austere asceticism was in strong contrast to the license of the "half-hearted clerics" and of Innocent III, who instigated the Albigensian war. The "champions of Christ" ravaged Raymond's county, and drove the Troubadours to the Italian cities, and ere

> within the Church's precincts they had raised a song,
> Chivalry had won acceptance in the ideal of sex
> and, blending with the worship of the Mother of God,
> assured the consecration of MARRIAGE, still unknown
> save to the Christian folk of Europe whence it sprang.
> Thus, as it came to pass, the second Essene War
> brought the New Life in which full soon Dante was born.[66]
>
> (iii, 734–40)

The poem proceeds with its analysis of love, showing that beauty is as necessary to Breed as to Selfhood in the evolution of animal instinct to spiritual emotion. With the growth of reason, man would have discarded physical love, "had he not learned in beauty to transfigure love." Science shies at such doctrine; it knows nothing of this beauty. But what does science know of color or sound?[67]

Bridges then asks how female beauty came to be the common "lure" in marriage. In animal mating the physical attractions, as they evolved with sense, took on beautiful forms, until beauty was recognized consciously and exploited by art. As beauty became spiritualized, love was idealized. The poet observes that as a result of the ideality of love, the lover must necessarily be disillusioned. In his first love physical beauty and spiritual beauty are inseparably mingled:

> . . . then is he seen
> in the ecstasy of earthly passion and of heavenly vision
> to fall to idolatry of some specious appearance
> as if 'twer very incarnation of his heart's desire,
> whether eternal and spiritual, as with Dante it was,
> or mere sensuous perfection, or as most commonly
> a fusion of both — when if distractedly he hav thought
> to mate mortally with an eternal essence
> all the delinquencies of his high passion ensue. (iii, 800–8)

Bridges' account of the sequence of earthly loves which a man experiences (and their relation to "an eternal essence") is similar to
that of Santayana: "A mother is followed by a boyish friend,
a friend by a girl, a girl by a wife, a wife by a child, a child by an
idea. A divinity passes through these various temples; they may
all remain standing, and we may continue our cult in them without outward change, long after the god has fled from the last into
his native heaven." [68]

Man is saved from ultimate disillusionment, however, by the
fact that hope is in itself a joy. That marriage should so rarely live
up to our expectations is no reason to discredit the institution itself. Since man cannot live like an animal,

> . . . there is no hope for him but to attune
> nature's diversity to a human harmony,
> and with faith in his hope and full courage of soul
> realizing his will at one with all nature,
> devise a spiritual ethic for conduct in life. (iii, 825–9)

A further allusion to the Essenes leads to the interesting observation, perhaps owing something to Schopenhauer,[69] that asceticism
is as natural to man as animal passion; that contempt of "fleshly
pleasur" is as near to his spirit as is love of it to his animal nature.

A reference to the story of Eve's creation leads Bridges to ask
what special function "fell sequestered out of Adam in his lost
rib," and he concludes that woman is more amenable to faith and

spiritual love than man, in whom the rational faculty is more
highly developed. But this faith, natural to woman, is necessary
to man if he would not succumb to the "inhumanity of nature's
omnipotence." He should remember that Reason and "spiritual
sense," which conspire to make him lose faith in nature, both come
to him from nature herself.

The third book closes with a long and beautiful passage on
Titian's picture "Sacred and Profane Love." [70] Bridges' earlier
assertion — that the efforts of painters to respiritualize art by
symbolism (in reaction to realism) were doomed to fail because
symbolism is "outfaced in the presence of direct feeling" — is
illustrated by the fact that Titian's "Sacred Love" "in pictorial
beauty suffereth defeat." Yet the painting does show

> . . . that as Beauty is all with Spirit twined,
> so all obscenity is akin to the ugliness
> which Art would outlaw. . . . (iii, 1119–21)

Bridges further interprets the painting as symbolizing the child's
first encounter with love. The child's love is moved by both the
sensuous and the spiritual, and the two kinds of love come together as he stirs their reflected images with his hand.

BOOK IV: ETHICK

The fourth book examines

> . . . that science, call'd Ethick, dealing with the skill
> and manage of the charioteer in Plato's myth. . . . (iv, 88–9)

An introductory passage on the evanescence of beauty in childhood is followed by an account of the origin of duty, and of the
two types of ethics (91–361). The relationship of pleasure to
happiness and virtue is then considered (362–594). This passage
is followed by a section on the relative importance of disposition
and education (595–721). Bridges then presents his theory of
mind (761–1137). A consideration of the nature and value of

prayer (1138–1267) leads to the traditional palinode and conclusion, in which the poet once more expresses his faith and summarizes the main conclusions of his poem (1268–1446).

The introductory passage has a marked Wordsworthian tone. "Beauty, the eternal Spouse of the Wisdom of God"

> attempteth every mortal child with influences
> of her divine supremacy, (iv, 4–5)

and where she finds response in "some richly favour'd soul"[71] the infant's desire is "purer and hath less of earthly tinge" than any later attainment of his understanding.[72] Yet without the aid of training,

> . . . this glimpse or touch of immanence,
> being a superlativ brief moment of glory,
> is too little to leaven the inveterate lump of life. . . . (iv, 58–60)

Nature has something "truly of her promise in all,'" yet, as Aristotle confesses, virtue cannot be taught to a mind not well disposed by nature, and those who receive the divine gift in plenitude are "truly fortunat." [73] But even those richly endowed with good disposition need some guidance: the science of ethics arose from this need.

Bridges begins his discussion of ethics with an account of the natural origin of the sense of duty — a sense so strong that some (Shaftesbury and Kant, for instance) have abstracted a special faculty "whereby the creature kenneth the creator's Will." The old myth of original sin is not untrue to life, since

> the imperativ obligation cannot be over-summ'd,
> being in itself the self-conscience of thatt Essence
> which is no other indeed than the prime ordinance
> that we call Law of Nature, — in its grade the same
> with the determin'd habit of electrons, the same
> with the determining instinct of unreasoning life,
> NECESSITY become conscient in man — whereto
> all insubordination is imperfection in kind.[74] (iv, 104–11)

This reference to "Necessity" as an "Essence" (like "Beauty" and "Order") leads to the first complete exposition of the "Ring of Being." The essences, such as Necessity or the Law of Nature, come from Universal Mind:

> Reality appeareth in forms to man's thought
> as several links interdependent of a chain
> that circling returneth upon itself, as doth
> the coil'd snake that in art figureth eternity.
> From Universal Mind the first-born atoms draw
> their function, whose rich chemistry the plants transmute
> to make organic life, whereon animals feed
> to fashion sight and sense and give service to man,
> who sprung from them is conscient in his last degree
> of ministry unto God, the Universal Mind,
> whither all effect returneth whence it first began.
> The Ring in its repose is Unity and Being:
> Causation and Existence are the motion thereof.
> Thru'out all runneth Duty, and the conscience of it
> is thatt creativ faculty of animal mind
> that, wakening to self-conscience of all Essences,
> closeth the full circle, where the spirit of man
> escaping from the bondage of physical law
> re-entereth eternity by the vision of God. (iv, 112–30)

Rather than argue the existence of his essences Bridges proceeds to his account of the natural origin of the moral sense in a passage apparently indebted to Darwin.[75] If he could ask the young black ouzel building her nest beside him why she did so, she would probably answer "I know not, but I MUST." If persuaded to desist from her action, she would come back a few days later, when it was time for her eggs to hatch, and look for her nest. If the poet again asked her, she would know a new word, "having made conscient passage from the MUST to the OUGHT."

In man, the sense of duty is extended from physical to moral ends; once again we observe the consciousness of instinct determining its evolution to higher ends:

And when and whereas Conscience transfigureth the Instincts
— to affection, as aforesaid, from motherly selfhood,
and to spiritual love from lust of breed —, we find
Duty therewith extended in the moral field. (iv, 159–62)

A reference to the relativist's claim that all morality is contingent
leads Bridges to distinguish between a higher and a lower ethics.
The following passage appears to be a defence of an absolute or
at least transcendent ethics: [76]

Altho' good disposition (as Aristotle hath it)
may be by beauty educated, and aspire
to theoretic wisdom (as Plato would teach)
and Ethick therewithal claim honor of the same rank
that ideal philosophy ascribeth to man,
yet, if for lack of faith he sink that claim, I see
a thing of hap without place in Reality. (iv, 208–14)

The lower type of ethics is "the one of social need," the "animal
sanction of virtue." This ethics, based on the customs and needs
of man, as it becomes strictly codified, tends to harden into preju-
dice and slavish observance of custom (225–31); hence the need
of teachers, seers and prophets who will call attention to a higher
and spiritual ethics. Bridges' distinction between the two types of
ethics is in general similar to that of Bergson.

The poet returns at this point to a familiar thesis: the futility
of any attempt to legislate virtue, of any ethics which tries to re-
form society rather than man. (In this, Bridges breaks completely
with romantic ethical theorists.) If socialists, who preach class-
hatred as the "enlighten'd gospel of love," were to seek scientific
ground for their theories, or examine history for any evidence of
progress as a result of "social virtue," they would be startled out
of their complacent belief that the evil lies in society rather than
in man. Their surprise would be like that of the archaeologist exploring Kish and Ur, when he came upon the bones of the king's
concubines and bodyguards, slaughtered to accompany him in
death, beside his own. (This allusion occasions a digression of

sixty lines on the archaeologist's findings [276–336], perhaps the
greatest passage of sustained lyricism in the poem.) If we are hor-
rified by this barbarism, we should examine more recent history.
Even today,

> See how cross-eyed the pride of our world-wide crusade
> against Nigerian slavery, while the London poor
> in their Victorian slums lodged closer and filthier
> than the outraged alien; and under liberty's name
> our Industry is worse fed and shut out from the sun. —
> In every age and nation a like confusion is found. (iv, 356–61)

The section as a whole is more impressive lyrically than philo-
sophically. If he has proved that social virtue is to be avoided,
since it has made no progress since the times of the Chaldees,
Bridges nevertheless deplores, in the final lines, that this virtue
has not prevailed. The passage began as an attack on equalitarianism; it ended by attacking a condition which only a certain amount
of equalitarianism could correct.[77]

Bridges then considers the problem of pleasure. "Life-Joy" results primarily from a harmony of impulses and instincts; from
a condition of life in which no valid impulse is denied its proper
expression. Yet while personal pleasure is intrinsically good,
hedonism is "confuted off-hand" because none will deny that
some pleasures are bad. How did pleasure, an intrinsic good, come
to appear "virtue's insidious foe"? Once again we are confronted
with the dualism of reason:

> As Pleasure came in man to the conscience of self,
> his Reason abstracted it as an idea, and when
> he found the pleasur increasing with the conscience of it,
> he dwelt thereon, and seeking more and more to enrich
> his conscious pleasur, and bloating it with luxury,
> invented and indulged vices unknown to brutes. (iv, 413–8)

Moralists "took fright" at this, and where they should have
been contented with a danger-signal, "posted a prohibition."[78]

Systematic repudiation of pleasure is wrong since all of man's activity is based on the "intrinsic joy of activ life." Yet man, vain of his reason, and eager to assert its independence, disclaims complicity with human emotion, and makes a distinction of kind between pleasure and happiness. Bridges defines happiness as merely a wider term "for the unalloy'd conditions of the Pleasur of Life," and asserts once more Santayana's doctrine of the continuity of the natural and the spiritual. We should see

> . . . Spiritual, Mental and Animal
> to be gradations merged together in growth and mix'd
> in their gradations, and that the animal pleasure
> runneth thru'out all grades heartening all energies. . . . (iv, 558–61)

The section on pleasure is concluded with the reflection that although some pleasures are definitely good and others bad, there are many types of pleasure not easily classified. Bridges agrees with Aristotle that in "that uncharted jungle" a good man will go right, "while an ill disposition will miss and go wrong."

The fourth book systematically examines the main problems considered in Aristotle's *Ethics*, and thus it naturally proceeds at this point to the question of disposition and education. After suggesting that the good in man outweighs the evil, Bridges finds man's imitative faculty to be the means used by nature to incline his disposition to the virtuous choice:

> "For Mimicry is inborn in man from childhood up:
> "and in this differeth he from other animals,
> "being the most imitativ: and his first approach
> "to learning maketh he in mimicry, and hath delight
> "in imitations of all kinds." [79] (iv, 608–12)

Each child has, as Santayana phrases it, "a birthright of beauty." [80] Thus the child will be

> . . . held by the inborn love of Beauty inconsciently
> of preference to imitate the more beautiful things.

And because Virtue is an activity, and lieth not
in doctrin and theory but in practice and conduct,
co-ordinating potencies into energy,
(and here 'tis Aristotle again speaketh, not I)
the preferential imitation of right action
is THE HABIT OF VIRTUE. . . .[81] (iv, 621–8)

The child bred in good environment will create an ideal for himself
which he will strive to attain. Because of his inborn love of beauty,

ther is nought in all his nurtur of more intrinsic need
than is the food of Beauty: as mammals milk to his flesh,
which admitteth no proxy, so Beauty is to his soul. (iv, 643–5)

The section on disposition and education is concluded with a
reflection on the old problem of whether those who achieve virtue
without great effort are more virtuous than those who survive
great temptations. Bridges concludes that although he must
deem "them the most virtuous who with least effort excell," the
problem is not an important one since all are tempted by carnal
pleasure: "the same incarnat traitor routeth in all hearts."

At this point Bridges resumes his study of the nature of the
mind. The ensuing section (761–1137), though largely a restate-
ment and further development of ideas already formulated, is one
of the most difficult of the entire poem. It begins by reminding
the reader of the interdependence of sensation and thought. All
human life depends upon a correlation of "living entities"; most
of these coordinations are "automatous." They result in "unify'd
organities," all of which act in response to external stimuli. Stimuli
affect even the "unconscious":

. . . thatt swarming intelligence where life began,
and where ideas wander at liberty to find
their procreativ fellowship; thatt fluid sea
in which all problems, spiritual or logical
aesthetic mathematic or practic, resolve
melting as icebergs launch'd on the warm ocean-stream:

and wheresoe'er this corporat alchemy is at best,
'tis call'd by all men GENIUS, and its aptitudes
like virtuous disposition may be inherited. (iv, 816–24)

This spontaneous life of essences owes nothing to reason.
Every essence has "its own Idea," but many of these are not the
contributions of Reason, whose peculiar idea is that of Order.
Yet since Order is her particular idea, reason naturally assumes
that all of the other ideas are subservient to hers,[82] and the consequent "assumed docility" — the human mind's willingness to
submit to the ordering of reason — "is by English moralists/
termed the 'Good Will.' "

Once again the reader is reminded of the relationship of mind
to body:

And of the body I think as the machinery
of our terrestrial life evolving towards conscience
in the Ring of Reality; and thence of the mind
as thatt evolved conscience. . . .[83] (iv, 888–91)

The doctrine of ideas and essences is then restated:

And human Intellect I see form'd and compact
of the essential Ideas, wherewith soever each man
hath come in contact personally. . . .

. . . Thus I come to think
that if the mind held all ideas in plenitude
'twould be complete, at one with natur and harmonized
with as good harmony as we may find in nature.

(iv, 893–5, 904–7)

The reader will find some difficulty in trying to distinguish between the terms *idea* and *essence*. In the second book Bridges describes Essences or Influences as "existences beyond" Reason's
grasp, "ever present influencing the unconscious mind." In the
fourth book, reason as an essence has the "idea of Order." The
obscurity is partly dispelled if it is recognized that Bridges' essences (which in 914 he unfortunately refers to as "ideas") are kin

to the essences of Santayana, and can therefore mean anything. Their presence is relative to the mind which perceives them; in any given mind they are

> . . . incomplete, being only such as that one man
> may hav happ'd on, and those only in the measure whereby
> he is tuned to take cognisance of them. . . . (iv, 915–7)

The character of these essences can hardly be understood without reference to "The Discovery of Essence," the ninth chapter of Santayana's *Skepticism and Animal Faith*:

Not only is the character of each essence inalienable, and, so long as it is open to intuition, indubitable, but the realm of essences is infinite. Since any essence I happen to have hit upon is independent of me and would possess its precise character if I had never been born, or had never been led by the circumstances of my life and temperament to comprehend that particular essence, evidently all other essences, which I have not been led to think of, rejoice in the same impalpable being — impalpable, yet the only sort of being that the most rugged experience can ever find.[84]

In the fourth book of *The Testament of Beauty* Bridges means by essence the essence which Santayana here defines; elsewhere in the poem he uses the term in a sense roughly equivalent to that of the Platonic Idea — something very different. Nowhere does he give a full and comprehensible definition of the term.

Bridges' application of his theory of essence is sufficiently clear, however. Since every man, according to his disposition and experience, will intuit ("possess," as he puts it) a different group of essences, all men are different. Beneath their differences, however, men are very much alike because the animal ideas (essences) are common property. Any deviation from this "greatest common measure of all mankind" will be determined by the intuition or possession of essences,

> for that the soul's nobility consisteth not
> in riches of imagination or intellect,
> but in harmony of Essences. . . . (iv, 945–7)

Obviously the essences "are a promiscuous company muster'd at random." It is the task of reason to remedy this disorder. If the ideas or essences work in harmony, a man will be "determin'd and consistent"; if they do not, he may be subject to "the tyranny of one idea."

The section on the mind is concluded by a definition of the position of reason in the "Ring of Being." This passage clarifies Bridges' conception of religion, and thus prepares for the final sections of the book. The religion described is, in its main outlines, the religion of Santayana and Spinoza. With its allusion to Santayana's *Life of Reason* the passage may indeed be regarded as an acknowledgment of the poet's general indebtedness to that philosopher:

> Reason (say I) wil rise to awareness of its rank
> in the Ring of Existence, where man looketh up
> to the first cause of all; and wil itself decree
> and order discreetly the attitude of the soul
> seeking self-realization in the vision of God,
> becoming at the last thatt arch-conscience of all,
> to which the Greek sage who possess'd it made appeal.
>   The attraction of this motion is our conscience of it,
> our love of wisdom and of beauty; and the attitude
> of those attracted wil be joyful obedience
> with reverence to'ard the omnificent Creator
> and First Cause, whose Being is thatt beauty and wisdom
> which is to be apprehended only and only approach'd
> by right understanding of his creation, and found
> in thatt habit of faith which some thinkers hav styled
> *The Life of Reason*; and this only true bond of love
> and reasonable relation (if relation ther be)
> 'twixt creature and creator, man and nature's God,
> the which we call *Religion*, — is fundamental,
> physically and metaphysically in fashion
> or force undistinguishable from Duty itself. . . . (iv, 1073–93)

Though religion has often degenerated into "dolorous superstition," we see today, even in the building of garden cities, a "han-

kering after lost Beauty." Thus there are many amid the blank
tyranny of ugliness who are plotting a recall of

> that old arrant exile who, for all her mischief,
> hid neath her cloak the master-key of happiness.[85] (iv, 1130–1)

There follows a long digression on prayer which requires no
elucidation. Bridges considers the salutary effect of prayer on
character, the difficulty of prayer, and the attitudes and gestures
which accompany it. Even if it had no other use, prayer would
be valuable as a means to "bind character, concentrate Will,/and
purify intention." As an afterthought to the section on prayer,
Bridges disposes of the problem of immortality in fifteen lines:

> Nor doubt I that as this thinking machinery
> perisheth with the body, so animal thought
> with all its whimper and giggle must perish therewith,
> with all shames, all vain ostentation and ugliness,
> and all personality of all other ideas;
> except it be that, like as in unconscient things
> whence conscience came, ther is also thru'out conscient life
> the same emergent evolution, persisting
> in our spiritual life to the goal of conscience.
> This mind perisheth with this body, unless
> the personal co-ordination of its ideas
> hav won to Being higher than animal life,
> at thatt point where the Ring cometh upward to reach
> the original creativ Energy which is God,
> with conscience entering into life everlasting. (iv, 1253–67)

This conception of immortality as depending upon the subject's
acquisition of sufficient "adequate ideas" is identical with that of
Spinoza. This immortality, whatever it is, belongs also to whoever
has mounted the topmost rungs of Plato's ladder, and has perceived the nature of Absolute Beauty or Absolute Love.

The one hundred and seventy eight lines which remain are in
the nature of a summary and conclusion. The poem ends as it was

begun, in a mood of ecstatic wonder. Having taken refuge from a mortal distress in the beauty of sunset, the poet fell into a "strange illusion"; though awake, he felt he was asleep and dreaming:

> for my tale was my dream and my dream the telling,
> and I remember wondring the while I told it
> how I told it so tellingly. . . . (iv, 1297–9)

And here, suspecting once more the speculations of formal reason, Bridges introduces the traditional palinode of medieval allegory:

> Verily by Beauty it is that we come at WISDOM,
> yet not by Reason at Beauty: and now with many words
> pleasing myself betimes I am fearing lest in the end
> I play the tedious orator who maundereth on
> for lack of heart to make an end of his nothings.
> Wherefor as when a runner who hath run his round
> handeth his staff away, and is glad of his rest,
> here break I off, knowing the goal was not for me
> the while I ran on telling of what cannot be told.
> For not the Muse herself can tell of Goddes love. . . .
> (iv, 1305–14)

God's love comes to the child from the mother's embrace; the child is therefore "apt to absorb Ideas in primal purity." With the growth of understanding, however, he would lose his faith, did not a second call

> of nature's Love await him to confirm his Faith
> or to revoke him if he is wholly lapsed therefrom. (iv, 1338–9)

And so mighty is this second vision that he calls it first love. Thus in his various earthly loves, "by near approach to an eternal presence,"

> man's heart with divine furor kindled and possess'd
> falleth in blind surrender; and finding therewithal
> in fullest devotion the full reconcilement
> betwixt his animal and spiritual desires. . . . (iv, 1358–61)

Or, as Santayana says, "Love is a true natural religion; it has a visible cult, it is kindled by natural beauties and bows to the best symbol it may find for its hope; it sanctifies a natural mystery; and finally, when understood, it recognizes that what it worshipped under a figure was truly the principle of all good." [86]

"Friendship is in loving rather than in being lov'd." Since a man loves self best, he looks in his friend and finds

> . . . his own better self, his live loveable idea,
> flowering by expansion in the loves of his life. (iv, 1376–7)

From the pagan assertion that there can be no friendship between God and man because of their unlimited disparity, man made escape in the worship of Christ, whose humanity is God's personality, and with whom communion "is the life of the soul":

> Our happiest earthly companionships hold a foretaste
> of the feast of salvation and by thatt virtue in them
> provoke desire beyond them to out-reach and surmount
> their humanity in some superhumanity
> and ultimat perfection: which, howe'er 'tis found
> or strangely imagin'd, answereth to the need of each
> and pulleth him instinctivly as to a final cause.
> Thus unto all who hav found their high ideal in Christ,
> Christ is to them the essence discern'd or undiscern'd
> of all their human friendships; and each lover of him
> and of his beauty must be as a bud on the Vine
> and hav participation in him; for Goddes love
> is inescapable as nature's environment,
> which if a man ignore or think to thrust it off
> he is the ill-natured fool that runneth blindly on death.
> (iv, 1408–22)

The last passage of the poem offers a truly Hegelian or Spinozist synthesis of all supposed opposites, a final refutation of dualism. The resemblance to Spinoza's general theory, in which the eternal and the temporal orders, substance and mode, active and passive

nature, God and the world, are all seen as coincident and synony-
mous, is striking:

> Truly the Soul returneth the body's loving
> where it hath won it . . . and God so loveth the world . . .
> and in the fellowship of the friendship of Christ
> God is seen as the very self-essence of love,
> Creator and mover of all as activ Lover of all,
> self-express'd in not-self, without which no self were
> In thought whereof is neither beginning nor end
> nor space not time; nor any fault nor gap therein
> 'twixt self and not-self, mind and body, mother and child,
> 'twixt lover and loved, God and man: but ONE ETERNAL
> in the love of Beauty and in the selfhood of Love. (iv, 1436–46)

CHAPTER THIRTEEN

The Testament of Beauty (III)

EADERS who have followed the foregoing summary with some care and who have consulted the notes for instances of resemblance and indebtedness will be impressed by Bridges' almost Ciceronian eclecticism. His refusal to cleave to a single well-defined system is likely to antagonize professional philosophers even more than his Platonic and Lucretian attempt to emotionalize philosophy. The rarity of such eclecticism among modern thinkers has, on the other hand, led some commentators to pigeon-hole Bridges' thought by emphasizing some of his ideas and ignoring others. As Larrabee says,

Some have seen in *The Testament* nothing but pure Platonism. To others the poem smacks of Aristotle, or of the Stoic sages, or of their rivals the Epicureans. The pantheism of Spinoza has inescapably been brought to mind by many. Bridges has been claimed for orthodox Anglicanism (whatever that may be ?) by not a few, while others comment on his Neo-Paganism, and hail him among the prophets of evolutionary materialism.[1]

It is not surprising, in view of Bridges' willingness and even determination to serve many masters, that his thought should resemble most closely that of George Santayana, the most eclectic professional philosopher of our time. Curiously enough, this resemblance was not noted by Nowell Smith in his *Notes on The Testament of Beauty*, the one extended commentary on the ideas and sources of the poem.[2] The probable influence of Santayana

on Bridges was first suggested to me by Robert Hillyer; my
opinion that Santayana was in fact the greatest single influence on
Bridges' poem was formed before I learned of the close friendship
of the two men.[3] Subsequently I read articles by Conrad Aiken [4]
and Harold A. Larrabee [5] expressing the same opinion.

Here particularly, however, one must be careful to distinguish
between resemblance and influence. The main outlines of Bridges'
thought — his idealism based on an evolutionary naturalism and
his aesthetic theory of life — were apparently arrived at independently; Santayana's volumes merely filled in those outlines
and gave them form. We have, fortunately, illuminating comments on the problem of influence and resemblance by the two
men concerned. In his review of Santayana's *Little Essays*, a book
of selections from his earlier volumes, Bridges describes the
American thinker's philosophy as one "which sets out to establish a high spiritual ideal of life on the basis of the emotions" [6]
and which takes "its most persuasive support from the idea of
beauty." [7] He adds this important comment:

The philosophy, as I understand it, is very consonant with my own
thought: there is no pretence of hiding the unsolved riddle of life.
The Sphinx lurks in all systems; different schools only hustle her from
pillar to post, and if she is to be driven into any corner where her
presence is obvious, her best refuge is the unsearchable atom. And this
is an honester method than that of dismembering her and seeking to
hide her mutilated fragments by dispersal, as a piano-tuner will dis-
tribute the error of his wolf all up and down the scale: for whatever
immaterial agency there may be, or even should we come to be convinced that all ultimate agency was immaterial, our minds would be
unable to conceive of its mode of action except in material terms.[8]

This review was first printed in 1920. Howgate, however, gives
us Santayana's opinion as expressed after the publication of *The
Testament of Beauty*:

Turning to the influence of Santayana upon Robert Bridges, we
see a relationship not of teacher and pupil but of contemporaries and

friends. Bridges was one of Santayana's most intimate friends in England, and long conversations upon life and philosophy served to bring out the discoveries and insights they held in common. . . .[9] It is Santayana's opinion, as expressed to the present writer, that most of Bridges' ideas were formed before he met Santayana, and his acquaintance with the latter merely served to corroborate and strengthen them. But Santayana's usual modesty in matters of this kind must be remembered.[10]

When these reservations have been made, much evidence for considerable real influence still remains. It is even possible that the writing of *The Testament of Beauty* was suggested to Bridges by his reading of Santayana's books. He discusses with interest Santayana's belief, expressed in *Three Philosophical Poets*,

that it is the function of poetry to emotionalize philosophy; and that the great poem must be the aesthetical exposition of a complete theory of human life, so far as that is understood; and that there is therefore at present a finer opportunity for a great poet than the world has hitherto offered.[11]

A full account of the philosophical conceptions shared by Bridges and Santayana would involve a laborious recapitulation of the two preceding chapters. Santayana's *The Life of Reason* may be described as an attempt to vindicate nature by showing that man's ideals have a purely natural foundation, and that everything in nature should have an ideal fulfillment. The life of reason is "a name for that part of experience which perceives and pursues ideals — all conduct so controlled and all sense so interpreted as to perfect natural happiness,"[12] or, as Bridges says,

> . . . thatt habit of faith which some thinkers hav styled
> *The Life of Reason.* . . . (iv, 1087–8)

Happiness is determined by the harmony of impulses which reason alone can establish; without the agency of reason, the friction of natural forces could not be placed at the service of ideal aspirations. These ideal aspirations, which find their firmest support in physical beauty, furnish the basis for a religion divorced from theological superstitions and fears: "Beauty is a pledge of the possible conformity between the soul and nature, and consequently a ground of faith in the supremacy of the good."[13] The five volumes of *The Life of Reason* are, as Edman says,

studies of the characteristic experiments by which are achieved those excellences and that harmony which constitute happiness. . . . They trace, too, the deviations and blindnesses, the pathetic, well-intentioned truancies from rational practice, which have led men astray. . . . The five books are reflections, in various contexts, of a single conception, the passage, often circuitous and oftener frustrated, from nature to the ideals which it suggests, and which, if efficaciously understood, it may come to incarnate.[14]

Although this description of Santayana's philosophy might be used unchanged to describe Bridges', evidence of influence lies rather in the arguments and illustrations used by the poet to support his theories. The first book of *The Testament of Beauty*, with its historical summary of the divagations of human reason and with its assertion of man's dependence on nature, seems modelled on *Reason in Common Sense*, while the third book, with its analysis of love, follows closely the first chapter of *Reason in Society*. Many passages on such problems as the relationship of existence to perception, the dualism of reason and the continuity of mind and nature, and the ideality of nature seem direct adaptations of passages in Santayana, but far less disputable evidences of influence are the lines which are almost paraphrased — the lines on the purgative value of skepticism, on Don Quixote, on the astronomer who tried to find heaven with a telescope, and on the categorical imperative, to mention only a few. Such instances of direct indebtedness are duly recorded in the notes to the preceding chapter.

The closest parallels to Bridges' thought in English poetry are found in George Meredith. Except for its belief that matter can become mind, Meredith's evolutionary naturalism and his ultimate idealism are identical with the main conceptions of Bridges and Santayana. The theme of "The Woods of Westermain" is the evolution of animal instinct to mind and spirit. Like Bridges, and unlike Tennyson, Meredith regarded man's heritage of animal instinct as valuable — provided it is put to proper use:.

> Wait, and we shall forge him curbs,
> Put his fangs to uses, tame.

"Brain" develops from "blood" and "spirit" from "brain." "Joy" meant for Meredith as for Bridges and Santayana a harmony of instinct, reason and spirit, in which all three find their proper fulfillment:

> Each of each in sequent birth
> Blood and brain and spirit, three
> (Say the deepest gnomes of Earth),
> Join for true felicity.
> Are they parted, then expect
> Some one sailing will be wrecked.
> Separate hunting are they sped,
> Scan the morsel coveted.
> Earth that triad is: she hides
> Joy from him who that divides;
> Showers it when the three are one
> Glassing her in union.

Were it not, however, for Meredith's use of *conscience* and *conscient* in the sense that Bridges uses them,[15] and for a brief passage in "Earth and Man" which the later poet adapted closely,[16] there would be no reason to believe that Meredith had influenced Bridges at all. Nearly all of Meredith's important ideas are to be found in Santayana.

I have already remarked that Bridges' "Ring of Being" seems to derive from Spinoza.[17] In commenting on Santayana's Platonism, Bridges once again seems to be describing himself:

it requires some attention to dispel the impression that we are dealing with a platonist . . . but whatever inspiration the author may owe to

Plato for his particular doctrine of Ideas, he recognizes Spinoza and Democritus for his immediate masters, and his philosophy might perhaps be described as a building up of idealism — that is, the supremacy of the imagination — on a naturalistic or materialistic basis.[18]

In Spinoza's system, man, as a result of his instinct of Selfhood, of his *conatus sese preservandi*, aspires to a knowledge of God through the medium of perfect self-knowledge. Reality, which is eternal, is obscured from man by the perversions of his fallible imagination: "Falsity consists in privation of knowledge which is involved by inadequate or mutilated and confused ideas."[19] God exists in two ways: finitely in individuals, and infinitely in himself. Therefore all distinctions between body and mind, matter and thought, are really secondary, since all these are alike parts of God. Since consciousness belongs to one attribute of God, *mind*, reason is necessary to attainment of vision of the eternal, or to attainment of that perfect self-knowledge which is equivalent to the love of God: "He who understands himself and his emotions loves God, and the more so the more he understands himself and his emotions."[20] Eventually, as the Platonic lover can forget the earthly Aphrodite, the human mind can discard whatever is finite: "The mind can bring it to pass that all the modifications of the body or images of things have reference to the idea of God."[21] This is the *amor intellectus Dei*: complete self-realization through complete loss of self in God.

Bridges' conception of Universal Mind may have its ultimate parentage in Vergil's famous lines in the sixth book of the Aeneid,[22] but its particular application seems to derive from the fifth part of Spinoza's *Ethics*, "Concerning the Power of the Intellect or of Human Freedom." In Bridges' poem, the mind achieves an ideal and impersonal immortality by acquiring sufficient adequate ideas; it perishes with the body unless

> the personal co-ordination of its ideas
> hav won to Being higher than animal life. (iv, 1263–4)

Or, as Spinoza writes, "The human mind in so far as it knows itself and its body under the species of eternity, thus far it necessarily has knowledge of God, and knows that it exists in God and is conceived through God."[23] The concluding lines of *The Testament of Beauty*, and the general conception that God loves himself through the loves of men, seem to be closely adapted from one of Spinoza's last propositions:

The mental intellectual love towards God is the very love of God with which God loves himself, not in so far as he is infinite, but in so far as he can be expressed through the essence of the human mind considered under the aspect of eternity, that is, mental intellectual love towards God is part of the infinite love with which God loves himself.[24]

As a geometric conception, Bridges' "Ring of Being" is identical with Spinoza's. With this in mind it is necessary to make certain very important reservations. Bridges described God "as activ lover of all" and argued the possibility of friendship between man and God, whereas Spinoza wrote that he "who loves God cannot endeavour to bring it about that God should love him in return."[25] Above all, the love which Bridges proposes is not a "mental intellectual love," but the love of traditional Christianity, with its ultimate rational surrender:

> . . . *Unless ye shall receive it as a child,*
> *Ye cannot enter into the kingdom of heaven.*   (iv, 1324–5)

Yet the essential tenets of the two religions are not irreconcilable. The ideal in both religions is individual self-perfection, and the lesson of *The Testament of Beauty* is nowhere better summarized than in Spinoza's final proposition: "Blessedness is not the reward of virtue, but virtue itself. . . ."[26]

Bridges naturally objected to Aristotle's as well as Spinoza's thinking God:

> . . . *the arch-thinker's heav'n cannot move my desire,*
> *nor doth his pensiv Deity make call on my love,*   (ii, 916–7)

and he is often guilty of a Wordsworthian anti-intellectualism far removed from Aristotle's rationalism. Bridges fluctuates continually in his consideration of reason, however, and it is precisely his dependence on Aristotle's *Ethics* in the fourth book of his poem which saves him from a romantic submission to natural law. The whole discussion of disposition and habit can hardly be appreciated without reference to the *Ethics*, which it frequently quotes. The most important of Aristotle's principles is emphasized by Bridges. This is the prime necessity of self-discipline; of controlling the animal instincts by the effort of the individual, rather than by social legislation.

Although Bridges' religion depends on a cosmology similar to Spinoza's, its spirit seems closer to the aspiring love of Plato than to the *amor intellectus Dei* of the later philosopher. Bridges' alteration of Plato's image of the soul of man illustrates, however, his very basic disagreement with the Greek philosopher; his rejection of any rigid dualism makes for a closer harmony with the Platonic tradition in English poetry than with the doctrines of Plato himself:

> In Nature and the language of the sense
> The anchor of my purest thoughts, the nurse,
> The guide, the guardian of my heart, and soul
> Of all my moral being.

Even the reader most distrustful of parallel passages cannot ignore the number of lines in Bridges' poem, recorded in the notes to the preceding chapter, which are similar in idea or phrasing to lines in *The Prelude*. These numerous similarities of thought and expression do not prove that Wordsworth influenced Bridges strongly so much as they show that the two poets belonged to a common poetic tradition. Bridges echoes or recalls Wordsworth most clearly in the passages on the spiritual supremacy of the child, on the manner in which God's love comes to the child through the mother's embrace, and on the pretensions and barrenness of formal reasoning.

A review of minor influences — the influences of Samuel Butler and Bergson, for instance — would lead us into endless and
unfruitful repetition. Bridges has, indeed, laid himself open to
far graver charges than those of eclecticism and lack of originality.
The most serious of these is undoubtedly the inconsistent use and
inadequate definition of basic terms. This weakness is fatally evident in the dark fluctuations of the term *essence*. Without a full
understanding of this term, Bridges' psychology and religion must
remain unexplained and incomplete. Yet a full understanding is
impossible. Even after the reader has mastered Santayana's elusive
essences, he will be bewildered to find these essences become, in
Bridges' poem, equivalent to the Platonic Ideas, to Kant's general
truths independent of sense experience, or to any forms of absolute Being. Describing the common flowers, Bridges says each
type is a "faultless essence of God's will. . . ." Sometimes he refers to his essences as Influences, sometimes as Ideas. The same
confusion surrounds the terms *nature* and *reason*. *Nature* is not
only used on occasion to represent the "ultimate Reality," but also
to mean "Reason," physical or external nature, the laws of nature,
instinct, and human nature. *Reason* may mean logical or geometric reasoning, the quality of reasonableness, consciousness or
awareness, and even the entire inner life of man.

To the present writer the poem seems to contain four serious
philosophical weaknesses: an occasional intrusion of Rousseauistic
primitivism, an attack on socialism which is often poorly reasoned
or inconsistent, a certain hesitancy in the condemnation of love
of war, and most of all, an incomplete and vacillating treatment
of the subject of religion. The first three of these weaknesses resulted from dangers likely to befall any philosopher who attempts
to formulate a thorough naturalism without sacrificing the benefits of a dualistic interpretation of life. The failure of past thinkers, such as Shelley and Wordsworth, to surmount these dangers,
seems to increase rather than lessen the many temptations.

Rousseauistic primitivism appears in the anti-intellectualism of the passages on reason and on science, and in the sections dealing, in a very Wordsworthian manner, with the alleged spiritual superiority of the innocent child. It was apparently impossible for Bridges to retain any conviction as to the authority of reason for more than fifty lines. In each of the four books he repeatedly discusses the dualism of reason: that it may not only guide our spiritual progress through its refinement of instinct, but also

> . . . delicatly and dangerously bedizen
> the rioting joys that fringe the sad pathways of Hell.
>
> (i, 60–1)

Bridges' repudiation of reason in art in the third book might have come from the pen of Shelley. The attack on formal intellectual training (iv, 688–721) seems to me equally dangerous, and while a warning against the pretensions of scientists, coming with particular force from a poet who was himself a scientist, has value as a corrective, it should be remembered that all one-sided attacks on the excesses of any discipline, such as the attacks of Molière on pedantry and medical quacks, tend not only to correct those excesses, but also to throw discredit upon the discipline itself. The most serious charge that may be brought against Bridges in his discussion of reason is that, instead of maintaining a temperate attitude which would at every point be aware of the virtues as well as the shortcomings of reason, he passed repeatedly from one extreme to the other, first accepting the authority of reason without question, then rejecting it without question. His repeated use of the sophistical argument — that only reason can judge of reason — is evidence of a further weakness.

Bridges' passages on the spiritual superiority of the child, if read with due attention to others on man's natural heritage of primitive savage instinct — that is, of original sin in the non-theological sense — will not seem particularly dangerous. But the fact remains that the tone and diction of these passages are borrowed from the romantic tradition of child-poetry of Vaughan,

Rousseau and Wordsworth. To a careless or hasty reader of his poem, Bridges will seem a member in good standing of this romantic school.

The inconsistency of Bridges' attack on socialism has already been indicated in the preceding chapter. In some ways his "fable of the bees" is as vicious as Mandeville's. He argues that "social virtue" should be discarded because it has seldom succeeded, and proves its failure by describing the poor living conditions of English industrial workers, conditions which he feels should be remedied by an application of the "social virtue" he has just condemned. His argument that material goods would disappear by subdivision is a familiar discovery of the adolescent mind. Finally, the same argument that he uses in refusing utterly to condemn love of war — that socialism frustrates man's instinctive impulses — is contradicted throughout the poem by passages insisting that certain instinctive impulses need to be restricted.

Bridges' religion has already been described at some length.[27] This religion depends to a great extent on the inexplicable theory of essences. Are these essences and influences natural forces generating in the "unconscious," or are they indeed implanted there by súpernatural agency? Is the Universal Mind from which they are said to emanate the whole of nature, or an Unknowable who is literally "activ Lover" of all? Was the friendship between God and man which Bridges deemed possible mere harmony between an animal and its environment, or the personal relationship of historical Christianity? These were questions which the poet, in the final analysis, refused to answer:

> For not the Muse herself can tell of Goddes love. . . .

It is at least certain that Bridges was less orthodox than his use of Christian figures would indicate. The unwary reader who studies the passages on nature and natural law without regard to their context will be surprised to find an apparent belief in purpose and design. But what we have in fact are the benefits of a teleological interpretation of nature without its scientific falsity. Whether or not the laws of nature — evolution, "necessity," and the like — were designed for our good, we can find in them the potential material for good; we can choose from them what we please. Insofar as they have made possible the appearance of that reason which can turn natural forces into ideal goods, the laws of nature have catered to the welfare and happiness of man.

Except for these occasional lapses, *The Testament of Beauty* represents a courageous and on the whole successful attempt to establish the truth of naturalism without sacrificing the inherited benefits of a dualistic ethics and without surrendering to the inexorable force of natural law. The failure to see that this sacrifice and this surrender were not inevitable undermined romantic ethical theory as well as much nineteenth and twentieth century political and economic doctrine. Even a mind so conscious of the power of the imagination as that of Henry Adams was persuaded that no force, no inheritance from the past, could combat the dynamo or the restless organism. Faced by such assertions that mind, having been deposed from her mythical and isolated throne, had lost her prerogatives of choice and will, many thinkers retreated into congenial superstitions or posited a dualism so rigid that it crippled as well as civilized the emotions of man. It is to his credit that Bridges adopted neither of these alternatives; that he accepted the "unconscious" without returning to dogmatic Christianity in search of the fugitive soul, and that he defended the autonomy of reason without, like the Neo-Humanists, pursuing rational control as an end in itself. In its recognition that the emotions, canalized by reason into fruitful action, are the main source of human happiness, Bridges' philosophy is more complete than that of Irving Babbitt; it is more complete than that of Spinoza as well.

It must be recalled once more, however, that this philosophy was by no means original with Bridges. To an Aristotelian conception of the life of reason it added a Spinozist cosmology which could be easily reconciled with the evolutionary theory of Darwin and a religion of beauty and love which could preserve the best ideals of historical Christianity. This particular amalgam had already appeared in Santayana's *The Life of Reason*. Whatever importance *The Testament of Beauty* may have in the history of ideas must rest not in its philosophy, but in the concreteness and vividness which it has given that philosophy; not in its many theories, but in the commentaries on human experience which those theories have provoked. The most lasting contributions are seldom distinguished by their originality of thought. In refuting the assertion that poetry and philosophy are incompatible, Santayana examines Lucretius, the exponent of materialism in science and humanism in ethics; Dante, the exponent of supernaturalism; Goethe, the exponent of romanticism — not one a truly original philosopher. "Can it be an accident," he asks, "that the most adequate and probably the most lasting exposition of these three schools of philosophy should have been made by poets?"[28]

The Testament of Beauty is on the whole least interesting where it deserts its broad philosophical conception, the naturalistic basis of idealism, to explore the obscurities of metaphysics and epistemology. It is most interesting where it records the poet's own impressions of human nature, the reactions of a highly-cultured mind to the permanent problems of human conduct. It is an autobiography, as well as the biography of the human intellect, yet the reader never feels that impatience with minute introspection which increases with each successive reading of *The Prelude*. Bridges tells us of himself through his lucid commentaries on historical movements and personalities, and through his opinions on art, science, education and war; on asceticism and hedonism and on love and marriage. To the reader of 1941, *The Testament of Beauty* seems to ignore only one central and eternal problem, the problem of government. It would be interesting to know what opinions Bridges would have today on this problem which as late as 1929 it still seemed possible to ignore.

Yet if it is true that the present political forces at work in the world are the fulfillment of nineteenth century organic theory, Bridges' survey of Western civilization may have more value as an historical document without a consideration of those new forces. Such a summary of the Graeco-Christian cultural tradition is of particular interest at the present time. *The Testament of Beauty*, by the ambitiousness of its subject as by its philosophical bias and discursive technique, announces itself as one of a long line of philosophical or semi-philosophical poems which this tradition has produced, a line which includes, in English literature, *The Faerie Queene*, *Paradise Lost*, and *The Prelude*. *The Testament of Beauty* is by no means the greatest poem in this long line, but it may be, as some conjecture, the last.

Whatever its value as a philosophical poem, *The Testament of Beauty* remains a personal triumph of style. Against the background of Bridges' earlier poetry, against the delicate flawlessness of the lyrics and the formal austerity of the plays, his final work stands in startling contrast. Its exuberance and formlessness, its playful digressions and uninhibited imaginative flights, find few counterparts in the *Shorter Poems* and plays. The sympathetic reader of Bridges must regard this belated freedom with mixed feelings. If it permitted an almost unparalleled vivification of wide learning, as in the great historical summaries of the first book or the later comments on art and poetry, it also admitted lines as pedestrian as any in English poetry:

> . . . the observed fertilization of plants,
> atomic mechanism with unlimited power
> to vary the offspring in character, by mutual
> inexhaustible interchange of transmitted genes. . . . (iii, 171-4)

The formlessness and disregard for the niceties of paragraph structure which invited spontaneous digressions rivalling the best of Milton's obscure many of the important philosophical passages.

That the general formlessness may have been as carefully calculated as that of *Tristram Shandy* in no way justifies it. A more careful structure and syntax, together with a more vertebrate meter, such as blank verse, would have helped the average reader considerably. One can only conjecture how much youthful gusto and imaginative fertility would have been lost by such a stronger discipline.

It is in any case certain that Bridges found in his purely syllabic meter the same fluid ease, the same amenability to periodic sentences, that Milton and Wordsworth had found in blank verse. The virtues and defects of this syllabic meter are obvious. The freedom of a line which required no specific number of accents or feet permitted Bridges to use an unusually large number of polysyllabic words which refuse more than a single accent. On the other hand, the absence of a fixed scheme of feet and accents deprived him of the opportunity to introduce the various subtle metrical substitutions which a poet working in blank verse, for instance, may use. The principle of perpetual variety in meter usually leads to monotony, and there are occasions on which the meter of *The Testament of Beauty* becomes very monotonous.

Yet the meter of the poem is normally successful. By various devices, Bridges succeeds in attaining the effects of normal metrical substitution, and he successfully avoids the chief temptation which a free twelve syllable line offers — the temptation to write it in four anapestic feet. In important passages Bridges accelerates the rhythm by the use of three of four colliding speech stresses, or by reverting temporarily to a strictly iambic, accentual-syllabic norm. He likewise calls attention to particular lines by the skillful use of rhyme, alliteration and assonance. The great majority of the lines are unrhymed, but both terminal and internal rhymes are sometimes used:

> to awake and *fill* and *thrill* their myriad-warbling throats. . . .(i, 70)

> and ever as to earth he *neareth*, and vision *cleareth*
> of all that he *feareth*, and the enemy *appeareth*. . . .(ii, 513–4)

Alliteration is used far more frequently than rhyme, and is one of the chief means used to strengthen the intrinsically invertebrate meter:

> Again where *r*eapers, bending to the *r*ipen'd corn,
> *w*ere *w*ont to *s*cythe in rank and *s*tep with measured *s*troke,
> a shark-tooth'd chariot rampeth *b*iting a *b*road way,
> and jerking its high swindging arms around in the air,
> *s*woopeth the *s*wath. Yet this queer Pterodactyl is well,
> that in the sinister torpor of the blazing day
> clicketeth in heartless mockery of *s*woon and *s*weat,
> as 'twer the salamandrine voice of all parch'd things:
> and the dry grasshopper wondering knoweth his God.
>
> (iii, 365–73)

Many readers will be disturbed in reading Bridges' poem, as they are disturbed in reading Milton, by the incantations of the rhythm, by the flow of a music whose rich orchestration lulls rather than excites the mind. Whatever the virtues and defects of the Vergilian style — that is to say, of a style whose polysyllabic diction and fluid meter tend to create a rhythm which overrides the barrier of line end and natural sense pause — its appearance in *The Testament of Beauty* is coincident with that of some of the greatest imaginative successes:

> . . . or old Methusalah
> who when the flood rose higher swam from peak to peak
> til, with the last wild beasts tamed in their fear, he sat
> watching the whelm of water on topmost Everest,
> as thatt too was submerged; while in his crowded ark
> Noah rode safely by: and sailors caught by storm
> on the wide Indian Ocean at shift of the monsoon,
> hav seen in the dark night a giant swimmer's head
> that on the sequent billows trailing silvery hair
> at every lightning flash reappeareth in place,
> out-riding the tempest, as a weather-bound barque
> anchor'd in open roadstead lifteth at the seas. (ii, 628–39)

The Miltonic qualities of Bridges' style will be appreciated by anyone who compares the preceding passage with the lines in *Paradise Lost* which probably suggested it:

> . . . or that sea-beast
> Leviathan, which God of all his works
> Created hugest that swim the ocean-stream.
> Him, haply slumbering on the Norway foam,
> The pilot of some small night-foundered skiff,
> Deeming some island, oft, as seamen tell,
> With fixèd anchor in his scaly rind,
> Moors by his side under the lee, while night
> Invests the sea, and wishèd morn delays.[29]

The tone of *The Testament of Beauty* owes as much to its diction and to its use of literary overtones as to its rhythms. Only five words — *grandesque, wonderfine, revelly, joybunches* and *emotionable* — do not appear in the Oxford English Dictionary, but there are many scientific terms and a fairly large number of obsolete words. Some of these — *pleasaunce, malease, illachrymable, random* (noun: rush of sound), *eterne* and *mappemond,* for instance — are justified by their associations and beauty of sound, but there are others, such as *misdoubting, approachment* and *abredged,* which are used for no particular reason.

Bridges' mastery of poetic language is evident not so much in his use of rare or archaic words, as in his ability to exploit all the historical and literary associations of a given word. Nowell Smith's *Notes on The Testament of Beauty,* while treating in a very inadequate manner the philosophical sources which Bridges used, makes an extensive catalogue of his literary allusions. Such allusions extend from actual quotations (quoted lines are italicized in the text of the poem) to distant allusions carrying only a slight aura of suggestion. Often, as in the following passage, Bridges uses various types of overtone within a few lines:

> . . . that lost garden regain'd,
> lost once thru' pride and now by long stooping regain'd, —
> a pictur and outward symbol of the comfort of them
> whose spirit dwell in the Eden that the Muse hath made,
> her garden of soul in the *golden lapses of Time*;
> and if, tracing to its source some Heliconian rill,
> its mossgrown cave is found in the black splinter'd rock,
> where thatt once cool'd and stay'd, a volcanic moraine
> to bank his blossom'd Paradise and feed his vines,
> ther-after to the poet all his joy will seem
> *a strange mysterious dream*, a thread of beauty eterne
> enwoven in mortal change, and he himself a flower
> fertilized awhile on the quench'd torrent of Hell. (iii, 521–33)

The allusion of the first two lines to *Paradise Lost* and *Paradise Regained* is obvious. "Lost once thru' pride" is a distant echo of Pope's lines beginning "In pride, in reasoning pride, our error lies" (*Essay on Man*, I, 123–8); the first italicized words recall the first line of Keats' sonnet, "How many bards gild the lapses of time," while the second italicized passage is a direct quotation from Milton (*Il Penseroso*, 147).

Nowell Smith identifies instances of quotation or paraphrase from Aristotle, Plato, Lucretius, Vergil, Thucydides, Ptolemy, Sophocles, the Bible, Vollandist *Acta Sanctorum*, St. Francis, St. Thomas, St. Augustine, Charles d'Orléans, Pascal, Descartes, Michelangelo, Goethe, Chaucer, Marlowe, Spenser, Shakespeare, Milton, Keats, Wordsworth and Tennyson. Perhaps the greatest single storehouse for verbal reminiscences used by Bridges is the King James Version; occasionally, as in the concluding lines of the first book, he introduces diction borrowed from the Bible in nearly every line.

The stylistic success of *The Testament of Beauty* resides, finally, in a certain joyful energy and imaginative fertility which is even more difficult to explain than its rhythm or diction. On every page the reader will find instances of poetic surprise, ranging from the humor of the epicure who "retireth with stomach Emeritus" to the most delicate and original of imagery:

> . . . when grave Night peacefully
> clearing her heavenly rondure of its turbid veils
> layeth bare the playthings of Creation's babyhood;
> and the immortal fireballs of her uttermost space
> twinkle like friendly rushlights on the countryside.   (i, 292–6)

The success of the intercalated nature lyrics, however, would not surprise the reader of Bridges' earlier poetry. The description which follows recalls by its tone, as well as by its acknowledged borrowing, Keats' "Ode to Autumn":

> Nay, whether it be in the gay apple-orchards of May,
> when the pink bunches spread their gold hearts to the sun,
> nor yet rude winds hav snow'd their petals to the ground;
> or when a dizzy bourdon haunteth the sweet cymes
> that droop at Lammas-tide the queenly foliage
> of a tall linden tree, where yearly by the wall
> of some long-ruin'd Abbey she remembereth her
> of glad thanksgivings and the gay choral Sabbaths,
> while in her leafy tower the languorous murmur
> floateth off heav'nward in a mellow dome of shade; —
> or when, tho' *summer hath o'erbrim'd their clammy cells*
> the shorten'd days are shadow'd with dark fears of dearth,
> bees ply the more, issuing on sultry noons to throng
> in the ivy-blooms — what time October's flaming hues
> surcharge the brooding hours, till passionat soul and sense
> blend in a rich reverie with the dying year. . . .   (ii, 345–60)

On a quite different key is the great description of the findings of Dr. Wooley and his colleagues in Mesopotamia,[30] which occurs in the fourth book. There are few passages in English poetry to rival this one for sustained and tragic eloquence:

> . . . and low hummocks of dust
> betray where legendary cities lie entomb'd,

Chaldaean KISH and UR; while for all life today
poor nomads, with their sparse flotilla of swarthy tents
and slow sand-faring camels, cruise listlessly o'erhead,
warreners of the waste: Now this man duly unearth'd
the walls whence Terah flitted, but beneath those walls
more walls, and the elder buildings of a dynasty
of wider rule than Abram knew, a nation extinct
ere he was born: where-thru' sinking deeper their shafts
the diggers came yet never on virgin soil, but still
wondering on earlier walls, arches and masonry,
a city and folk undremt of in archeology,
trodden-under ere any story of man began; and there,
happening on the king's tomb, they shovel'd from the dust
the relics of thatt old monarch's magnificence —
Drinking vessels of beaten silver or of clean gold,
vases of alabaster, obsidian chalices,
cylinder seals of empire and delicat gems
of personal adornment, ear-rings and finger-rings,
craftsmen's tools copper and golden, and for music a harp;
withal in silver miniatur his six-oar'd skiff,
a model in build and trim of such as ply today
Euphrates' flowery marshes: all his earthly toys
gather'd to him in his grave, that he might nothing lack
in the unknown life beyond, but find ready to hand
his jewel'd dice and gaming board and chamber-lamp,
his toilet-box of paints and unguents — Therefore 'twas
the chariot of his pride whereon he still would ride
was buried with him; there lay yet the enamel'd film
of the inlaid perish'd wood, and all the metal gauds
that had emboss'd the rail: animal masks in gold,
wild bulls and lions, and twin-figured on the prow
great panther-heads to glare in silver o'er the course,
impatient of their spring: and one rare master-work
whose grace the old warrior wist not should outliv the name
and fame of all his mighty doings, when he set it up
thatt little nativ donkey, his mascot on the pole.
    'Twas he who dug told me of these things and how,

finding himself a housebreaker in the home of men
who sixty hundred years afore, when they left life,
had seal'd their tombs from sacrilege and there had lain,
till from the secresy of their everlasting sleep
he had torn the coverlet — his spirit, dazed awhile
in wonder, suddenly was strick'n with great horror;
for either side the pole, where lay the harness'd bones
of the yoke-mated oxen, there beside their bones
lay the bones of the grooms, and slaughter'd at their post
all the king's body-guard, each liegeman spear in hand,
in sepulchred attention; and whereby lay the harp
the arm-bones of the player, as there she had pluck'd her dirge,
lay mingled with its fragments; and nearby disposed,
two rows of skeletons, her sisterly audience
whose lavish ear-pendants and gold-filleted hair,
the uniform decoration of their young service,
mark'd them for women of the harem, sacrificed
to accompany their lord, the day when he set forth
to enter into the presence of the scepter'd shades
congregated with splendour in the mansions of death. (iv, 279–337)

CONCLUSION

The Nature of the Traditional Poet

CONCLUSION

The Nature of the Traditional Poet

HE TRIPARTITE DIVISION into which this book has necessarily fallen may have several unfortunate consequences. The reader unwilling to allow dates to stand between him and a direct appreciation of the poet's work may have been given the impression that the division of the book was strictly chronological, and that Bridges gave up writing lyrics before turning to the plays, and that immediately upon finishing the plays he began work on *The Testament of Beauty*. Again, he may have been given the equally false impression that Bridges wrote the three types of poetry — lyric, dramatic and philosophical — from the beginning to the end of his long career. We have, as a matter of fact, to deal with the rather unusual circumstance of two fairly distinct careers, separated by a period of relative silence which lasted almost a quarter of a century. Although the first *Poems* appeared in 1873 and *New Verse* in 1925, the majority as well as the best of Bridges' lyrics were written between 1875 and 1900, while eight of his ten plays were written between 1882 and 1888. *The Testament of Beauty* was published in 1929. After 1900, and before he began his philosophical poem, Bridges engaged in various activities which contribute little to his final stature as a poet: experiments in classical prosody, studies of Milton's prosody, the preparation of essays and anthologies, investigations for the Society for Pure English which he had founded.

The reader who has just finished the fairly extensive study of

The Testament of Beauty may have forgotten the first of these two careers; he may have forgotten the importance of the *Shorter Poems* and the usually unsuspected importance of the plays. The lyric and dramatic poetry have indeed much more in common than either has with *The Testament of Beauty*; the former seem the product of a classical youth, uncompromisingly flawless, austere and restrained; the latter seems the work of a romantic age, energetic and uninhibited, impatient with the trammels of form. To many who felt that the lucid simplicity of the *Shorter Poems* provided a much needed corrective for the radical innovations of the age, the chaotic formlessness and real difficulty of Bridges' philosophical poem must have come with something of the shock of unexpected betrayal. The betrayal — the sacrifice of an ideal of artistic perfection to the diversity which freedom allows — was in a sense a real one, yet even the most conservative critic should recognize that *The Testament of Beauty* displays two characteristics which distinguished the early lyrics and plays: a cautious yet experimental traditionalism, and a concern with universal human problems. It is here, in their rich traditionalism and their wide moral pertinence, that the two careers become one.

Sainte-Beuve defined a "true classic" as one who, among others things, "has spoken to all in his own peculiar style . . . a style new without neologism, new and old, easily contemporary with all time." [1] Most critics today would find little to commend in such a classic. Many ages have looked to the methods and accomplishments of a century or so before and proudly announced, "Nous avons changé tout cela," but it is doubtful if any age has really changed so much, broken so radically with the traditional subjects and poetic techniques of the past, as our own. Surely the most dramatic triumphs of a hundred or a hundred and fifty years ago — Hugo's escape from the couplet's rigid rules or Wordsworth's rejection of the honored Augustan legacies — are tame indeed compared with the accomplishments of the last fifty years, compared even with the attenuated strain of French Symbolism which dominates English poetry today. Even though such movements as Dada have each had but a few years of grace, and even though such a poet as Ezra Pound has found no successful imitator, the fact remains that we are farther away from the old themes and the old music, from Milton and Wordsworth and Tennyson, than were ever the "Free Verse" leaders of the last generation:

> Nightingales, Anangke, a sunset or the meanest flower
> Were formerly the potentialities of poetry,
> But now what have they to do with one another
> With Dionysius or with me?

Of the many legacies from French Symbolism and kindred movements, three at least have almost universal currency today. Poetry must have new forms and new rhythms to express a new age. As Eliot has written, "Perhaps the conditions of modern life (think how large a part is now played in our sensory life by the internal combustion engine!) have altered our perception of rhythms." [2] Again, poetry, which no longer appeals to the understanding but only to the sensibility, must deal with the isolated moment and the fragmentary experience, and not with those fictions of the past — the whole emotion, the formed pattern of beauty, the rounded character. Finally, poetry must do penitence for the glibness and lyricism of the romantics: it must shun the conventional, traditional effect; the abstract lucid statement; the euphonious phrase. It must be tortuous, allusive, oblique, indirect: it must waver and circle with the waverings and circlings of the poet's mind. It must make no intellectual and therefore false impositions of order and form.

Odell Shepard has written that during "a period in which the most representative poet has been Walt Whitman, the apostle of shuffle and sprawl and warm wet wallowing, the Laureate has maintained according to his abilities the standards of the poet who was born in Mantua just two thousand years ago." [3] It would per-

haps be more accurate to say that he had maintained these standards during a period in which the most representative poet has
been Jules Laforgue, the apostle of romantic irony in feeling and
eccentricity in style. But against either background — the primitivism which runs from Whitman to William Carlos Williams,
or the self-concious, penitent and ironic art of the Symbolists and
T. S. Eliot — Bridges has remained, in company with the later
Yeats and Robert Frost and a few others, an isolated figure with
some of the naïve sweetness of Sainte-Beuve's "classic." By so
doing he has, it seems to me, showed us the strength or weakness
of the genuinely traditional poet in any age.

Two temptations await the consciously and speciously traditional poet. He may consider the tradition as something exotic,[4]
and regard the poetry of his predecessors merely as the source for
recondite allusions or startling echoes. Surely the Cantos of Ezra
Pound resemble nothing so much as a graduate student's Midsummer Night's Dream! On the other hand, he may be slavishly
obedient to the tradition, or more often to a particular master,
and merely copy the forms, meters and language of an earlier
day, without recognizing the perceptual value of those forms and
meters or the true meaning of that language. From the many
imitators of T. S. Eliot during the last decade two or three really
important poets have emerged — and a much larger number who
repeated only the familiar formulae: the broken rhythms and the
esoteric learning, the inhibited characters and the startling juxta-
positions of mood. Robert Bridges either escaped or conquered
both these temptations — self-conscious traditionalism and slavish imitation — with remarkable success.

The tradition was not something exotic, but rather a climate in
which it was natural for him to move. It is significant that Bridges
ignored chronological arrangement in both of his anthologies,
The Chilswell Book of English Poetry and The Spirit of Man. In
Milton's Prosody he writes of the earlier poet's experiments as
though he were writing of his own, analyzing the motives for

an innovation and weighing carefully the alternatives which offered themselves. As for allusions and echoes, they are merely part of a poet's language: "the immense stores of our historic vocabulary gain in recognition and significance by being a still living tradition in unbroken continuity of actual growth." [5] In a passage intended to convey an old-fashioned Protestantism, it is only natural to borrow Milton's "grim wolf with privy paw"; in a poem on nightingales, to have overtones from the longing of Milton, Keats and Arnold. But the echoes are never used to startle the reader by the incongruity of their appearance or by their evidence of wide learning. The few lyrics which are wholly based on earlier poems show in fact a catholic education (the originals run from an anonymous Sicilian *nona rime* stanza to a translation of Thomas Moore by Gautier), but is evident that the models were selected for their intrinsic worth and for their appropriateness to the feeling which Bridges wished to convey. The abundance of acknowledged echoes and borrowed lines in *The Testament of Beauty* very nearly rivals that of *The Waste Land*, yet they always appear to confirm rather than ironically discredit the poet's own original emotion. The nightingale

> that woke poetic eloquence
> alike in Sophocles and the sick heart of Keats

is introduced to show that the tradition of song is an unbroken one; not to make still more tawdry the plight of an Apeneck Sweeney.

The distinguishing characteristic of Bridges' traditionalism is its critical and selective quality. In his lyrics, Bridges studied Milton and Heine and Herbert as a painter or composer studies an earlier master, analyzing and mastering their technical experiments and valuable innovations; trying, above all, to understand the emotions and mental attitudes which their styles conveyed. It was necessary, perhaps, for him to understand the cynicism which Heine had failed to overcome or the skepticism which Arnold had failed to overcome before he could master these emotions in himself. Similarly, a study of Milton and Herbert may have aided him to achieve that reconciliation of divergent claims, of two contradictory goods, which the fully civilized man must achieve. Bridges' emotional and moral experience was enriched by every poet he studied; or, to be more exact, by every poet of whom he became a part. That some of his early sonnets should have represented *pastiche* rather than imitation was perhaps inevitable. But eventually the mannerisms and particular voice of Milton, for instance, were left behind, and there remained only a valuable and now wholly personal element of style. The reader who wishes to see the various stages through which Bridges' education, in a particular case, passed, has only to compare the unmistakably Miltonic blank verse of the opening of *Prometheus the Firegiver* with the pure and unmannered blank verse of *Achilles in Scyros*. The individuality as well as the richness of this later blank verse could have been achieved, however, only after the study of Milton, Shakespeare and other great masters in the form.

In the plays this critical and selective traditionalism is even more marked. None of the plays is wholly original; each is based on mythology, history, or an earlier story or play. Bridges' significant contribution, however, lies not so much in his transmutation of old material, as in his skillful exploitation, in a single play, of various dramatic traditions and forms. That is, he makes use of good dramatic conventions found in Elizabethan tragedy, for instance, while ignoring stage conventions of Elizabethan tragedy which no longer have any value; in the same play he makes similar use of dramatic conventions from Greek and Spanish Renaissance drama, again rejecting those which had a purely transitory significance. In the best of his plays — *The Christian Captives*, *Achilles in Scyros* and the two plays on *Nero* — he thus mediated between various dramatic traditions, and achieved a form combining valuable elements from each. Whether or not, his own experiments in this direction were successful, they point an interesting alternative road to the modern contemporary dramatist who feels that a dramatic convention, once it has become obsolete, can never be used again.

In *The Testament of Beauty*, this critical and selective traditionalism appears in the diversity of philosophical sources rather than in the structure of the verse. In contrast to modern professional philosophers, with their desperate cleaving to one or another particular and narrow school, Bridges formulated a philosophy which could embrace the ethical dualism of Aristotle and the naturalism of Spinoza, Darwin's theory of evolution and the best ideals of historical Christianity, a Neo-Humanist insistence on self control and a Bergsonian contempt for purely conventional morality. The poem is not, however, the product of an unthinking eclecticism. Its only serious obscurities result from a theory of essences which is never clearly defined.

Like every genuinely traditional poet, Bridges was a conscious experimentalist. The cautious nature of his metrical experimentation has a particular force today, when poetry has not yet recovered from the excesses of free verse. He recognized that the possibilities for variation in certain meters had been exhausted, and that new rhythms would have to be found. But he also knew that a subtle extension of the rules of blank verse, for instance, would in the end be more rewarding than the abolition of all formal meters. The difference between radical experiment divorced from all past attainment and cautious experiment to enrich old rhythms is illustrated by a comparison of sprung-rhythm or sprung-meter as used by Gerard Manley Hopkins and Bridges. By introducing sprung feet into every line, Hopkins arrived at a fevered rhythm capable of conveying only intense excitement. Bridges, on the other hand, used sprung meter as an occasional resource for variation or counterpoint in standard accentual and accentual-syllabic poems. In his hands, it became a particularly valuable means of introducing momentary excitement, of calling sharp attention to a particular word or phrase. As a result of Bridges' experiments, many poets are today able to use sprung-meter occasionally with

rewarding effect. But a successful imitator of Hopkins has yet
to appear.

The first important characteristic which appears in all of Bridges'
poetry, its traditionalism, is not unrelated to the second, its wide
moral pertinence, its concern with universal human problems. At
a time when nearly all serious poets seem dedicated to the proposition that life cannot be understood, the conception of poetry as a
means of establishing order in the emotional life of man seems to
have fallen into fairly complete abeyance. To the reader of *The
Waste Land* and the latest psychological textbook, the generaliza-
tions of *The Testament of Beauty* and the rounded character studies
of Bridges' plays must seem as quaint and factitious as the subjects
of his lyrics — scenes of the English countryside, clearly defined
conflicts between reason and desire, ordinary grief and joy, simple
and unfrustrated love. Many poets, indeed, seem bent on out-
doing the psychologists in their systematic reduction of the soul
to a bundle of reflexes; of an hour's living to a congeries of unrelated sensations. The Shandean conception of human character is
of course much older than Jung, Adler and Freud — certainly as
old as the medieval interpreters of dreams — but it has penetrated
poetry only in recent years. Since much of human experience is
fragmentary, automatic and little understood, poets regard any
lucid record of an experience and any shaped and patterned emotion as fictions of the truant intellect. Perhaps the strongest prohibition of contemporary criticism of poetry is the one it has
posted against any appearance of the rational intellect, with its
ancient tendency to use simple exposition and abstract language.

The critic who regards with alarm this submergence of the intellect, this surrender of the poet to the raw material of his poetry,
runs the danger of blinding himself to the enormous value of
recent psychological discoveries and to the very real value of
recent poetic experiments. Had Irving Babbitt been successful
in forbidding the poet and novelist to explore the subconscious
and the abnormal, he would have rendered impossible some of the

chief masterpieces of our day. He should rather have complained of poets and novelists who were not philosophers as well as psychologists; who refused to understand (and therefore control) experience in the way that an ordinary civilized man understands and to a certain extent controls his experience.

The lucid, exact and complete evaluation of human experience in Bridges' lyrics is the ultimate reason for their greatness, as it is the ultimate reason for the greatness of Milton's and Shakespeare's. The best of the *Shorter Poems* define and give life to a series of attitudes toward some of the central difficulties of man: the struggles of faith and skepticism, of reason and instinct, of individual happiness and the laws of a mechanistic civilization. They define and vivify these attitudes not by precept or disinterested description, but by the actual presentation and molding of experience. The completeness of the definition is indissociable from the problem of poetic form. Poetic perception — the act of willing, seeing, or understanding something — is also the act of giving shape to something; of defining it through all the resources at the artist's command: meter and total structure as well as image and abstract language. The poet who succumbs to the more extreme types of organic form, and allows his subject-matter to dictate its own embodiment, sacrifices the best parts of his inherited language. He becomes, as Bridges never became, the meek stenographer of half-understood sensations and impressions. In the last analysis, Bridges' greatness as a stylist cannot be separated from his "masterly control of the material" with which he deals. And it should not be forgotten that this material is, in the best lyrics, the normal experience of the civilized human being.

If the lyrics represent successful attempts to understand the poet's own experience through the definition of impulses and attitudes, the plays represent the more detached studies of a philosopher. Not since the Elizabethans, perhaps, has English drama concentrated so successfully on the study of human character as in Bridges' two plays on Nero. Whether these plays can ever be acted is a matter of small importance beside the richness of their psychology. As Charles Lamb observed, the qualities which we most admire in Shakespeare's tragedies can seldom be transferred to the stage. Particularly today, with the professional theater so utterly devoid of serious content or intellectual interest, the actability of a profound psychological tragedy can hardly be used as a standard by which to measure its value. It seems to me that the characterizations of Nero and Seneca in Bridges' two Nero plays are among the most impressive in English dramatic literature. In Seneca we have a rich and living study of the decay of the power of judgment as a result of a life of continual moral compromise; in Nero we have a pendant study of the disintegration of personality as a result of self-indulgence and an uncontrolled lust for power. The other plays are less interesting psychologically, but nearly all of them contain passages of great lyric beauty. The reader interested only in Bridges' style cannot afford to ignore the masques *Achilles in Scyros*, *Prometheus the Firegiver* and *Demeter*, for in them he will find some of the firmest and richest blank verse in English poetry. The indifference in which Bridges' plays are held can be explained only by the fact that almost no one has read them.

The active effort to understand and illumine human experience is most easily seen, of course, in *The Testament of Beauty*. The fact that Bridges' philosophy — an idealism erected on naturalistic foundations — closely resembles that of George Santayana in no way impairs its value. Although its occasional pedestrian and amateurish explorations of minor epistemological problems contribute little, the poem represents a courageous attempt to reconcile the truth of naturalism with a necessary respect for reason and the ethical heritage of dualistic philosophies. How can man control and refine his animal nature without sterilizing the emotions which make for his happiness? How can he preserve freedom of will in a world he never made? How can he assert and maintain the autonomy of reason without setting up consciousness and rational control as objects of worship, as ends rather than means? *The Testament of Beauty* attempts to solve these problems. That they were the problems which chiefly concerned the most thoughtful Victorians, and that they are now largely ignored, does not alter the fact that they are our problems, problems which have to be answered. "The army of unalterable law" has indeed marched in a way which Meredith could scarcely have predicted, and a ruthless imperialism and theory of the state has been rightly described as "organic." The central subject of *The Testament of Beauty* is the possibility of directing and controlling, rather than passively accepting, the organic and dynamic forces of life.

In all these ways, but especially in his insistence on the autonomy of human imagination and reason, on their power to understand and control experience, Bridges is a truly traditional poet; in Sainte-Beuve's words, "a true classic." Like many traditional poets with the same ideals, he has been accused of two serious faults: limitation of range and poverty of emotion. Although it belongs to the jargon of contemporary criticism, the term *range* is seldom defined. If range is measured by the varieties of human action with which an artist deals, Bridges' range is small. One could likewise say that the range of Flaubert is smaller than that of Zola, or, to make an extreme case, that the range of Wordsworth is smaller than that of Southey. But this kind of range — this diversity of physical experience — is unimportant beside the range of a Thomas Mann or a Henry James. Mann and James show little or none of James Farrell's familiarity with the *mores* of the lowest classes, yet they explore far more deeply the mind and heart of man. The concern of the great artist is with depth rather than breadth of experience. If range is measured by this depth, the novels of Jane Austen exhibit as wide a range as those of Scott. In this sense, the range of Bridges is also very wide. If he was isolated from the realms of experience which a full social documentation of his time would have required, and if he largely ignored the criminal or abnormal mind, he more than compensated for these limitations by his full understanding of the experience of the civilized man. And this understanding was, as I have said, at every point lucid, sound, complete.

Only the critic who demands incoherence could accuse Bridges of poverty of emotion. He effected, in fact, an unusually successful compromise between the extreme romantic's unformed and incoherent emotionalism and the sterile restraint of the Neo-Classic. The fresh and honest joy of the *Shorter Poems*, their uninhibited acceptance of beauty and love, would indeed have seemed shamefully "romantic" to the emotionally starved creatures of Eliot's *Waste Land*. In the love poems, we have the calm purity of Jonson's songs rather than the meaningless intensity of Shelley's "Indian Serenade"; in the more sombre lyrics, the tragic accent of Donne's "A Hymn to God the Father" rather than the violent hysteria of Thompson's "The Hound of Heaven." More than any poetry of the last century, Bridges' lyrics are the product of a sensibility which has been enriched and civilized without being crippled or destroyed.

APPENDIXES

APPENDIX A

Bridges' Prosody

A FULL ACCOUNT of Bridges' prosody would require a volume at least as large as the poet's own *Milton's Prosody*. In the present appendix I shall merely describe a few of the outstanding features of Bridges' practice in the four meters which he employed: *accentual-syllabic meter* (in which the line is divided into a fixed number of feet with a fixed number of accented and unaccented syllables: the commonest meter in modern English poetry), *accentual meter* (in which the line has a fixed number of accented syllables, and an indeterminate number of unaccented syllables), *syllabic meter* (in which the line has a fixed number of syllables, and an indeterminate number of accents) and *quantitative meter* (in which the line is divided into a fixed number of feet, which are described by the length or quantity of their component syllables). Much confusion has been caused by the failure of prosodists to distinguish clearly between the first three of these meters. Bridges himself failed to distinguish, in his terminology, between the syllabic and accentual-syllabic types, which he indiscriminately described as "syllabic." In his own poetry, however, he discriminated carefully between the two types.[1]

I. ACCENTUAL–SYLLABIC METERS

At the outset it is necessary to define *metrical accent*, perhaps the most widely misunderstood of all literary terms. It is commonly assumed that a syllable is accented if it is emphasized in any way — by speech stress through energy of utterance, by duration, or by rise in pitch. In accentual-syllabic meter (in blank verse, for instance) the accent is determined *only* by rise in pitch, the characteristic of vocalization least varied by the peculiar habits of a given reader. Thus in the line,

Absént thee fróm felícitý awhíle,

the eighth syllable is accented because it represents a rise in pitch over the seventh syllable, and in spite of the fact that it is very short in duration and receives little speech stress or energy of utterance. In this connection, the rule of degree of accent must be remembered: that accentual-syllabic lines are divided into feet as rigidly as the lines of the Latin hexameter, and that a syllable is therefore accented or unaccented in relation to the other syllable or syllables of the foot in which it appears, not in relation to syllables which appear in the rest of the line. The fact that the line from *Hamlet* contains only three marked speech stresses does not alter the fact that it has five accents: the prosodial explanation of a line defines its basic structure, not the way in which it is read. Prosody merely describes the underlying norm against which several types of counterpoint may be introduced. Bridges gives a good example of two lines whose rhythm is nearly identical, but whose prosodial explanation (because of the rules of elision) is different:

> The image / of God
>
> The sav / our of death.[2]

If the rule for degree of accent is preserved, we can discover in Bridges' lyrics many beautiful lines which appear to offer pyrrhic and spondaic feet. Actually, the italicized feet in the lines which follow are all regularly iambic:

> How well my eyes remem*ber the dim path*! (*N. P.*, 4)*
>
> Pillar'd the portico *to that wide walk*. . . . (*N. P.*, 4)
>
> Therein a wooden sta*tue of rude style*. . . . (*N. P.*, 26)
>
> Like steadfast stars *in the blue vault* of night. . . . (*L. P.*, 1)

In these lines Bridges has attained the effect of pyrrhic and spondaic feet by making the unaccented syllable of one foot more strongly ac-

* The following abbreviations, referring to volumes forming separate parts of the 1936 *Poetical Works*, or to plays, are used: S. P. (*Shorter Poems*; roman numeral indicates book; arabic, the number of the poem); G. O. L. (*The Growth of Love*); N. P. (*New Poems*); L. P. (*Later Poems*); P. C. P. (*Poems in Classical Prosody*); Oct. (*October, and other poems*); N. V. (*New Verse*); T. O. B. (*The Testament of Beauty*); Prom. (*Prometheus the Firegiver*); Dem. (*Demeter*) Achilles (*Achilles in Scyros*); Ulysses (*The Return of Ulysses*).

cented than the accented syllable which immediately precedes it. A somewhat similar effect may be achieved by permitting combative accent; by using a quantitatively long syllable which is not accented before a quantitatively short syllable which receives the metrical accent. The first two syllables of the following line, considered by themselves, form a strictly iambic foot, although the unaccented syllable "Nay" is much longer in duration than the syllable "bar-" which, because of its rise in pitch, receives the accent:

> Nay, bár / ren are those mountains and spent the streams.[3]

The feet italicized in the following lines are likewise strictly iambic; their beauty lies in the conflict between accent and quantity:

> *See, whirl* / ing snow / sprinkles / the starvèd fields. . . . (*S. P.*, V, 7)

> Space and / *Time, Beau* / ty and God / — Praise we / his name! (*Oct.*, 27)

> Where the / *straight al* / leys hide / me, wall'd / between. . . . (*L. P.*, 1)

> In the / *high sum* / mer tide. . . . (*N. V.*, 12)

In the first two lines we may also observe the other two familiar types of variation in accentual-syllabic meter. The foot "sprinkles" is an instance of *metrical inversion*; that is, a trochee has been substituted for an iamb; the foot "ty and God" represents substitution by the introduction of a third and extrametrical syllable.

Bridges achieved effects of great beauty by using in succession three syllables of almost equal quantitative value:

> While yet the *móon's cold fláme* was hung between. . . . (*S. P.*, II, 3)

> Now in the *hígh beams básk*ing as we sped. . . . (*G. O. L.*, 38)

In the following line the last four syllables are of almost equal duration, yet they constitute two regular iambic feet:

> With the *new yeár's full móon*. . . . (*S. P.*, V, 15)

Bridges' use of sprung meter in his accentual-syllabic lyrics has already been discussed.[4]

The student of Bridges' blank verse, which was consciously modelled on Milton's, should read with care the first part of the final revised edition of *Milton's Prosody*, "On the Prosody of Paradise Lost." This part of the treatise analyzes Milton's variations on the normal blank verse line, and formulates a list of rules of elision based on Milton's practice.

The subject of elision is fundamental to a study of Bridges' poetry, since it is an important part of the prosody of his accentual-syllabic and syllabic poems, and unless the rules of elision are applied, his lyrics, blank verse, and syllabic poetry will appear to be metrically incorrect. Bridges reminds his readers that elision in English is not true Greek elision; that is, in English elision may occur within a word as well as at its end, and the elided syllable is *not cut out*.[5] In the practice of Milton and Bridges two things must be remembered: first, *elision is always optional* (the syllable may or may not be metrically elided); second, *elided vowels or syllables are not necessarily cut out of the pronunciation.* Failure to understand these two basic principles has resulted in two types of misunderstanding: readers who do not account for the elisions or do not apply the rules of elision invariably feel that Bridges' blank verse does not scan; readers who apply these elisions to the scansion and also apply them to the pronunciation read the lines barbarously. These remarks apply to the syllabic poetry as well. Because he does not recognize the four elisions in the following line, Nowell Smith describes it as having sixteen syllables: [6]

> illimitable unsearchable and of heavenly import. . . . (*T. O. B.*, i, 76)

But if the reader applies the rules of elision, eliminating prosodially four syllables, and allows his scansion to guide his pronunciation, he would say:

> illimita-blun-searcha-bland-of-hevn-limport,

which makes intolerable an already rather indifferent line.

Bridges uses in his blank verse all of the types of elision which he found in Milton's:

Vowel-elisions of common speech. "Y-glide": "To live not brutally though without *fire*. . . ." (*Prom.*, 96). "W-glide": "Fair above other *flowers*, as she is fairest. . . ." (*Dem.*, 39). Common speech elisions where the contiguous vowels make neither a diphthong nor a disyllable: "Its *radiant* revelry and. . . ." (*Dem.*, 8).

Poetic elision of vowels. Bridges distinguishes six types: (1) "y-glide" with first vowel stressed; (2) "y-glide" with second vowel stressed; (3) "y-glide" with neither vowel stressed; (4) "w-glide" with first vowel stressed; (5) "w-glide" with second vowel stressed; (6) "w-glide" with neither vowel stressed. There follow examples from Bridges' blank verse of the six types:

(1) Heaven's dial, sisterly mirror of night. . . . (*Prom.*, 7)
(2) This variegated ocean-floor of the air. . . . (*Prom.*, 5)
(3) By the complaints against the imperial household. . . . (*Nero*, I, 2955)
(4) A place in power, she has striven to force a title. . . . (*Ibid.*, 436)
(5) Uprisen in rebellion to overthrow. . . . (*Prom.*, 36)
(6) Rather by swath and furrow, or where the path. . . . (*Prom.*, 13)

A distinct type is elision through consonantal *h*:

To have done / this thing / had tried / me; to have / attempt(ed it). . . .
(*Nero*, I, 3004)

The line has, in addition to its two elisions, two extrametrical terminal syllables.

Poetic elision of the semi-vowels. There follow examples of elision through *r*, *l*, and *n*:

The flash of mastering fire, and it have borne. . . . (*Prom.*, 83)

gustily, and with garish bows laughing o'erarch. . . . (*T. O. B.*, i, 287)

His cruelty, his effeminate, blundering passion. . . . (*Nero*, II, 56)

Like Milton, Bridges frequently treats the final syllabic semi-vowel *n* as asyllabic; this is the least arbitrary elision of all:

A prisoner I bring them stolen from heaven. . . . (*Prom.*, 82)

A large number of the elisions by which Bridges keeps his blank verse decasyllabic are purely theoretical; thus the feet involved often have the perceptual value of real trisyllabic feet:

Is walled with corn *I am found*, by trellissed vine. . . . (*Prom.*, 14)

There are, however, various other means of breaking the regular blank verse pattern.

Many writers of blank verse frequently employ one or two extrametrical unaccented syllables at the end of the line; this is an accepted convention of dramatic blank verse:

> To talk of subsidies hurts no man's conscience. . . . (*Nero*, I, 2953)

> Unjustly. In times of greatest liberty. . . . (*Nero*, I, 2986)

The most obvious prosodial difference between Bridges' Miltonic blank verse, as represented by *Prometheus the Firegiver* and *Demeter*, and his calmer dramatic blank verse, as found in the other plays, is the greater relaxation of the latter. The first hundred lines of *Prometheus* show only four extrametrical terminal syllables, while in the first hundred lines of *The First Part of Nero*, Act V, Scene 2, there are thirty-eight such extrametrical syllables. In Shakespeare an analogous extra-metrical syllable often occurs within the line; Milton used this device in *Comus*, but not in *Paradise Lost*. Bridges uses it occasionally:

> Drowned 'neath the waters. Yet on the mountain-tops . . . (*Prom.*, 61)

Extrametrical syllables may be introduced likewise through the use of real trisyllabic feet. Such trisyllabic feet — feet in which the extra syllable cannot be accounted for in any of the ways already considered — are extremely rare in Bridges' blank verse. Two examples follow:

> The Fates' decrees and bends the wills *of the gods.* (*Prom.*, 3)

> Outcast *in the scorn* of all his cringing crew. . . . (*Prom.*, 31)

The following line, divided between three speeches, shows both a midverse extrametrical syllable and a trisyllabic fifth foot:

> *Mess.* We thought her drowned.
> *Nero.*   *Ha!*
> *Mess.*   But by the grace *of the gods.* . . .
>   (*Nero*, I, 2997)

Bridges employs metrical inversion frequently and with great skill. As he says,

Inversions of accent in all places except the first disturb the rhythm so as to call attention to the word which carries the irregular accent or stress: they are, therefore, used primarily in relation to the sense. . . . Inversion is most common in the first foot, next in the third and fourth, very rare in the second, and most rare in the fifth.[7]

These examples are typical of Bridges' practice:

Thíckets and woods, the windings of the glade, (Achilles, 96)

Whose throat séems the white mountain and its passion. . . . (Prom., 1159)

The morning mist lífted, and lo, a sight. . . . (Achilles, 516)

And smallest point of time various and broad. . . . (Nero, I, 3201)

To have said outright — Good, honest, Príscus. . . . (Nero, I, 62)

The example given of inversion of the fifth foot — the only one in Bridges' verse — is doubtful. Prosodially it may be so described, but the effect on the rhythm is so negligible as to warrant a different explanation. The line may be plausibly described as a four-foot line with an extrametrical syllable in the first foot and an extrametrical unaccented terminal syllable. True inversion in the fifth foot is very striking, as these lines from Paradise Lost show:

Beyond all past example and fúture. . . . (x, 840)

Which of us who beholds the bright súrface. . . . (vi, 472)

II. ACCENTUAL METERS

Theoretically the problem is this, whether in poetry the speech as determined by its accent and rhythm can be made so persistently beautiful in form as to dispense with all the subtle assistance which it derives from interplay with a fundamental metrical form, which while never relaxing its conscious guidance gives special significance to every deviation from it, and overriding all irregularities blends them into a consistent whole; or whether, in renouncing this it must not, if it should do well, create a prosody of its own?[8]

The fourth part of Milton's Prosody (ed. 1921) consists of an attempt to formulate such a prosody. There are seven main rules[9] to be followed by the writer of accentual verse: (1) the stress governs the rhythm; (2) the stresses must be all true speech stresses (conventional metrical stresses are eliminated); (3) a stress has more carrying power (or power of attraction) over the syllable next to it than it has over a syllable removed from it by an intervening syllable; (4) a stress has a peculiarly strong attraction toward verbal *unity and for its own proclitics and enclitics*; (5) *a stress will not carry a heavy syllable which is removed from it by another syllable*; (6) *a stress will not carry more than one heavy syllable or two light syllables on the same side of it*; (7) *a stress may be said to be distributed over four unstressed syllables which occur together*.

These rules permit certain combinations of syllables to form feet, and forbid others. A heavy syllable means a syllable which is quantitatively long; a light syllable, one which is quantitatively short. I shall use the following symbols in scanning accentual verse: ˘ indicates a short unstressed syllable, as in *gĕntlў*; − indicates a long (or as Bridges terms it, heavy) unstressed syllable, as in *hīgh tówer̄s*, the acute accent indicating the stressed or accented syllable. It will be seen from the rules that the following combinations are possible in accentual feet as defined by Bridges: the bare stress without any complement: ´; second, the two rising disyllabic feet; ˘´, −´; third, the two falling disyllabic feet: ´˘, ´−; fourth, the midstress trisyllabics: ˘´˘, −´˘, ˘´−, −´−; fifth, the falling and rising trisyllabics (dactyl and anapest): ´˘˘, ˘˘´; sixth, the quadrisyllabics: ˘´˘˘, −´˘˘, ˘˘´˘, ˘˘´−; seventh, the five-syllable foot: ˘˘´˘˘. In "The Nightingales," one of Bridges' most successful accentual experiments (though the poem may be scanned, with some wrenching, on an accentual-syllabic basis) eleven of the sixteen possible feet are employed:

Beáutĭful / mŭst bé / thĕ moúntaĩns / whénce / yĕ cóme,
Aňd bríght / iň thĕ frúitfŭl / vállĕys / thĕ stréams, / whĕrefróm
      Yĕ leárn / yoŭr sóng:
Whére arĕ / thōse stárrў / woóds? / Ō míght / Ī wándĕr / thére,
  Ămóng / thĕ flówer̄s, / whĭch iń that̆ / héavĕnlў / aír
    Blóom thĕ / yeār lóng.

Nāy, bárrĕn / arĕ thóse / moúntaĩns / aňd spént / thĕ stréams:
Oŭr sóng / iš thĕ voíce / ŏf dĕsíre, / that̆ háunts / oŭr dréams,
    Ă thróe / ŏf thĕ heárt,
Whōse píniňg / vísiŏns / dím, / fŏrbíddĕn / hópes / prŏfóund,
  Nō dýiňg / cádĕnce / nŏr lóng / sígh / căn sóund,
    Fŏr áll / oŭr árt.

Alóne, / ăloúd / iñ thĕ ráptŭred / eár / ŏf mén
Wĕ póur / oŭr dárk / nŏctúrnăl / sécrĕt; / añd thén,
　　　Aŝ níght / iŝ wìthdráwn
Frŏm thése / sweēt-spríngĭng / meáds / añd buŕstĭñg / boúghs / ŏf Máy,
Dréam, / whíle / thĕ iñnuḿbĕ̆rable / chóir / ŏf dáy
　　　Wélcŏme / thĕ daẃn.

It should be noted that in this poem the longer feet are used sparingly: there is only one five-syllable foot, and there are only three quadri-syllabic feet. Bridges' success in early accentual poems, such as "The Nightingales," is evident; he faced much greater difficulties when he attempted heavier accentual meters. In the "Ode on the Tercentenary Commemoration of Shakespeare, 1916" he seems to be going deliberately as far as his rules will permit. The result is that many of the rules are broken. The first and tenth lines of the first stanza refuse syllables in the fourth foot, thus destroying verbal unity; in the last foot of the second line a single word is distributed over two feet, and the stress is a conventional metrical one. There are at least five instances of conventional metrical stress:

> And smiting / the fetters / of slav / ery. . . .
>
> To world wide / brother / *hood*. . . .
>
> Of the shows / of etern / ity. . . .
>
> In echoing / chant / and cadenced / lit / any. . . .
>
> *His* / presence / hath startled / me. . . .

In five of the thirty-six lines of "Melancholy" Bridges overloaded his stresses. The first three examples illustrate infractions of rule 5; the fourth and fifth, infractions of rule 6. The overloaded feet are italicized:

> Aŝ whén / *ŏn ăn Aútŭmn plāin* / thĕ stórm / lāys lów / thĕ whéat. . . .
>
> Itŝ blóodstrēam / *faíntĕd dōwn* / tŏ thĕ slóthfŭl / wéarў / béat. . . .
>
> *Márkĭng tíme* / twìxt dárk / Hĕreáftĕr / añd Lóng- / bĕfóre. . . .
>
> Iñ ré / cŏncílemĕnt / ŏf Deáth, / añd Vánitў / *ŏf āll néeds*. . . .
>
> Mў héart gāve wāy / tŏ thĕ stráin, / rĕnoúncĭng / móre / añd móre. . . .

In these two poems, then, Bridges has broken not only the rule concerning the overloading of stresses, but has also, by allowing conventional stresses, broken the fundamental rule of his prosody: that the stress must determine the rhythm, and that all the stresses must be true speech-stresses. It is evident that the rules outlined by Bridges are at best merely descriptions of what is generally satisfying to the ear, and cannot be considered binding.

The Feast of Bacchus is written in an accentual measure whose rules [10] are very similar to those outlined in *Milton's Prosody*. The normal line has six speech-stresses, and no stress is allowed to carry more than one long syllable with it. The result is a curious mixture of rhythms so unpredictable that the ear takes up and rejects a new metrical norm with every line:

> Ménedémus, although our acquáintance has béen but shórt,
> And ónly dátes from the dáy you bóught this píece of lánd,
> And cáme to líve close bý me: for líttle or nóught but thát
> Occásioned it, ás you knów: yét my respéct fór you,
> Or else your béing a néighbour, for thát itsélf, I táke it,
> Coúnts in sóme sort as fríendship, mákes me bóld and frée
> To gíve you a piéce of advíce: the fáct is you séem to mé. . . .
>
> *(Feast of Bacchus, 24–30)*

On several occasions, later in the play, Bridges reverts to a line of six iambic feet, and the chief effect of these transitions is to show the manifest superiority of the stricter accentual-syllabic prosody.

Of the various types of heavier accentual meters, such as we find in the Shakespeare Ode, "Melancholy," and *The Feast of Bacchus*, the most pertinent criticism is that made by William Johnston Stone: "The fatal objection to this form of verse . . . is the incomparable ease with which lines can be reeled off by anybody." [11] The heavy six-stress line is only one of several "carry-all" meters which Bridges worked out and then discarded during his long career. His final solution of the problem was the twelve-syllable line of *New Verse* and *The Testament of Beauty*, but first he spent several years working in classical prosody.

III. QUANTITATIVE METERS

Bridges' experiments in classical prosody, which represent perhaps the most rigorous poetical effort of his career,[12] were undertaken to test the theories of William Johnston Stone, which were first proposed in his pamphlet "Classical Metres in English." Stone's quantitative prosody differs from that of other English theories in the same field in its strict adherence to the classical model. Stone denied that accent should be allowed to determine quantity (as Matthew Arnold had insisted it should),[13] and consequently he recommended the classical liberty of combative accent. The reader who is interested in Stone's classification of English vowel quantities should consult "Classical Metres in English Verse," printed with the 1901 edition of *Milton's Prosody*; he should also consider Bridges' objections to various of Stone's strictures in *Ibant Obscuri*.[14] As in Latin, vowel sounds are long not only by nature; many short vowels may be lengthened by position, the principal rule being that a short vowel followed by two or more consonants makes a long syllable, when one at least of the consonants is sounded with it.

The reader accustomed to ordinary accentual-syllabic verse will find it extremely difficult to scan Bridges' quantitative poems. Bridges himself experienced great difficulty in learning to "think in quantity" with English words. The first seven lines of "Wintry Delights" are scanned below according to Stone's rules, and show no false quantities. The long vowels are marked thus: *Mȳ*; the short, *tŏ thĕ*. It should be observed that combative accent is employed in all lines except the second. I have italicized the syllables in which the accent falls on short vowels:

Nōw ĭn *wĭn* / trȳ dē̆ / lights, ānd / lōng fire / side mĕdĭ / tātĭŏn,
'Twīxt stūd / iēs ānd / rōutine / pāyĭng dūe / cōurt tŏ thĕ / Mŭsĕs,
Mȳ *sŏlăce* / ĭn *sŏlĭ* / tŭde, whēn / brōkĕn / rōads bărrĭ / căde mē
Mūdbōund, / ūnvĭsĭt / ĕd fŏr / mōnths wĭth / mȳ mĕrrȳ / chĭldrĕn,
Grātefŭl / t'wārd *Prŏvĭd* / ēnce, ānd / hēedĭng ă̄ / slāndĕr ă̄ / gāinst mē
Lēss thăn ă̄ / rhēum, *thĭnk* ŏf / mē tŏ- / dāy, dēar / Lĭōnĕl, / ānd tāke
Thĭs *lĕttĕr* / ās *sŏme* ă̄ / ccōunt ŏf / Wĭll Stōne's / vĕrsĭfĭ / cātĭŏn.

("Paying" in line 2 is elided; "a/ccount" is so divided, because the geminated consonant here counts as a single letter.)

Two main objections are usually raised against the introduction of the classical system into English poetry: first, that the language is too monosyllabic, and is thus not fitted "for the long sonorous roll of the hexameter"; [15] second, that the language is "lamentably deficient in pure long vowels." [16] As a result of the monosyllabic character of the language it is often necessary to end lines with one-syllable words, and this at once departs from Latin practice and prohibits the unbroken periods of the best Latin hexameters.

In trying to capture the effects of Latin hexameters, Bridges employs an extraordinary proportion of unusual polysyllabic words. The result is not always gratifying to the ear:

> As to defy Ideas of imperative cerebration. . . .
>
> Her metamorphoses transmuting by correlation. . . .
>
> In the flat accretions of new sedimentary strata. . . .

Bridges was on the whole more successful in the lighter classical meters, but in his translation of lines from Vergil, "Ibant Obscuri," he wrote a few passages which do no injustice to the original: [17]

> They wer' amid the shadows by night in loneliness obscure
> Walking forth i' the void and vasty dominyon of Ades;
> As by an uncertain moonray secretly illumin'd
> One goeth in the forest, when heav'n is gloomily clouded,
> And black night hath robb'd the colours and beauty from all things.

Even the most successful of Bridges' *Poems in Classical Prosody* serve chiefly to emphasize the limping meter of the majority of the poems. There are certain insuperable obstacles to the composition of quantitative verse in English, of which the difficulty of learning to think in quantities is the greatest. If, as he claimed, Tennyson knew the quantitative value of every English word except *scissors*,[18] he was very exceptional indeed. At least so far as the heavier forms of quantitative verse are concerned, the conclusion reached long ago by Nashe would seem to be true:

The Hexamiter verse I graunt to be a Gentleman of an auncient house (so is many an English beggar) yet the Clyme of ours he cannot thrive in; he goes twitching and hopping in our language like a man running upon quagmires, up the hill in one syllable, and down the dale in another, retaining no part of that stately smooth gate which he vaunts himself with amongst the Greeks and Latins.[19]

IV. SYLLABIC METERS

We come now to the meter which has been the most discussed and the least understood of all those used by Bridges: the "Neo-Miltonic syllabics" [20] of *New Verse* and *The Testament of Beauty*. In *The Testament of Beauty* Bridges refers to his meter as his "loose alexandrines," [21] and this description has no doubt commended itself to readers as meaning that the verse had no fixed number of syllables. The *only* rule is line-length, and all of the regular lines have twelve syllables. The line is thus similar to the French alexandrine. (There are about thirty-five ten-syllable lines; these are appropriately indented.) The division into feet is abandoned, and since accents can be ignored or combined at will, the verse is purely syllabic. Nowell Smith describes the metrical norm as a line of twelve syllables with six stresses on the even syllables; actually the number or position of the stresses is wholly indeterminate. Smith also remarks that many lines have supernumerary syllables. Actually, no line in the poem has more than twelve syllables. Wherever there is the appearance of a greater number, the line is reducible by elision. The rules for this elision are the same as those of Milton as recorded by Bridges, with a few minor exceptions.[22]

Bridges' own account of the origin of this meter is given in "New Verse: Explanation of the Prosody of My Late Syllabic 'Free Verse.' " [23] In revising *Milton's Prosody* for its last edition, Bridges observed "that Milton had freed every foot in his blank verse . . . except the last: and that he had done this by excluding extrametrical syllables within the line . . . and that the reason why he had not freed the last foot also was that he allowed it still to carry an extrametrical syllable." [24] A foot is "free," according to Bridges, when there is no place in which any syllable must be necessarily accented or unaccented. It was thus possible for Milton to invert any foot in the first four. But since he still allowed extrametrical syllables at the end of the line, it was impossible for him to invert the last foot regularly. Since the reader's ear would become accustomed to feminine endings which were extrametrical (bringing the line up to eleven or twelve syllables), a ten-syllable line with the ninth syllable accented and the tenth syllable unaccented would appear to be "a line deficient in one syllable with an extrametrical ending." [25]

Seeing then that to free the last foot it was only needed to forbid the terminal extrametrical syllable, and that Milton had, with so great effect, excluded it from every other place . . . it seemed to me that the next step that he would have taken (had he continued his work) would have been to forbid it also in the last place.

I naturally wondered what the effect would be, and determined to experiment on it. [26]

The result of this experiment was "The Flowering Tree." This poem is written in sixes; that is, in twelve-syllable lines with a mid-line caesural break. The first stanza follows fairly strictly an accentual-syllabic pattern of six iambic feet, but in the second stanza wholly different rhythms appear:

> The sunlight was enmesh'd
> in the shifting splendour
> And I saw through on high
> to soft lakes of blue sky:
> Ne'er was mortal slumber
> so lapt in luxury.
> Rather — Endymion —
> would I sleep in the sun
> Neath the trees divinely
> with day's azure above. . . .

This poem (dated November 7, 1913) was followed on November 28, 1913, by "Noel: Christmas Eve, 1913," written in the same meter (with the caesural break) but without rhyme. For some years after this Bridges "felt no call to poetry," [27] but in 1921 he had "some months of good disposition" [28] and wrote several poems in this meter, "all of them experiments to discover its relation to rhyme." [29] These form the first part of New Verse.

In preparing Milton's Prosody Bridges observed the twelve-syllable lines in Samson Agonistes (which may be interpreted also as ten-syllable lines with two extrametrical syllables), and noticed that in these lines, as in the unquestionable twelve-syllable lines of the Nativity Ode, Milton discarded the caesural break at the middle of the line character-istic of earlier twelve-syllable lines. Bridges greatly admired Milton's lines,[30] and determined to experiment in the meter, writing according to the rules of Milton's blank verse (with regard to elision), but forbid-ding any extrametrical syllables at the end of the line:

I had no notion how the thing would hold together when thus apparently freed from all rule. It was plainly the freest of free verse, there being no speech-rhythm which it would not admit; and I saw also that all the old forms of 12-syllable verse, the Greek iambic, the scazon, the French alexandrine, etc., would be admitted on equal terms. It was partly this wish for liberty to use various tongues that made me address my first experiment to a parrot, but partly also my wish to discover how a low setting of scene and diction would stand; be-cause one of the main limitations of English verse is that its accentual (dot and go one) bumping is apt to make ordinary words ridiculous; and since, on theory at least, there would be no decided enforced accent in any place in this new metre, it seemed that it might possibly escape from the limitations spoken of. And thus I wrote *Poor Poll*.[31]

There follow typical lines from this earliest poem written in *The Testament of Beauty* meter:

> I am writing verses to you & grieve that you should be
> *absolument incapable de les comprendre,*
> *Tu, Polle, nescis ista nec potes scire:*
> Alas! Iambic, scazon and alexandrine,
> spondee or choriamb, all is alike to you —
> my well-continued fanciful experiment
> wherein so many strange verses amalgamate
> on the secure bedrock of Milton's prosody. . . .

The poem which follows "Poor Poll," "The Tapestry," not only has a more serious subject but shows a greater facility in the new medium. Already there are lines which would not dishonor *The Testament of Beauty*:

> My tale is but a fable of God's fair tapestry
> the decorated room wherein my spirit hath dwelt
> from infancy a nursling of great Nature's beauty
> which keepeth fresh my wonder as when I was a child.

Such is the joy of the eye, that dark conduit whereby
the swift creative ray, offspring of heavenly fire,
steals to the mind, wakening in her secret chamber
vast potencies of thought which there lie slumbering
in the image of God.

It should be observed, of course, that Bridges did not arrive at his syllabic alexandrine simply by forbidding extrametrical syllables and by using a twelve rather than a ten-syllable norm. Miltonic blank verse would retain its division into feet if these changes, and no others, were made. The *differentia* of Bridges' meter is its abandonment of the accentual-syllabic division of the line into feet.

APPENDIX B

Sources and Analogues

THE PASSAGES cited below offer instances·of conveyance or striking resemblance not quoted in the text or notes, but which for various reasons deserve quotation:

1. Discese nel mio cor, se come manna,
    Amor soave, come in fior rugiada,
    Che m'e piu dolce assai che mel di canna.
    D'esso mon parto mai, dovunque vada.
    Suolio io sempre mai gridar usanna;
    Amor eccelso, ben fa chi te lauda:
    Assavora' lo quando innamorai.
    Niente, sanza lui, fue ne fie mai;
    Ne sanza lui non vo'che mi cor gauda.
    — F. Trucchi, ed., *Poesie italiane inedite de dugento autori* (Prato,
        1846), pp. 10–11. Anonymous poem.

Love on my heart from heaven fell,
Soft as the dew on flowers of spring,
Sweet as the hidden drops that swell
Their honey-throated chalicing.

But never from him do I part,
Hosanna evermore I cry:
I taste his savour in my heart,
And bid all praise him as do I.

Without him noughtsoever is,
Nor was afore, nor e'er shall be:
Nor any other joy than his
Wish I for mine to comfort me.
    — *Shorter Poems*, IV, 11. See Note, *Poetical Works of Robert Bridges*,
        II, 262.

2. Gli occhi miei vaghi delle cose belle,
   E l'alma insieme della sua salute,
   Non hanno altra virtute
   Ch'ascenda al ciel, che mirar tutte quelle.
   Dalle più alte stelle
   Discende uno splendare,
   Che 'l desir tira a quelle;
   E qui si chiama amore.
   Nè altro ha gentil core,
   Che l'innamori e arda, e che 'l consigli,
   Ch'un volto che ne gli occhi lor somigli.
   — *Le rime di Michelangelo Buonarroti* (ed. Guasti, Florence, 1863),
   Madrigali, VIII, p. 33.

   Ravished by all that to the eyes is fair,
   Yet hungry for the joys that truly bless,
   My soul can find no stair
   To mount to heaven, save earth's loveliness.
   For from the stars above
   Descends a glorious light
   That lifts our longings to their highest height
   And bears the name of love.
   Nor is there aught can move
   A gentle heart, or purge or make it wise,
   But beauty and the starlight of her eyes.
   — George Santayana, *A Hermit of Carmel: And Other Poems* (London, 1903), p. 143.

   My eyes for beauty pine,
   My soul for Goddës grace:
   No other care nor hope is mine;
   To heaven I turn my face.

   One splendour thence is shed
   From all the stars above:
   'Tis namèd when God's name is said,
   'Tis love, 'tis heavenly Love.

   And every gentle heart,
   That burns with true desire,
   Is lit from eyes that mirror part
   Of that celestial fire.
   — *Shorter Poems*, IV, 9. The poems of Santayana and Bridges are
   independent translations of Michelangelo's madrigal.

3. Since all my words thy beauty doth indite,
   And love doth hold my hand and makes me write.
   > — Sir Philip Sidney, quoted in *Oxford Book of Sixteenth Century Verse*, p. 170.

   Baffled but not dishearten'd she took flight
   Scheming new tactics: Love came home with me,
   And prompts my measured verses as I write.
   > — Bridges, *Growth of Love*, 56.

4. That wondrous pattern, whereso'er it be,
      Whether in earth laid up in secret store,
   Or else in heaven. . . .
   > — Spenser, *Foure Hymnes*, II, 36–8.

   Almighty wondrous everlasting
   Whether in a cradle of astral whirlfire
   Or globed in a piercing star thou slumb'rest
      The impassive body of God. . . .
   > — Bridges, *October*, 6.

5. Shall I come, sweet Love, to thee,
      When the evening beams are set?
   Shall I not excluded be?
      Will you find no feigned let?
   Let me not, for pity, more
   Tell the long hours at your door.
   > — T. Campion, quoted in *Oxford Book of Sixteenth Century Verse*, p. 841.

   Long are the hours the sun is above,
   But when evening comes I go home to my love.

   I'm away the daylight hours and more,
   Yet she comes not down to open the door.
   > — Bridges, *Shorter Poems*, I, 11.

6. O Love! they wrong thee much
   That say thy sweet is bitter,
   When thy rich fruit is such
   As nothing can be sweeter.
   Fair house of joy and bliss,
   Where truest pleasure is,
      I do adore thee:

I know thee what thou art,
I serve thee with my heart,
      And fall before thee.
            — Anon. Madrigal (1605), *Chilswell Book of English Poetry*, No. 119.

But when again thou smilest,
      And love for love returnest,
And fear with joy beguilest,
      And taketh truth in earnest;
Then, though I sheer adore thee,
The sum of my love for thee
Seems poor, scant, and unworthy.
            — *Shorter Poems*, I, 6 (second stanza).

7.   . . . as the wakeful Bird
Sings darkling, and in shadiest Covert hid
Tunes her nocturnal note.
            — Milton, *Paradise Lost*, III, 38–40, quoted in *Spirit of Man*, No.
            130.

Alone, aloud in the raptured ear of men
We pour our dark nocturnal secret. . . .
            — *Shorter Poems*, V, 12.

8. The Atoms of Democritus
   And Newton's Particles of Light
   Are sands upon the Red Sea shore,
   Where Israel's tents do shine so bright.
            — Blake, "Mock on, mock on, Voltaire, Rousseau."

   Thy spirit, Democritus, orb'd in the eterne
Illimitable galaxy of night
Shineth undimm'd where greater splendours burn
Of sage and poet: by their influence bright
We are held; and pouring from his quenchless urn
Christ with immortal love-beams laves the height.
            — *October*, 27.

9. And full grown lambs loud bleat from hilly bourn. . . .
            — Keats, "Ode to Autumn."

   the newborn lambs
Within their strawbuilt fold beneath the hill
      Answer with plaintive cry their bleating dams.
            — *Shorter Poems*, V, 9.

10. Perhaps the self-same song that found a path
    Through the sad heart of Ruth. . . .
        — Keats, "Ode to a Nightingale."

So through my heart there winds a track of feeling,
   A path of memory, that is all her own. . . .
       — *Shorter Poems*, I, 2.

11. The oak Leviathans, whose huge ribs make
    Their clay creator the vain title take
    Of lord of thee, and arbiter of war.
        — Byron, *Childe Harolde*, iv, 212-4; *Chilswell Book of English
          Poetry*, p. 102.

The fabled sea-snake, old Leviathan,
Or else what grisly beast of scaly chine
That champ'd the ocean-wrack and swash'd the brine,
Before the new and milder days of man,
Had never rib nor bray nor swindging fan
Like his iron swimmer of the Clyde or Tyne,
Late-born of golden seed to breed a line
Of offspring swifter and more huge of plan.
    — *Growth of Love*, 27.

12. And I have loved thee, Ocean! and my joy
    Of youthful sports was on thy breast to be
    Borne, like a bubble, onward: from a boy
    I wanton'd with thy breakers — they to me
    Were a delight; and if the freshening sea
    Made them a terror — 'twas a pleasing fear,
    For I was as it were a child of thee,
    And trusted to thy billows far and near,
    And laid my hand upon thy mane — as I do here.
        — *Childe Harolde*, iv, 235-243; *Chilswell*, p. 103.

On such a stony, breaking beach
My childhood chanced and chose to be:
'Twas here I played, and musing made
My friend the melancholy sea.
   He from his dim enchanted caves
With shuddering roar and onrush wild
Fell down in sacrificial waves
At feet of his exulting child.

Unto a spirit too light for fear
His wrath was mirth, his wail was glee: —
My heart is now too fixed to bow
Tho' all his tempests howl at me. . . .
— *Shorter Poems*, IV, 27.

13. The woods decay, the woods decay and fall,
The vapours weep their burthen to the ground.
— Tennyson, "Tithonus."

The wood is bare: a river-mist is steeping
The trees that winter's chill of life bereaves. . . .
— *Shorter Poems*, I, 2.

14. My very spirit faints and my whole soul grieves
At the moist smell of the rotting leaves.
— Tennyson, "A spirit haunts the year's last hours."

The trees that winter's chill of life bereaves:
Only their stiffened boughs break silence, weeping
Over their fallen leaves.
— *Shorter Poems*, I, 2.

15. Charge once more, then, and be dumb!
Let the victors, when they come,
When the forts of folly fall,
Find thy body by the wall!
— Arnold, "The Last Word."

Fight, to be found fighting: nor far away
Deem, nor strange thy doom.
Like this sorrow 'twill come
And the day will be to-day.
— *Shorter Poems*, V, 19.

16. And if the driver lose his way,
Or the reins sunder, who can say
In what blind paths, what pits of fear
Will plunge the chargers in their mad career?
Drive well, O mind, use all thy art,
Thou charioteer. . . .
— Paraphrase from *Katha-Upanishad* in P. E. More, *A Century of Indian Epigrams*; quoted in Irving Babbitt, *Rousseau and Romanticism*, p. 261.

'tis faith alone can keep the charioteer in heart —
Nay, be he but irresolute the steeds wil rebel,
and if he looketh earthward they will follow his gaze;
and ever as to earth he neareth, and vision cleareth
of all that he feareth, and the enemy appeareth. . . .
    — *The Testament of Beauty*, II, 510–4.

17.   Quand la Perdrix
       Void ses petits
En danger, et n'ayant qu'une plume nouvelle,
Qui ne peut fuir encor par les airs le trépas,
Elle fait la blessée, et va traisnant de l'aisle,
Attirant le Chasseur, et le Chien sur ses pas,
Détourne le danger, sauve ainsi sa famille,
Et puis quand le Chasseur croit que son Chien la pille,
Elle, luy dit adieu, prend sa volée, et rit
De l'homme, qui confus des yeux en vain la suit.
    — Lafontaine, "Discours à Madame de la Sablière."

    It is pretty to mark
a partridge, when she hath first led forth her brood to run
among the grass-tussocks or hay-stubbles of June,
if man or beast approach them, how to usurp regard
she counterfeiteth the terror of a wounded bird
draggling a broken wing, and noisily enticeth
or provoketh the foe to follow her in a vain chase;
nor wil she desist from the ruse of her courage
to effect her own escape in loud masterful flight,
untill she hav far decoy'd hunter or blundering hoof
from where she has bid her little ones to scatter and hide.
    — *T. O. B.*, ii, 114–24.

18. While the mother bird is feeding or brooding over her nestlings, the maternal instinct is probably stronger than the migratory, and at last, at a moment when her young ones are not in sight, she takes flight and deserts them. When arrived at the end of her long journey, and the migratory instinct ceases to act, what an agony of remorse each bird would feel if, from being endowed with great mental activity, she could not prevent the image continually passing before her mind of her young ones perishing in the bleak north from cold and hunger.
    — Darwin, *The Descent of Man*, chapter IV. Quoted in Santayana, *The Life of Reason*, I, 263. Santayana refers incorrectly to chapter III.

Ther is a young black ouzel, now building her nest
under the Rosemary on the wall, suspiciously
shunning my observation as I sit in the porch,
intentiv with my pencil as she with her beak:
Coud we discourse together, and wer I to ask for-why
she is making such pother with thatt rubbishy straw,
her answer would be surely: "I know not, but I MUST."
Then coud she take persuasion of Reason to desist
from a purposeless action, in but a few days hence
when her eggs were to hatch, she would look for her nest;
and if another springtide found us here again,
with memory of her fault, she would know a new word,
having made conscient passage from the MUST to the OUGHT.
— *T. O. B.*, iv, 134–46.

19. And order, high discourse,
And decency, than which is life less dear,
She has of him: the lyre of language clear,
Love's tongue and source.
— Meredith, "Earth and Man." [*Him* refers to earth or nature.]

Not emotion or imagination ethic or art
logic of science nor dialectic discourse,
not even that supersensuous sublimation of thought,
the euristic vision of mathematical trance,
hath any other foundation than the common base
Of Nature's building. . . .
— *T. O. B.*, i, 365–70.

APPENDIX C

The Dates of Some of Bridges' Lyrics*

AT MY REQUEST Mrs. Robert Bridges very kindly looked through her husband's papers for material which might aid in the dating of his lyric poems. She found a loose-leaf notebook containing fifty-eight poems in manuscript, and allowed me to transcribe the dates affixed to them by their author. The years in which twelve of these poems were written may be found in the Oxford Standard Authors edition of Bridges' poems (1936); the dates of the other forty-six are given below.

First words	MS. date	First words	MS. date
All-ador'd	1910	Love on my heart	Feb., 1890
As our car	1921; corrected	Lo where the virgin	1904
	1925	Man hath with man	1899
At dead of unseen	1902	Mazing around	April, 1913
Beneath the wattled	1895	Mortal though I	"1905 or
Crown Winter	1889		earlier"
Folk alien	1914; dated 1904	My delight and thy	Aug. and Nov.,
	in printed text		1896
From a friend's	1921	No country know I	1917
How should I be	1921	O Love, I complain	1896
How well my eyes	1899	On a mournful day	1916
I climb the mossy	Dec., 1895	One grief of thine	1900
I have lain	1911 or 1912	Over the warring	1916
I have sown	1899	Power eternal	Finished May
In still midsummer	1910; one word		16, 1898
	corrected, 1919	Riding adown	1899
It's all up	1902; corrected	See, Love, a year	1902
	1920	Since I believe	1912
Joy, sweetest lifeborn	1879	Sweet pretty	Feb., 1913
Look down the river	1897	The day begins	Jan., 1894

* Reprinted from *Modern Language Notes*, LV, 3, March, 1940.

First words	MS. date	First words	MS. date
The saddest place	1899	What happy bonds	1902
The sea keeps not	1899	What voice	Jan., 1892
These grey stones	1902–3	When to my lone	1902
To my love	1895	Who goes there?	Feb., 1913
'Twas mid of the moon	1921	Why hast thou nothing	1899
Two demons thrust	1913	Would that you were	1902; corrected 1920,
Voyaging northwards	1899		

Mrs. Bridges also allowed me to transcribe from her husband's copy of the 1873 *Poems* the dates which he had entered in pencil. This is Robert Bridges' earliest volume, and only seventeen of its fifty-three poems were reprinted in later volumes. Bridges' memory, like that of so many poets, was not infallible. N. C. Smith writes: "Of his first volume, published in 1873, he himself wrote that he 'went to the seaside (Seaford) for two weeks and wrote it there.'" † The book itself contains an "Advertisement" saying: "The foregoing poems, with the exception of a few that have their proper dates affixed, were written between the summers of seventy-two and seventy-three." The dates of only four of the poems (here enclosed by parentheses) were printed in the 1873 *Poems*.

First words	Date	First words	Date
A boy and a girl *	Sept., 1872	For too much love *	July, 1873
A lady sat high *	Aug., 1872	Happy the man *	(1868)
All women born	Aug., 1873	Her eye saw *	July, 1872
An Abbot once lived *	Sept., 1872, Seaford	His poisoned shafts	July, 1873
		I found to-day	June, 1872
An idle June *	July, 1873	I heard a linnet	(1869)
A poor old *	Sept., 1872	I made another song	1873
A poppy grows	June, 1872	In my most serious *	July, 1873; lines 5–10, 1868
As in our arbour *	1872		
Assemble, all ye	Aug., 1873	In ten years hence *	Jan., 1873
Clear and gentle	Aug., 1873	Into thy young heart *	July, 1873
Come gentle Death *	1873	In wooing and in *	Aug., 1873
Dear Lady, when thou	Feb., 1873	I sat one winter's *	1873
Deep in the inner *	Feb., 1873	I shall not see *	July, 1873

* Not reprinted in later volumes.

† "Robert Bridges," *Dictionary of National Biography*, 1922–30.

First words	Date	First words	Date
I will not let thee go	July, 1872	Since thou dost bid *	July, 1872
Long are the hours	Aug., 1872	Sometimes when	Aug., 1872
Love is up *	1862; corrected 1873	The cliff-top	June, 1872
		The humble bee *	1872
Love, that is king *	1873	The King of a *	1873
Night by night *	Seaford, 1873	The merry elves *	1873
Oh how have I of-		The wood is bare	1872
fended? *	March, 1873	'Twas midnight *	June, 1872
Old Thunder is dead *	(1869)	Two beds there were *	1872; Parts II,
O trust the eyes *	Aug., 1872		III in 1873
Parted so long *	Feb., 1873	When first we met	Aug., 1873
Poor withered rose	July, 1872	When I sit to write *	(1869)
Shame on his name *	Sept., 1872	When King Darius *	1873
She is coming *	Not dated	Who has not walked	Sept., 1872
Sick of my *	1865; rewritten 1873	Woe to the friend *	July, 1873

* Not reprinted in later volumes.

NOTES

PART ONE

CHAPTER ONE

1. *Spectator*, no. 160.
2. L. Binyon, "Robert Bridges and the Poetic Art," *Bookman* (London), LIV (1918), 144.
3. *A Defense of Poetry*.
4. *Three Friends: Memoirs of Digby Mackworth Dolben, Richard Watson Dixon, Henry Bradley* (London, 1932), p. 17.
5. *Collected Essays, Papers, etc.* (London, 1927–36), VI, 212. Hereafter referred to as *Essays*.
6. *Essays*, IV, 77.
7. *Ibid.*, IV, 91.
8. *Ibid.*, IV, 92.
9. *Essays*, XXVII, 185.
10. *The Oxford Book of Modern Verse* (London, 1936), p. xx.
11. *Three Friends*, p. 130.
12. Y. Winters, "Robert Bridges and Elizabeth Daryush," *The American Review*, VIII (1937), 335.
13. *Three Friends*, p. 139.
14. "Pure, Ornate, and Grotesque Art in English Poetry," in *Literary Studies*.
15. F. E. Brett Young, *Robert Bridges: A Critical Study* (London, 1914), p. 14.
16. *Three Friends*, p. 114.
17. *The Academy*, XXXVIII (1890), 496–7.
18. *The Letters of Gerard Manley Hopkins to Robert Bridges*, ed. C. C. Abbott (London, 1935), "Introduction," p. 19. Hereafter referred to as *Letters*.
19. "Wintry Delights."
20. *Essays*, II, 37.
21. *Three Friends*, p. 139.
22. M. Arnold, "Preface to the Poems of 1853."
23. Y. Winters, *Primitivism and Decadence: A Study of American Experimental Poetry* (New York, 1937), p. 71.
24. *Three Friends*, p. 17.
25. *Poems* (1873), no. xxix. Not reprinted.
26. *Ibid.*, no. XIV. Not reprinted.
27. *Aeneid*, VI, 595–6. The phrase "bulk incredible" is thoroughly Miltonic.
28. *Poems* (1873), no. XLVI. Not reprinted.

29. Letter from Muirhead quoted by T. H. Warren in *Robert Bridges: Poet Laureate* (Oxford, 1914), p. 14. A published lecture.

30. *The Oxford Book of Modern Verse*, p. xviii.

31. See Appendix C, p. 294.

32. *Poems* (1873), no. IV. Not reprinted.

33. *Ibid.*, no. XXII. Not reprinted.

34. *Ibid.*, no. IX. Reprinted as *Shorter Poems*, I, 2.

35. *Ibid.*, no. XLVIII. Not reprinted.

36. *The Academy*, V (1874), 53.

37. *Ibid.*, XIX (1881), 352. Unsigned review.

38. *Letters*, p. 123.

39. *The Academy*, XXXVIII (1890), 496–7.

40. "The Poetry of Robert Bridges," *The Quarterly Review*, CCXIX (1913), 232.

41. *The Academy*, XXXVIII (1890), 496–7.

42. *Symposium*, 211.

43. C. S. Lewis, *The Allegory of Love* (Oxford, 1936), p. 5.

44. George Santayana, *Little Essays: Drawn from the Writings of George Santayana*, ed. L. P. Smith (New York, 1920), p. 41.

45. *Letters*, p. 37.

46. *Ibid.*, p. 38.

47. *Essays*, XXX.

48. *Letters*, p. 152.

49. *The Academy*, XIX (1881), 352.

50. *Robert Bridges: Poet Laureate*, p. 28.

51. These plays are discussed in Part II.

52. *Eros and Psyche* (ed. 1885), p. 157.

53. See pp. 37–41.

54. *Eros and Psyche* (ed. 1885), p. 156.

55. C. S. Lewis, *The Allegory of Love*, p. 298. According to Lewis, Malecasta and Busirane represent false love, or Courtly Love, opposed to Britomart, representing Chastity, which for Spenser meant married love.

56. *The Poets and the Poetry of the Century* (ed. A. H. Miles), VIII (London, 1892), 115–6.

57. *New Studies in Literature* (London, 1895), p. 72.

58. *The Academy*, LIII (1898), 155.

59. *The Poetical Works of Robert Bridges*, 6 vols. (London, 1898–1905), II, 294. Hereafter referred to as *Poetical Works of Robert Bridges*, as distinguished from the one-volume *Poetical Works of Robert Bridges Excluding the Eight Dramas* (Oxford, 1936), which will be referred to as *Poetical Works*.

60. "La Gloire de Voltaire."
61. "To Robert Burns, An Epistle on Instinct."
62. *The Journal of Education*, XLV (1913), 574.
63. Quoted in "Robert Bridges, Poet Laureate," *The Dial* (Chicago), LV (1913), 70.
64. F. R. Leavis, *New Bearings in English Poetry: A Study of the Contemporary Situation* (London, 1832), p. 237.
65. *Robert Bridges*, p. 19.
66. "Robert Bridges and Elizabeth Daryush," p. 355.
67. *Poetical Works*, p. 408.
68. *Ibid.*, p. 474.
69. "New Verse," Appendix to "Letter to a Musician on English Prosody," *Essays*, XV, 88–9.
70. *Ibid.*, p. 89.
71. *Ibid.*, p. 78.

CHAPTER TWO

1. *Conjectures on Original Composition.*
2. *Letters*, p. 291.
3. *Three Friends*, p. 116.
4. *Essays*, XXVIII, 238.
5. *Ibid.*, II, 54–5.
6. *Ibid.*, III, 66.
7. *Ibid.*, VI, 211.
8. *Ibid.*, VI, 209.
9. *Milton Prosody* (ed. 1921), p. 100.
10. *Letters*, p. 206.
11. *Essays*, XIV, 41–2.
12. *Eros and Psyche*, February 27; *Faerie Queene*, VII, vi, 50.
13. *T. O. B.*, I, 268–70. Cp. Matthew Arnold's translation (in "Pagan and Medieval Religious Sentiment"):

> Praised be my Lord for our mother the earth, the which doth sustain us and keep us, and bringeth forth divers fruits, and flowers of many colours, and grass.

14. "To Francis Jammes."
15. "Who has not walked upon the shore."
16. "Recollections of Solitude."
17. *Eros and Psyche* (ed. 1885), pp. 156–7.

18. *   *Bridges*   *Apuleius*

       March   *Metam.* Book IV, Sects. 28–31
       April   IV, 32–end
       May   V, 1–6
       June   V, 7–14
       July   V, 15–24
       August   V, 25–7
       September   V, 28–end
       October   VI, 1–5
       November   VI, 6–10
       December   VI, 10–16
       January   VI, 16–21
       February   VI, 21–4

19. Douglas Bush, *Mythology and the Romantic Tradition in English Poetry* (Cambridge, Mass., 1937), p. 434. The reader is referred to Prof. Bush's book for an interesting criticism of the poem.

20. *Eros and Psyche*, June 19.

21. L. Apuleius, *Metamorphoses*, Loeb Classical Library (New York, London, 1915), V, 12.

22. *Ibid.*, V, 10.

23. *Ibid.*, V, 34.

24. *Ibid.*, V, 22.

25. *Ibid.*, V, 24.

26. *Ibid.*, V, 28.

27. *The Poetical Works of Robert Bridges*, II, 292.

28. T. Moore, *The Epicurean . . . and Alciphron* (London, 1839), Alciphron, p. 50.

29. T. Gautier, *Poésies complètes*, 2 vols., II (Paris, 1875–6), 230.

30. See p. 72.

31. "All earthly beauty hath one cause and proof" derives partly from Michelangelo's Madrigal xix, as Bridges acknowledges (*The Poetical Works of Robert Bridges*, II, 292). The first quatrain of "Ye blessed saints, that now in heaven enjoy" is from Michelangelo's Madrigal "Beati voi" (*ibid.*, I, 292). Bridges also translated Michelangelo's "O nott', o dolce tempo benche nero" in a pamphlet (1882), not reprinted. For the fourth lyric, see Appendix B, p. 286.

32. See Appendix B, pp. 287–8.

33. Cp. "Epithalamion," lines 42–3, 131–2, 218–22.

34. *F. Q.*, II, vi, 7.

35. From "Suns of the world may stain when heaven's sun staineth" (Sonnet 33).

36. See *Essays*, XII, 22.

37. *Ibid.*, XIII, 31.

38. See Chapters VI, IX and Appendix A.

39. Compare the fourth stanza of Bridges' elegy with the Nativity Ode, XIII.

40. Quoted in *Chilswell Book of English Poetry*, p. 64.

41. *Essays*, IV, 162.

42. *Ibid.*, IV, 161.

43. "The Wreck of the Deutschland."

44. "The Starlight Night."

45. *Letters*, p. 243.

46. *Ibid.*, p. 93.

47. *Ibid.*, p. 96.

CHAPTER THREE

1. *T. O. B.*, I, 318–9.

2. Quoted as epigraph for F. R. Leavis, *New Bearings on English Poetry*.

3. *The Laocoon*, Chapter VII, *passim*.

4. *Eros and Psyche*, November 12.

5. *T. O. B.*, I, 15–6.

6. "A Note on the Verse of John Milton," *Essays and Studies by Members of the English Association*, XXI (1936), 35.

7. The following analysis owes much to a classroom lecture by Robert Hillyer.

CHAPTER FOUR

1. I. Babbitt, *Rousseau and Romanticism* (Boston, 1919), p. 291.

2. *Ibid.*, p. 312.

3. G. Rostrevor Hamilton, *Poetry and Contemplation* (Cambridge, 1937), p. 147.

4. I. A. Richards, *Practical Criticism* (New York, 1929), p. 320. My position is little different from that of Matthew Arnold in his essay on "Wordsworth."

5. "Robert Bridges and Elizabeth Daryush," p. 357.

6. "The Thanksgiving."

7. "The Holy Scriptures."

8. "Gratefulness."

9. *T. O. B.*, IV, 1439–46.

10. *Ibid.*, III, 326–30.

11. *Prometheus Unbound*, III, iii.

12. P. E. More, *On Being Human* (Princeton, 1936), p. 147.

13. Italics mine.

14. *Poems* (1873), III. Dated 1868. Not reprinted.

15. W. Pater, *The Renaissance: Studies in Art and Poetry* (London, 1920), p. 218.

16. *Rousseau and Romanticism, passim.*

17. Winters, *Primitivism and Decadence*, p. 5.

18. That wondrous pattern, whereso'er it be,
     Whether in earth laid up in secret store,
     Or else in heaven . . . . (*Foure Hymnes*, ii, 36–8.)

Cp. Bridges' "Epistle to a Socialist" (ll. 195–204), *T. O. B.*, I, 174–6, and this interesting passage: ". . . the thoughts of men are not mere earthly notions born in his animal brain . . . but are eternal essences or influences that come to him from without." (*Essays*, XXIX, 245.)

19. Cp. Santayana, *Little Essays*, p. 16.

20. The Ring of Being is most clearly defined in *T. O. B.*, IV, 1262–7.

21. *Ibid.*, I, 204–6.

22. "Ode to the West Wind."

CHAPTER FIVE

1. L. W. Miles, "The Poetry of Robert Bridges," *Sewanee Review*, XIII (1905), p. 130.

2. Y. Winters, "Robert Bridges and Elizabeth Daryush," p. 235.

3. The sadness of the nightingales is that of the poets who are supposed to be happy. For an interesting interpretation of the poem, see C. Brooks and R. P. Warren, *Understanding Poetry* (New York, 1939), pp. 198–200.

4. *Oxford Book of Sixteenth Century Verse*, p. 322.

5. *Summa Theol. Prima Secundae*, xxxiv, Art. 1. I am indebted to C. S. Lewis, *The Allegory of Love*, p. 16, for this reference.

6. *F. Q.*, II, xi, 1.

7. I am indebted to Yvor Winters' *Primitivism and Decadence* for some of the methods of analysis used in the following pages. The debt is too great to be acknowledged in less general terms.

8. See *Primitivism and Decadence*, p. 70.

9. *Supra*, pp. 34–6.

10. F. O. Matthiessen, *The Achievement of T. S. Eliot* (Boston and New York, 1935), p. 10.

11. T. S. Eliot, *Selected Essays: 1917–1932* (New York, 1932), p. 246.

12. Matthiessen, *op. cit.*, p. 80.

13. *Ibid.*, p. 67.

14. "The Study of Poetry."

15. *Hy. V*, II, ii, 78–143.

16. *Lear*, IV, vii, 60–71.

17. *Ant. and Cleop.*, V, ii, 280–98.

18. *Essays*, IV, 99.

19. "Sleep and Poetry."

20. *Essays*, IV, 99.

21. Matthiessen, *op. cit.*, p. 42.

22. Winters, *Primitivism and Decadence*, p. 77.

23. Eliot, *Selected Essays*, p. 248.

24. This chapter was written before the author had had an opportunity to read Winters' article on "T. S. Eliot: The Illusion of Reaction," *The Kenyon Review*, III (1941), 7–30, 221–39.

CHAPTER SIX

1. Winters, *Primitivism and Decadence*, p. 100.

2. *Ibid.*, p. 101. The two hexameter lines, 2 and 9, are reducible by elision. There are trisyllabic substitutions in lines 7, 8, 9, 10, 11, 14, 16, 18, 20, 21.

3. *Essays*, XV, 77–8.

4. "Lycidas."

5. *Poetical Works*, p. 474.

6. "New Verse," Appendix to *Essays*, XV, 89.

7. *Essays*, III, 68.

8. "A Note on the Verse of John Milton."

9. *Paradise Lost* is "a curruption of the language, . . . accomodating itself to greek and latin inversions and intonations." (*The Letters of John Keats*, ed. M. B. Forman [New York, 1935], letter 156, p. 425.)

10. *Essays*, IV, 109.

11. *Ibid.*, II, 53.

12. *Ibid.*, IV, 151.

13. *Ibid.*, III, 67.

14. *Ibid.*, XXVIII, 225.

15. Pope, "Essay on Criticism."

16. *Essays*, IV, 158.

PART TWO

CHAPTER SEVEN

1. *Poetical Works of Robert Bridges*, III, 262.

2. *The Humours of the Court* was produced in 1930 by the Oxford University Dramatic Society. *Prometheus* was "acted at a boy's grammar school near Newbury" (*Letters*, p. 160); *Demeter* was written for the students of Somerville College, Oxford, and acted by them on June 11 and June 22, 1904, and by the Frensham School (New South Wales) in 1933.

3. *Demeter* was written to order in a single month, and does not indicate a renewed dramatic ambition. All of the plays with the exception of *Nero* were dated by their author in the first editions: *Prometheus the Firegiver*, 1882; *Palicio*, 1883; *The Return of Ulysses*, 1884; *The Christian Captives*, 1886; *Achilles in Scyros*, August, 1887; *The Humours of the Court*, 1888; *The Feast of Bacchus*, June, 1885. A revised edition of the last named play appeared in 1894.

4. Friedrich Wild, *Die Englische Literatur der Gegenwart . . . Drama und Roman* (Wiesbaden, 1928), p. 107.

5. Yvor Winters, "T. Sturge Moore," *The Hound and Horn*, VI (1933), 542.

6. *Poetical Works*, III, 262.

7. "On the Tragedies of Shakspere Considered with Reference to Their Fitness for Stage Presentation." Lamb believed that "the plays of Shakspere are less calculated for performance on a stage than those of almost any other dramatist whatever. Their distinguished excellence is a reason that they should be so."

CHAPTER EIGHT

1. According to Mühlbach there appeared 59 plays about Nero (in all languages) between 1600 and 1906, but only one of these — Racine's *Britannicus* — has been widely acknowledged as a great play. Mühlbach omits from his list *Nero: A Tragedy* by R. Comfort (Philadelphia, 1880). (E. Mühlbach, *Die Englische Nerodramen des XVII Jahrhunderts insonderheit Lees Nero* [Leipzig, 1910].)

2. J. S. Roberts, "Nero in Modern Drama," *The Fortnightly Review*, New Series, LXXIX (1906), p. 95.

3. Bridges probably suggested to Phillips the fidelity of Actè, and he was the only dramatist before Phillips to present Britannicus' fatal banquet on the stage.

4. *The Works of Thomas Gray*, ed. E. Gosse, 4 vols. (London, 1884), I, 101–3.

5. *Letters*, p. 257.

6. *Ibid.*, p. 302.

7. *Annals of Tacitus* (ed. W. J. Broadribb), XIII, 21.

8. Compare, for instance, the speech of Flavus in *Nero: Part II* (V, iii) with the version of the same speech given by the 1624 dramatist (IV). The two speeches are close paraphrases of Tacitus' record in *Annals*, XV, 67.

9. *The Tragedy of Nero* (II); *Nero: Part II* (III, ii). Both scenes may derive from the meeting of the conspirators in Brutus' orchard in *Julius Caesar* (II, i).

10. Racine, *Britannicus* (II, ii).

11. *Annals*, XV, 57.

12. Thrasea's leaving the Senate without voting (*First Part of Nero*, I, i) is recorded by Tacitus in *Annals*, XIV, 12 (A.D. 59); that is, *after* the death of Agrippina. The trial (*Nero: Part II*, V, iii), which lasted for several days and preceded by some time the death of Seneca, is compressed into a single day, and on that day Seneca also dies (V, v). Tacitus records the trial in *Annals*, XV, 56-9, and the death of Seneca in *Annals*, XV, 60-3. The final confident lines spoken by Nero in Bridges' play (V, iv) are hardly consonant with the Emperor's alarm as recorded by Tacitus in *Annals*, XV, 58-9.

Bridges makes Otho reluctant to introduce his wife to Nero. This interpretation of his character is considerably at variance with that of Tacitus, who suspects that Otho praised his wife in front of Nero "in the hope of adding to his own influence by the further tie which would arise out of the possession of the same woman." (*Annals*, XIII, 12.)

13. *Poetical Works*, IV, 302.

14. *Ibid.*, V, 295.

15. The original of this fine passage is translated by D. S. M'Carthy as follows:

> My soul is full of some mysterious fear; —
> That Fate frowns darkly is my fixed belief;
> For since I saw fair Lisbon disappear,
> Its well-known heights fast fading one by one —
> Of all the thoughts that haunt me Death is chief!
> Scarcely had we our enterprise begun,
> Scarce had our ships commenced their onward chase,
> When, in a paroxysm, the great sun,
> Shrouded in clouds, concealed his golden face,
> And angry waves in foaming madness wreck'd
> Some of our fleet. Where'er I look I trace
> The same disaster; — O'er the sea project

A thousand shadows; — If I view the sky
Its azure veil with bloody drops seems fleck'd; —
If to the once glad air I turn mine eye,
Dark birds of night their mournful plumage wave; —
If on the earth, my fall doth prophesy
And represent my miserable grave.

Dramas of Calderón, trans. D. F. M'Carthy, 2 vols. (London, 1853), I, 23.

CHAPTER NINE

1. Vz. *supra*, pp. 4–5.
2. *Letters*, p. 217.
3. T. Sturge Moore, *Selected Poems* (London, 1934), p. 200.
4. For instance, "Bridges has avoided all symbolism, all allegory, in his *Prometheus*." (E. E. Kellett, "The Poems of Robert Bridges," *The London Quarterly Review*, CXXIV [1915], 243.)
5. *Prometheus Unbound*, I, 697.
6. *Ibid.*, I, 387.
7. An anonymous play entitled *Prometheus the Fire-Giver* (London, 1877) contains several passages which indicate Bridges might have read it. Cp. for instance,

Forethought forearms me, I forsee the worst . . . (*Prom. the Fire-Giver*, p. 46)

with Bridges'

in knowledge is all my power,
And what prevention in foreknowledge lies. (*Prom. the Firegiver*, l. 700.)

8. *Prometheus Unbound*, Shelley's Preface.
9. *Ibid.*
10. Brett Young, *Robert Bridges*, p. 190.
11. *Demeter* (ed. 1905), p. 57.
12. Cp. Shelley:

It doth repent me: words are quick and vain;
Grief for awhile was blind, and so was mine.
I wish no living thing to suffer pain. (*Prom. Unbound*, I, i, 303–5.)

13. Compare these lines with similar ones in *The Testament of Beauty*:

— whether 'twer lark or lion, or some high antler'd stag
in startled pose of his fantastic majesty
gazing adown the glade. (*T. O. B.*, I, 213–5.)

14. See, for instance, *The Athenaeum*, no. 3872 (1902), p. 40, and John Bailey, "The Poetry of Robert Bridges," *The Quarterly Review*, CCXIX (1913), 236.

15. *The Library*, Lib. III, xiii, 8.
16. *Ibid.*, Loeb Classical Library, *Apollodorus*, II, 73–5.
17. *Ibid.*, II, 74, footnote 1.
18. *Achilles in Scyros*, ll. 572–88.
19. *Ibid.*, ll. 1468–82. Cp. *P. C. P.*, I, 28–30; *T. O. B.*, I, 653–8.
20. Bridges acknowledges his indebtedness to Calderón in *Poetical Works*, III, 264. A comparison with the original, as translated by M'Carthy (*The Constant Prince*, I, i) may be of interest:

> First (so many a fair illusion
> Oft the wandering seaman mocks),
> I could not determine truly
> Whether they were ships or rocks;
> For, as on the coloured canvas
> Subtle pencils softly blend
> Dark and bright, in such proportions
> That the dim perspectives end —
> Now, perhaps, like famous cities,
> Now, like caves or misty capes,
> For remoteness ever formeth
> Monstrous and unreal shapes.
> Thus, athwart the fields of azure
> Lights and shades alternate fly. . . .
>
> First they seemed to us uplifting
> High in heaven their pointed towers,
> Clouds that to the sea descended,
> To conceive in sapphire showers,
> What they would bring forth in crystal. . . .
>
> For the sails, when lightly shaken,
> Fanned by zephyrs as by slaves,
> Seemed to us like outspread pinions,
> Fluttering o'er the darkened waves;
> Then, the mass, approaching near,
> Seemed a mighty Babylon,
> With its hanging gardens pictured
> By the streamers floating down.
> But, although our certain vision
> Undeceived, becoming true,
> Showed it was a great armada,

For I saw the prows cut through
Foam, that, sparkling in the sunshine,
Like the fleece of snow-white flocks,
Rolled itself in silver mountains,
Curdled into crystal rocks.

21. Rowe's *Ulysses* has, like Lee's *Nero*, a very marked Spanish tone. Telemachus loves "Semanthe," the daughter of Eurymachus, and when he kills Eurymachus in defending his mother, Semanthe is torn between her love for Telemachus and her "honour." She compromises by promising to love Telemachus always, but she herself goes back to Samos. Stephen Phillips' *Ulysses* which passes freely from Olympus to Hades, is about as bad as his *Nero*. Zeus speaks these remarkable lines:

I to no higher wisdom make pretence
Than to expound eternal sapience.

22. *Poetical Works*, IV, 303.
23. Alfred Gilde, *Die dramatische Behandlung der Rückkehr des Odysseus bei Nicholas Rowe, Robert Bridges und Stephen Phillips* (Königsberg, 1903), p. 31.
24. *Letters*, p. 217.
25. W. B. Yeats, *Ideas of Good and Evil* (London, 1896), p. 157.
26. Gilde, p. 33.

CHAPTER TEN

1. *Poetical Works*, VI, 276.
2. *Ibid.*
3. Brett Young, *Robert Bridges*, p. 172.
4. In *Heautontimorumenos*, Chremes' son is Clitipho; in *The Feast of Bacchus* his name is Pamphilus, and Clitipho is the name assumed by the disguised Clinia. The following passages are translated or are closely adapted from Terence:

		The Feast of Bacchus	Heautontimorumenos (ed. Bentley)	
Act I	Lines	12–15	I, i	36–40
		24–60	I, i	1–36
		60–130	I, i	41–106
		145–155	I, i	107–115
		262–278	I, ii	25–37
Act II		496–519	II, i	Whole scene
		520–530	II, ii	Whole scene
		531–536	II, iii	15–20

	547–567		II, iii	33–67
	577–601		II, iv	1–29
Act III	918–925		III, i	11–16
	995–1004		III, i	47–52
Act IV	1076–1160		IV, i	Whole scene
	1160–1161		IV, iv	3–15
	1226–1230		V, i	6–10
	1237–1239		V, iv	10–11
	1288–1300		V, iii	1–11
Act V	1341–1345		IV, viii	1–3
	1397–1399		V, i	1–2
	1402 ff.		IV, viii	Whole scene

5. See Appendix A.

6. *Poetical Works*, V, 296. The main characters in *El secreto à voces* are the same as those of *The Humours of the Court*, though some of the names are changed. Where these are changed, they come from *El perro del hortelano*. Diana is Countess of Belflor in Lope's play, but Flerida, Duchess of Parma, in Calderón's; Ricardo's name comes from Lope, while Calderón calls him Enrique.

PART THREE

CHAPTER ELEVEN

1. "In the Pages of the Testament of Beauty," *Boston Evening Transcript*, February 21, 1930.

2. Bridges' explanation of the prosody of his syllabic verse (*Essays*, XV, Appendix, 87–91) is dated December 1923, and this "account of the origin of its metre was written some two years before *The Testament of Beauty* was definitely begun. A fragment of fourteen lines exists, however . . . dated Christmas 1924 — of which the initial seven lines form the beginning of the poem." It is certain that the poem was begun by February 1927, and completed by September 1929. A rough draft of the poem was printed, in installments, for Bridges' convenience in revising his work. This rough draft has been withheld from the public, and the only copies extant, to my knowledge, are in the possession of Mrs. Bridges and Mr. Kenneth Sisam of the Clarendon Press. The colophon of this rough draft gives some idea of the period of composition: "The first draft of THE TESTAMENT OF BEAUTY was privately printed for the convenience of the Author: Book I (25 copies) in February 1927; Book II (25 copies) in Septem-

ber 1927; Book III (25 copies) in May 1928; Book IV lines 1–1135 (25 copies) in February 1929; and the end of Book IV 4 copies in September and 17 copies in October 1929." This colophon is reproduced with the permission of Mr. Sisam, from whose copy it was transcribed.

3. *T. L. S.*, October 24, 1929.

4. Hillyer, *op. cit.* Sir Frederick Pollock, who considered *The Testament of Beauty* "the only great philosophical poem" in English, agrees with Mr. Hillyer that we must go back to "Lucretius himself" to find a comparable poem. Mr. Justice Holmes disagreed strongly: "It seemed to me the Cosmos arranged to suit polite English taste." See *Holmes-Pollock Letters* (Cambridge, Mass., 1941), II, 261–4, a reference for which I am indebted to Miss Dorothy Greenwald.

5. *Spectator*, CXLIII (1929), 635.

6. *Saturday Review of Literature*, VI (1930), 913.

7. *Atlantic Bookshelf* (April 1930), p. 24.

8. *Bookman*, LXXI (New York, 1930), 153.

9. *Nation and Athenaeum*, XLVI (1929), 287.

10. *New Republic*, LXII (1930), 164.

11. *Poetry*, XXXVI (1930), 96.

12. "Wintry Delights," ll. 71–2.

13. *Ibid.*, ll. 169–72.

14. *Ibid.*, ll. 199–203.

15. *Ibid.*, ll. 212–4.

16. J. Gordon Eaker, "Robert Bridges' Concept of Nature," *PMLA*, LIV (1939), 1194. See the *Critique of Judgment*, section 87.

17. "Wintry Delights," ll. 345–54.

18. "To a Socialist in London," ll. 251–2.

19. "Come Se Quando," ll. 89–90.

20. *Ibid.*, ll. 197–201.

21. Nowell Charles Smith, *Notes on The Testament of Beauty* (London, 1931), xxxvi.

22. Doubled consonants with the phonetic value of a single letter are often reduced to their true form, as in "wil" for "will." Usually the demonstrative "that" is distinguished from the relative by doubling the final consonant, but Bridges' practice is not consistent. Compare, for instance, lines 24 and 38 of the first book. The ordinary spelling of the word "nature" is retained "except in those places where it suffers liquid synaloepha in the prosody." (*T. O. B.*, "Publisher's Note on the Text.")

23. *Essays*, XIX, 162.

24. *De Rerum Natura*, I, 936–45.

25. *Essays*, XIX, 144.
26. George Santayana, *The Life of Reason*, 5 vols. (New York, 1905-6), I, 3.
27. *Phaedrus*, 246.
28. Spinoza, *Ethics*, Part V, Prop. XXXVI. In *Ethics and De Intellectus Emendatione*, trans. A. Boyle (London, Everyman's ed., 1910), p. 219.
29. *Essays*, XIX, 149.
30. Lionel Stevenson, *Darwin among the Poets* (Chicago, 1932), p. 343.

CHAPTER TWELVE

(*References are to the text of the first edition of "The Testament of Beauty"*)

1. A conscious reminiscence of the opening lines of Dante's *Inferno*. (Nowell Smith, p. 1.) Wherever identification of a source, analogue or reference is made by Smith, acknowledgment will be made in the notes. Duplication has been avoided except in cases where the information contributes to an understanding of the poem or of the poet's method.
2. With lines 8 and 36, cp. *Prelude*, ed. de Selincourt (Oxford, 1926), 1805 version, I, 1-115.
3. Cp. *Prelude*, VIII, 626; XIII, 62-5; XVII, 370-9; also "Lines Composed above Tintern Abbey."
4. Cp. Tennyson: "Procuress to the Lords of Hell," *In Memoriam*, liii (Nowell Smith, p. 2).
5. The philosophy of relativism suggested here should not be confused with Berkeley's absolute idealism. Bridges' point of view is the same as Santayana's: "If a thing were never perceived, or inferred from perception, we should indeed never know that it existed; but once perceived or inferred it may be more conducive to comprehension and practical competence to regard it as existing independently of our perception. . . ." (*Life of Reason*, I, 113.)
6. Vz. *Oedipus Coloneus*, 17-8, 670-8.
7. Cp. *T. O. B.* (*Testament of Beauty*), I, 223-5; II, 88; III, 702-3, 977-80; also "Wintry Delights," 396-404.
8. The capitalized words acknowledge a conscious recollection of Pope's *Essay on Man*, I, 294.
9. Cp. *Prelude*, II, 208-10, 214-5; XI, 123-8.
10. The same argument is used in "Wintry Delights," line 427. Passages on the fallibility of reason appear throughout the poem, and form a Wordsworthian and Kantian critique of the intellect. Cp. *T. O. B.*, I, 135-44, 713-5; II, 697-707, 722-3, 864-8; III, 986-90; IV, 1025, 1062-4, 1073-80.

11. The use of "tickle" in this sense recalls *Faerie Queene*, VII, i; *M. for M.*, I, ii, 177; *2 Hy. VI*, I, i, 216.

12. "Consciousness is the mere surface of our minds, of which, as of the earth, we do not know the inside but only the crust." *World as Will and Idea*, trans. R. H. Haldane, J. Kemp, 3 vols. (London, 1891), II, 328.

13. One of the main assumptions of the poem. Cp. *T. O. B.*, II, 462–3, 493–4, 497–8; III, 310–1, 743–6, 809–10, 991–4; IV, 221–4, 460–2, 601–4, 621–2. Cp. also *Growth of Love*, 52, and *Prelude*, VIII, 87.

14. Cp. *T. O. B.*, I, 52–6, 630–2; II, 771–3, 915–6; III, 760–3, 944–8; IV, 538–43.

15. Vz. *supra*, p. 180. Also note 16 to Chapter XI.

16. Bridges is not, in the strict sense of the term, a materialist. He does not believe that matter *becomes* consciousness. This is one of the central passages in the poem. The belief thus outlined is expressed throughout the four books, and finds its closest parallel in the philosophy of Santayana: "The world, instead of being a living body, a natural system with moral functions, has seemed to be a bisectible hybrid, half material and half mental, the clumsy conjunction of an automaton with a ghost. . . ." (*Life of Reason*, I, 211.) It was such a division of the world into a "bisectible hybrid" — the conception of one substance underlying matter, another underlying mind — that Spinoza objected to in the Cartesian philosophy. The natural basis of thought and ideals, and, in general, the continuity of mind and matter is propounded frequently by George Meredith. In "Earth and Man" there is a close parallel in thought and diction to Bridges' lines. See Appendix B. Cp. also Swinburne's "Hertha" and Meredith's "The Woods of Westermain."

17. Cp. Pope's "A being darkly wise and rudely great."

18. Cp. Santayana: "Skepticism is harmless when it is honest and universal; it clears the air and is a means of reorganizing life on its natural foundations." (*Life of Reason*, V, 308.)

19. "Pure Reason" is apparently used advisedly, with reference to Kant. According to Kant, "pure reason" means knowledge that does not come to us through our sense-experience, knowledge coming to us because of the inherent nature and structure of the mind: "General truths, which at the same time bear the character of an inward necessity, must be independent of experience, — clear and certain in themselves." (*Critique of Pure Reason*, preface.) Hence "essential principles" (essential propositions) — i.e., premises or propositions which predicate in a subject something implied in its definition.

20. "Reason" here means "reasonable." Cp. Pascal: "Verité au deça des Pyrénées; erreur au delà."

21. The lines owe something to Masefield's sonnet "The Lemmings."

22. It is evident from his allusions to St. Bernard and Eleanor of Aquitaine that Bridges has confused or telescoped the first and second crusades.

23. Ulfilas, Gothic translator of the Bible; Theoderic (Nowell Smith, p. 9).

24. Cp. *Prelude*, XII, 280–6.

25. "Laughter also has this subtle advantage, that it need not remain without an overtone of sympathy and brotherly understanding; as the laughter that greets Don Quixote's absurdities and misadventures does not mock the hero's intent. His ardour was admirable, but the world must be known before it can be reformed pertinently. . . ." (*Life of Reason*, V, 91.)

26. Cp. last line with *Prelude*, X, 642–5.

27. Proverbs, ix. 1. (Nowell Smith, p. 11.)

28. Cp. Wordsworth,

> . . . this I speak
> In gratitude to God, who feeds our hearts
> For his own service. . . . (*Prelude*, XII, 274–6)

29. Spinoza's *conatus sese preservandi* is certainly the *locus classicus* for the idea of Selfhood: "Everything, in so far as it is in itself, endeavours to persist in its own being, etc." (*Ethics*, III, 6, 7.)

30. Cp. Schopenhauer: "Plants have at most a very weak analogue of consciousness; the lowest species of animals only the dawn of it. But even after it has ascended through the whole series of animals to man and his reason, the unconsciousness of plants, from which it started, still remains the foundation. . . ." (*The World as Will and Idea*, II, 337.)

31. See Appendix B.

32. "The Temple of Nature," Canto II, Section 2. Quoted in J. W. Beach, *The Concept of Nature in Nineteenth-Century English Poetry* (New York, 1936), p. 229.

33. Beach, *idem*.

34. See the lines beginning

> Blest the infant Babe
> (For with my best conjectures I would trace
> The progress of our Being) blest the Babe. . . . (*Prelude*, II, 238 ff.)

35. In his *Fable of the Bees*, Mandeville showed a society falling into apathy because it possessed all the virtues; Bridges shows the society of the bees, who originally "wer fully endow'd with Reason," falling into apathy (Reason becoming atrophied) because it pursued an equalitarian ideal. Bridges may also have had in mind the fourth book of Vergil's *Georgics*.

36. Cp. *T. O. B.*, IV, 270–2 and "Epistle to a Socialist," ll. 354–417.

37. Plato denied family life only to the guardian class (*Republic*, 460), as Nowell Smith observes (*op. cit.*, p. 17).

38. Cp. Wordsworth

the soul
Remembering how she felt, but what she felt
Remembering not, retains an obscure sense
Of possible sublimity. . . . (*Prelude*, II, 334–7.)

39. *Phaedrus*, 249–50.

40. Santayana, *Little Essays*, pp. 268–9.

41. Cp. *Prelude*, I, 420–4.

42. *St. John*, vii, 37; iv, 13.

43. See Appendix B.

44. This fanciful notion of Methuselah surviving the flood was probably suggested by the Samaritan text of Pentateuch. All texts agree that he died at 969. According to the Samaritan text he was 67 at the birth of Lamech, and 120 at the birth of Noah, who was 600 at the flood. The whole passage echoes a similar one in *Paradise Lost*. See pp. 247–8.

45. Cp. Santayana: "Whoever it was that searched the heavens with his telescope and could find no God, would not have found the human mind if he had searched the brain with a microscope." (*Little Essays*, p. 49.)

46. Cp. *T. O. B.*, I, 135–44, 713–5; II, 722–3, 864–8; III, 986–90; IV,1073–80.

47. Cp. *Prelude*, XII, 370–9, and Santayana: "Reason as such represents a single formal interest, the interest in harmony." (*Life of Reason*, I, 267.) Also *T. O. B.*, II, 826, 899; IV, 78–9, 601, 1027–8.

48. The quotation is from *Tamburlaine*, V, i. (Nowell Smith, p. 26.) Compare the whole passage with the concluding paragraph of Santayana's *The Sense of Beauty* (London, 1896), pp. 269–70.

49. In this passage *conscience* means, as usual, *consciousness* or *awareness*. This meaning must be particularly kept in mind in line 871.

50. "And saw Virtue in her shape how lovely," (*P. L.*, IV, 847–8; [Nowell Smith, p. 28]).

51. Cp. Santayana, *Little Essays*, p. 42.

52. *Psalms*, xxxiv, 14.

53. *Hamlet*, IV, iv, 38–9. (Nowell Smith, p. 29.)

54. *Life of Reason*, II, 3–34.

55. *Ibid.*, II, 9.

56. *Ibid.*, II, 8.

57. *Ibid.*, II, 3–7.

58. *Ibid.*, II, 4–5.

59. Cp. Santayana: "All this makes the brightest page of many a life, the

only bright page in the thin biography of many a human animal. . . ." (*Life of Reason*, II, 15.)

60. *De Rerum Natura*, I, 22–3.

61. Cp. Plato, *Symposium*, 183–4.

62. Santayana, *op. cit.*, II, 9.

63. "Whatever circumstances pave the way, love does not itself appear until a sexual affinity is declared. When a woman, for instance . . . asks herself whether she really loves her mate, or merely accepts him, the test is the possibility of awakening a sexual affinity." (*Ibid.*, p. 21.)

64. The theory of the origin of the idealization of women in the Troubadour poetry suggested in 639–40 is, of course, not accepted by scholars in the field.

65. The Cathari. (Nowell Smith, p. 44.)

66. That Christianity was responsible for the perfection of man's love is one of the poem's central assumptions. Thus Bridges naturally emphasizes the place of the Virgin in the history of human ideals. An interesting summary of the theory opposed to this one is given by C. S. Lewis: "The fall of the old civilization and the coming of Christianity did not result in any deepening or idealization of the conception of love. . . . That Christianity in a very general sense by its insistence on compassion and on the sanctity of the human body, had a tendency to soften or abash the more extreme brutalities of the ancient world . . . may be taken as obvious. But there is no evidence that the quasi-religious tone of medieval love poetry has been transferred from the worship of the Blessed Virgin: it is just as likely . . . that the colouring of certain hymns to the Virgin has been borrowed from the love poetry." (*Allegory of Love*, p. 8.)

67. Other passages on the fallibility of science include II, 680–4; III, 964; IV, 671–3, 858–60.

68. Santayana, *op. cit.*, II, 29.

69. Cp. Schopenhauer's *Essay on Women*.

70. "Modern critics reject the interpretation of the picture implied by this title, supposing the subject to be taken from classical mythology." (Nowell Smith, p. 53.)

71. Cp. Wordsworth:

> furnish'd with that kind
> Of prepossession without which the soul
> Receives no knowledge that can bring forth good. (*Prelude*, VIII, 458–60.)

72. An interesting attack, from the Catholic point of view, on this exaltation of the child's intuitions is found in R. W. Rauch, "Intimations of Mortality: A Note on the Poetry of Childhood," *The American Review*, VIII (1937), 297–308.

73. Aristotle: "Some think that men become good by nature, others think it is by habit, others by teaching. Now the gift of nature does not depend upon us, but for some divine cause or other belongs to those who are truly fortunate." (*Ethics*, X, ix, 6, [Nowell Smith, p. 57].)

74. The reference in the first line is to Kant's "categorical imperative." Cp. Santayana, "There is no categorical imperative but only the operation of instincts and interests more or less subject to discipline and mutual adjustment." (*Little Essays*, p. 178.)

75. See Appendix B, pp. 291–2.

76. The faith referred to here would be faith in "theoretic wisdom"; in absolute eternal moral principles.

77. Cp. "Epistle to a Socialist."

78. In seeking a motive for asceticism, Bridges neglects the value attached by Aristotle and others to the restriction of impulse as a means of disciplining the soul.

79. Paraphrase of Aristotle, *Poetics*, I, iv.

80. *Little Essays*, p. 114.

81. Cp. Aristotle, *Ethics*, II, iv.

82. Cp. Bacon, " . . . the human understanding, from its peculiar nature, easily supposes a greater degree of order and regularity in things than it really finds." (*Novum Organum*, I, 45.)

83. Cp. Santayana: "Now the body is an instrument, the mind its function, the witness and reward of its operation. Mind is the body's entelechy, a value which accrues to the body when it has reached a certain perfection, of which it would be a pity, so to speak, that it should remain unconscious; so that while the body feeds the mind the mind perfects the body, lifting it and all its natural relations and impulses into the moral world, into the sphere of interests and ideas." (*Life of Reason*, I, 206.)

84. *Skepticism and Animal Faith* (London, 1927), p. 76.

85. *Psalms*, xlii. The "exile" is religion.

86. *The Life of Reason*, I, 32.

CHAPTER THIRTEEN

1. Harold A. Larrabee, "Robert Bridges and George Santayana," *Faculty Papers of Union College*, II (1931), 88.

2. Mabel V. Hughes, *Everyman's Testament of Beauty: A Study in The Testament of Beauty of Robert Bridges* (London, 1932), is a work of religious propaganda, sympathetic but naïve in its interpretations.

3. On their friendship, see Odell Shepard, "Robert Bridges," *Bookman*, LXXI (1930), 151–6.

4. Review of *The Testament of Beauty*, *New Republic*, LXII (1930), 164.

5. Larrabee, *op. cit.*

6. *Essays*, XIX, 156.

7. *Ibid.*

8. *Ibid* , 164.

9. George W. Howgate, *George Santayana* (Philadelphia, 1938), p. 289.

10. *Ibid.*, p. 291.

11. *Essays*, XIX, 162.

12. Santayana, *The Life of Reason*, I, 3.

13. Santayana, *The Sense of Beauty* (New York, 1896), p. 270.

14. I. Edman (ed.), *The Philosophy of Santayana: Selections from the Works of George Santayana* (New York, 1936), xvi–xvii.

15. See "The Test of Manhood" in *A Reading of Life*.

16. See Appendix B, p. 292.

17. Vz. *supra*, pp. 188–9.

18. *Essays*, XIX, 147.

19. Spinoza, *Ethics*, Part II, Prop. XXXV.

20. *Ibid.*, Part V, Prop. XV.

21. *Ibid.*, Part V, Prop. XIV.

22. *Aeneid*, VI, 724 ff.

23. Spinoza, *Ethics*, Part V, Prop. XXX.

24. *Ibid.*, Part V, Prop. XXXVI.

25. *Ibid.*, Part V, Prop. XIX.

26. *Ibid.*, Part V, Prop. XLII.

27. Vz. *supra*, pp. 188–90.

28. Santayana, *Three Philosophical Poets* (New York, 1910), Introduction.

29. *Paradise Lost*, I, 200–8.

THE NATURE OF THE TRADITIONAL POET

1. "What is a Classic?" Quoted in J. H. Smith and E. W. Parks, *The Great Critics, an Anthology of Literary Criticism* (New York, 1932), p. 546.

2. Quoted in Edmund Wilson, *Axel's Castle;* in M. D. Zabel, *Literary Opinion in America, A Book of Modern Critical Essays* (New York, 1937), p. 192.

3. Odell Shepard, *op. cit.*, p. 154.

4. Cp. Winters, *Primitivism and Decadence*, p. 74.

5. *Essays*, XIV, 42.

APPENDIX A

1. I am much indebted to Yvor Winters' masterful analysis of English meters in *Primitivism and Decadence*.

2. *Milton's Prosody, with a Chapter on Accentual Verse and Notes* (Oxford, 1921), p. 36.

3. This example is used by Winters in *Primitivism and Decadence*, p. 98.

4. Vz. *supra*, pp. 50, 107–8.

5. *Milton's Prosody* (ed. 1921), p. 10.

6. Nowell Smith, *Notes on The Testament of Beauty*, p. xxxvi.

7. *Milton's Prosody* (ed. 1921), p. 40.

8. *Ibid.*, p. 87.

9. *Ibid.*, pp. 92–105.

10. *The Poetical Works of Robert Bridges*, VI, 277.

11. "Classical Metres in English," in *Milton's Prosody* (ed. 1901), p. 130.

12. Vz. *supra*, pp. 27–8.

13. "On Translating Homer."

14. *Ibant Obscuri, an Experiment in the Classical Hexameter* (Oxford, 1916), pp. 154–8.

15. *Milton's Prosody* (ed. 1901), p. 153.

16. *Ibid.*

17. *Aeneid*, VI, 268–72.

18. *New Verse, Written in 1921* (Oxford, 1925), vii.

19. *Foure Letters Confuted.*

20. *New Verse*, Preface.

21. *T. O. B.*, 841.

22. For the exceptions see "New Verse," Appendix, *Essays*, XV, 91.

23. *Ibid.*

24. *Ibid.*, p. 87.

25. *Ibid.*, p. 88.

26. *Ibid.*

27. *Ibid.*, p. 89.

28. *Ibid.*

29. *Ibid.*

30. *Milton's Prosody* (ed. 1921), p. 60.

31. "New Verse," Appendix, *Essays*, XV, 90.

APPENDIX C

1. "Robert Bridges," *DNB, 1922–1930*, pp. 116–7.

2. Bridges, *Poems* (London, 1873), p. 126.

INDEX

INDEX

(Notes and authors quoted but not mentioned in the text are not indexed.)